Competing Claims to Recognition in the Nigerian Public Sphere

Competing Claims to Recognition in the Nigerian Public Sphere

A Liberal Argument about Justice in Plural Societies

John Boye Ejobowah

LEXINGTON BOOKS

A division of
ROWMAN & LITTLEFIELD PUBLISHERS, INC.
Lanham • Boulder • New York • Toronto • Plymouth, UK

LEXINGTON BOOKS

A division of Rowman & Littlefield Publishers, Inc.
A wholly owned subsidiary of The Rowman & Littlefield Publishing Group, Inc.
4501 Forbes Boulevard, Suite 200
Lanham, MD 20706

Estover Road
Plymouth PL6 7PY
United Kingdom

British Library Cataloguing in Publication Information Available

Library of Congress Cataloging-in-Publication Data
Ejobowah, John Boye, 1962–
   Competing claims to recognition in the Nigerian public sphere : a liberal argument
about justice in plural societies / John Boye Ejobowah.
      p. cm.
   Includes bibliographical references (p. 189–202) and index.
   1. Minorities—Nigeria—Political activity. 2. Federal government—Nigeria.
3. Nigeria—Ethnic relations. 4. Nigeria—Politics and government. I. Title.
JQ3086.M5 E38 2001
323.1'669—dc21   2001038566

   ISBN-13: 978-0-7391-0313-5 (cloth : alk. paper)
   ISBN-10: 0-7391-0313-X (cloth: alk. paper)
   ISBN-13: 978-0-7391-2683-7 (pbk. : alk. paper)
   ISBN-10: 0-7391-2683-0 (pbk. : alk. paper)

Printed in the United States of America

♾™ The paper used in this publication meets the minimum requirements of American
National Standard for Information Sciences—Permanence of Paper for
Printed Library Materials, ANSI/NISO Z39.48–1992.

Contents

Acknowledgments

This book is a heavily revised version of my doctoral dissertation. The revisions were made in response to questions raised during the defense, and to comments made at various international conferences where most of the chapters were presented. I am especially grateful to Joseph Carens, my supervisor, for encouraging me to publish my work. From him I learned the true meaning of an academic adviser.

I also thank Melissa Williams for her incisive and perceptive comments on various parts of the manuscript. Jonathan Barker, Dickson Eyoh, and Richard Simeon—all members of my dissertation committee—provided critical comments on various parts of the work. I thank them all.

Richard Sklar, my examiner, made written comments and suggestions for improvement. Will Kymlicka provided extensive comments on a section of the manuscript and Arend Lijphart drew my attention to my initial misreading of some aspects of his consociational theory. Mary Liston read the entire work, pointed out stylistic problems in some sentences, and also ensured that materials cited were listed in the bibliography. Patti Lenard took time to prepare the index even though she had moved from the University of Toronto to Oxford. Melissa McNitt and Paul State of Lexington Books proofread the manuscript with a great deal of attention. I am grateful to all of them. My special thanks also go to Jennifer Nedelsky for introducing me to Serena Leigh, the executive editor of Lexington Books, during the annual American Political Science Association (APSA) meeting in Washington D.C., August 2000.

The University of Toronto and the Rockefeller Foundation gave me good doctoral and research fellowship support. The Political Science Department of the University of Toronto also provided some grant money for this book. I appreciate their support greatly.

A small section of chapter 6 was published in *Africa Today* 47, no. 1 (winter 2000): 29-47. Another section of that same chapter was published in the *Journal of Third World Studies* 18, no. 1 (spring 2001): 143-60. A large part of chapter 7 was published in *Nationalism and Ethnic Politics* 6, no. 3 (fall 2000): 1-18.

Introduction

This book explores two matters: first, it is about the nature of the theoretical principles that should guide the design of political arrangements conducive to peace and unity in a multiethnic society such as Nigeria; second, it is about how theoretical principles are shaped and limited by the concrete experiences of a particular society. These two issues are interconnected. Theoretical principles that serve as guides for political action grow out of practical experiences, but these principles are in turn reshaped by the political arrangements they generate or try to remold (Raz 1986: 3).

Nigeria provides a good example of the intersection between theory and practice. Composed of several ethnic groups, the country remains deeply divided by ethnic, religious, and sectional differences despite various constitutional designs in the twentieth century to meet these competing group claims to equal recognition.[1] This book embodies an attempt to establish a linkage between theoretical principles about justice and democracy in plural societies and practical claims to equality and fairness in the Nigerian polity. To achieve this goal, the teachings and insights of many political thinkers are employed to present an inventory of the merits and drawbacks of the competing group claims made in the various successive phases of Nigerian political history. In the course of making this inventory, principles of justice drawn from these thinkers are used in order to evaluate the desirability (or otherwise) of the constitutional arrangements that were put in place during each of the various phases of Nigerian history as well as what alternatives were best and most practicable. The book, then, is both theoretical and empirical and is prescriptive from start to finish. This distinguishes it from most writings about ethnic accommodation in Africa, which are either conducted from an empirical viewpoint, narrate events and conclude with prescriptions, or make prescriptive arguments by drawing on the policies and lessons of other states.

In African studies, the literature on ethnicity dwells on the importance of identity in politics, argues for the political recognition of groups, or evaluates policies that have been used by some states to accommodate

groups in order to extract positive models for others to adopt.[2] The literature criticizes strategies adopted by some states but does not spell out the
range of possible alternatives that could have been adopted and implemented.[3] Very often, the literature does not consider contending group
claims that have to be balanced or the sociohistorical circumstances that
state officials ought to consider to arrive at particular strategies. Criticisms tend to be negative, in that they condemn and reject, rather than
corrective, by presenting alternatives reflecting conditions on the
ground.[4]

This work goes beyond critique to make normative judgments regarding the respective merits of opposing group demands and to consider
possible feasible alternative constitutional arrangements required by justice. It listens to and evaluates conflicting claims the way a judge or jury
hears and deliberates opposing claims in a civil suit. From this range of
alternatives, it then presents the solution that best reflects the interests of
the opposing parties. Thus, the project brings a perspective that comple-
ments the empirical literature on democratic arrangements and the reduction of ethnic conflict in African states.

Contemporary liberal philosophical literature on group recognition,
on the other hand, offers key principles for reorganizing societies to accommodate cultural difference. These principles, like all philosophical
principles, are supposed to be universally valid but might be informed by
experiences that are contextually specific to the West and therefore may
render them inadequate if applied to non-Western states. This book tries
to generate awareness about the requirements of theory by using the Nigerian case regarding political accommodation of groups to reveal some
weaknesses in the philosophical literature. It therefore uses a particular
case to criticize general principles in order to elicit a better understanding
of a theory that cuts across cultures.

The Issues

To date, Nigeria has adopted no fewer than four constitutional approaches to accommodate its diverse groups at different historical periods. The first approach, spanning the 1940s through to the 1957-58
Willink Commission, developed from a series of debates held in Nigeria
and Britain. It recognized the three most numerous ethnic groups through
the division of the country into three political regions, as well as several
constitutional arrangements for a federal system, but it denied recogni-

tion to several other smaller groups despite their expressed fears about majoritarian domination.

A second approach, spanning the early 1960s through 1969, paid more attention to difference. This formula involved adopting a quota system for appointments into national bodies and redivided the country into twelve states to represent and include the smaller groups that were previously denied recognition. This occurred under the contingencies of Biafra's attempted secession and the subsequent civil war in Nigeria.

After the civil war, a new set of constitutional debates and government inquiries produced yet another approach. The third approach, beginning from the mid-1970s through the early 1980s, involved the adoption of a "federal character" strategy. It consisted of two elements, the first being a further division of the country into a greater number of states to account for ethnic ties (without explicitly acknowledging ethnic recognition as the purpose of the new states' formation). The second element set a requirement that the composition of national bodies reflect the constituent states of the federation, which were assumed to be synonymous with ethnic composition, and that elections to the highest offices of state be based on a plurality of votes but distributed over wide areas. This strategy proved inadequate as federal power remained under the firm control of one ethnic region and the reemergence and consolidation of military dictatorship during the 1980s further froze political control.

The mid-1980s marked the beginning of still another set of debates and negotiations that continued into the 1990s. A fourth approach emerged that was largely a revision of the "federal character" strategy of the 1970s. This revision involved further division of the country into a greater number of states and local government units to more adequately reflect ethnicity. It also involved an agreement on the proportional representation of parties (assumed to reflect ethno-regional interests) in the executive cabinet and on the rotation of the highest offices of state between ethnic regions. However, some of these innovations were not only compromised by the continuation of military rule but also were reversed in 1999 when the military finally disengaged from the political sphere.

Each of these four approaches to group accommodation involved a combination of a number of devices worked out by constitutional negotiators and local political experts. I identity five such devices, the first being the creation of states and the equitable distribution of national revenue among them. State boundaries were formally geographic but in practice followed ethnic group territories very closely with the effect that ethnic groups were in fact granted state status. In effect, then, a distribution of resources from the center to the states turned out to be a distribution of resources to groups.

The second device was the distribution of positions within federal institutions among states' representatives. With this measure, appointments and recruitment into national institutions were made to reflect the component states. The overall goal was to avoid domination within national institutions by a few groups. In the 1960s, this device took the form of a quota system of appointments and in the 1970s it was incorporated into the federal character strategy.

The third device was political representation within the central legislature. It involved the drawing of legislative districts to follow quite closely the boundaries of ethnic communities with a view to ensuring group representation. This device was derived from the 1957 constitutional agreement by which the country was divided into 312 equal constituencies whose boundaries followed colonial administrative boundaries, which themselves helped define ethnic groups and subgroups.

The fourth device was that of a rotational presidency in which geo-ethnic areas were structured to ensure the circulation of the presidency among groups. The division of the country into geo-ethnic areas was for the exclusive purpose of circulating the office of the president. This device was crafted in the 1990s but was quickly abandoned.

The fifth was local government status within states where positions in local civil service and agencies as well as social infrastructure projects were distributed equitably among the local government units that were assumed to reflect ethnic or subethnic membership. With this device, the office of the governor in each state would also circulate among the local government units.

These devices combined in a variety of ways to produce the continuously changing constitutional approaches mapped out earlier. The mutability of the strategies and the regular reoccurrence of violent conflicts raise the question of what political arrangements can produce a stable and just political union in this ethnically plural country.

My book attempts to answer this question by conducting a critical evaluation of the key debates in Nigeria, from the immediate post-World War II period to the present, over the question of how ethnic claims ought or ought not to be reflected in political arrangements. The debates are grouped into four historical sets (as discussed above) each identified by the issues that were at stake and the constitutional approaches that were adopted. Competing group claims advanced in each set are evaluated for their normative importance while accounting for their strategic character. Constitutional arrangements adopted in response are then evaluated for their desirability and fairness, given the normative importance of the claims, and in light of the requirements of justice derived from political thinkers who have grappled with similar ethical and empirical issues. If the arrangements were seen not to be fair and desirable, alternative approaches that were feasible under the same conditions are considered.

Group-based claims are sometimes strategic in character. They can be smokescreens behind which deeper economic or political agendas lie. For example, post-1999 claims by northern Muslim elites for state adoption of sharia as public law could be seen as a strategy for reintegrating the old North and regaining or maintaining control of national political power. Or, contemporary demands for the creation of states could be conceived as rationalizations made by elites to justify their quest to obtain power and resources. Although I recognize the ideological character of group-based claims, at the same time I go beyond ideology to assess these claims for their normative merit. Ideologies are advanced because they have some qualities and merits that may be acceptable to a wider public. For example, arguments made by key Yoruba elites in the 1950s for regrouping the country into ethnic regions may have been based on rationalizations for their political interest in expanding the territorial area of the Western Region to include Yorubas in the North and Lagos on the coast while, at the same time, also constituting a strategy to reduce the Northern and Eastern Regions to more insignificant sizes. However, the arguments about regrouping the country according to ethnic regions appealed to non-Yorubas as well. Thus, this book does not dismiss competing group claims because they were strategic; rather, it critically evaluates them to determine their merit and normative relevance. The evaluation of claims for their merit generates a range of alternative political arrangements. Such claims, in turn, are evaluated in light of principles drawn from normative and empirical political theorists to determine the arrangement that would have been most desirable and practicable given circumstances on the ground and in keeping with Nigeria's historical experience.

An evaluation and determination of the most desirable and feasible arrangements during the four moments in Nigeria's political history lead, in turn, to an evaluation and criticism of the prescriptive arguments of the political thinkers in light of the empirical Nigerian experience.[5] Prescriptive arguments are often developed in a general fashion and are sometimes fed by cultural assumptions that may not be truly relevant for some countries. Unanticipated difficulties arise when such prescriptions are finally implemented. Evaluating the arguments of political theorists in light of the empirical Nigerian experience will reveal the practical difficulties they are likely to generate. For example, one strand of normative philosophy prescribes special rights for minorities but, in countries outside North America, there are countless minority groups whose recognition would raise the issue of institutional instability. Also, the benefits of special rights would prompt majority subgroups to subdivide and thereby to make their own claims for minority status, thus further raising the political costs. It is this type of empirical reality that is employed in this book to reveal the difficulties of the prescriptive arguments.

The central thesis of this work, then, is that theoretical arguments for group recognition are meaningful for the Nigerian political context and would support both minority and majority claims for the expression of difference. However, where groups are multiple or prone to differentiation, as is the case in Nigeria, the constitutional recognition of groups risks generating institutional and social instability. On the other hand, structures that deny recognition promise intense conflict and lesser stability than do those that give recognition. Given this dichotomy, I conclude that recognition does not generate fundamental tension between the need for the expression of difference and the need for stability; rather, recognition has to be worked out to ensure unity between the two.

Theoretical Foundations

I draw on two literatures, both providing prescriptive arguments from which are derived the principles of justice that are applied to the four successive phases of Nigeria's constitutional history. One stream is philosophical and debates the principles required to accommodate ethnic pluralism in contemporary states around the world. These debates are conducted from a liberal perspective and, although cases are drawn from immigrant countries such as the United States and Canada, nonetheless, there are still good reasons to examine these types of cases in the Nigerian context.

One reason to use the philosophical literature is that the arguments therein are made in a universal manner to apply to all multiethnic states. This universal focus has to do with the upsurge of political claims by ethnic groups and the near breakdown of the techniques of accommodation that liberal democracy has relied upon over the years (Williams

1994: 34). It also concerns the threats intrastate ethnic conflicts bring to world peace, and the need to prevent destabilizing conflict by designing modes of accommodation that will ensure justice among groups.[6]

The second reason for drawing on theoretical and universalist arguments is the culture of toleration that is central to liberalism. Liberal philosophers from John Stuart Mill to Ronald Dworkin have argued for tolerance at the individual level but have not applied this thinking to groups. Individuals were regarded as equal by virtue of their human qualities and capacity to lead a good life, which meant that few grounds existed for legitimately criticizing the preferences or life choices of others. Although Mill (1972) emphasized the autonomy of the individual and used it to criticize received practices and ideas, his defense of personal freedom rested on the idea that plurality of thought and of life-styles were the main engines of societal progress. In contemporary theory, this liberal value of toleration entails respect for cultural difference. Theorists like Michael Walzer, Charles Taylor, and Will Kymlicka each propound a revised account of traditional liberal democracy and they are united by the common argument that the toleration of cultural difference is a requirement of justice in multiethnic societies. It is the latter set of arguments about toleration and justice upon which this work draws.

It might be objected that it is inappropriate to use a core Western value as a standard for judging other societies and that doing so amounts to cultural imperialism. In response to this criticism, I would note that there is nothing wrong if the value is itself inherently good and societies to be judged ascribe to it either implicitly or explicitly. While respect for cultural difference derives from the culture of tolerance that is central to liberalism, it is not completely external to non-Western societies. In Africa, the pre- and postindependence political claims of ethnic groups were not different from the sorts of claims that prompted arguments for the respect of difference in today's multiethnic states of Europe and North America. Most of the secessionist movements and uprisings that broke out after independence were expressions of active resistance either to nation-building projects that sought to assimilate groups or to hegemonic projects that limited political power to the elites of one group while excluding the elites of several other groups. The type of liberal tolerance I invoke, then, is not at odds with contemporary group claims for equal recognition in most African states and I would argue that this value is also internal to many of these cultures.

The second literature that provides general principles is empirical and it presents arguments for the design of inclusive political arrangements in Africa. This literature contains important normative prescriptions for the type of democratic arrangements that are required in ethnically plural states. For example, consociational theorists use empirical facts to demonstrate that the proportional distribution of political offices and resources among groups makes for moderate and cooperative behavior. This argument differs from the Anglo-American democratic practice of allocating offices on the basis of plurality votes and its theoretical underpinnings. Donald Rothchild and Donald Horowitz each argue that a federal system is necessary to accommodate societal cleavages, disperse power to those that would not have had the chance of exercising it, and ensure the equitable distribution of societal goods. Consociationalists make similar arguments. This also marks a shift from the dominant liberal view that argues for the necessary separation of the state from ethnicity. In the empirical literature, there is a general consensus that African states have to rewrite the rules of liberal democracy to reconcile ethnic cleavages.

Apart from these two literatures, there is a third that is empirical and analyzes the invention of ethnic identities. This work explores and accepts the idea of identities as fluid and contingent upon circumstances, but it does not reject them outright. Instead, it argues for their political salience by showing that they constitute a dense network within civil society, that they overlap in both the private and public spheres, and that they have always been essential to and part of state construction in Africa. The social constructionist literature is sympathetic to the neo-Marxist view that groups prone to differentiation are subject to manipulation by elites who are in search of power and privileges. But, even as the literature accepts this Marxist insight, it goes beyond it to argue that the personal interests of elites do, in fact, intersect with their communities' interest in having access to power and resources. In fact, very often communities establish their own schools in order to produce their own share of future elites who can bring power closer to home. As Richard Joseph (1987: 54) has rightly noted in the case of Nigeria: "the fundamental social process . . . is one in which these two propositions—(a) I want to go ahead and prosper, and (b) my group (ethnic, regional linguistic) must go ahead and prosper cannot logically be separated, whether in the context of behavior, actions or consciousness."

On the other hand, acceptance of the post-modernist idea of continuous ethnic change poses a fundamental challenge to the theoretical and empirical arguments contained within the first two sets of literature. This challenge is not dismissed; rather, it is used to identify the difficulties that prescriptive arguments will encounter if they travel from the domain of theory to that of policy implementation. Difficulties include endless claims to recognition and continuous fragmentation of social institutions. This problem is reflected in the thesis I formulated above.

The Outline

Given the approach as discussed above, each chapter of the book has a two-part structure. Chapter 1 reviews the contemporary debate among normative liberal theorists about the potential relevance of cultural and ethnic differences to politics. It also critically discusses the empirical literature on ethnic difference in politics and democratic institutional arrangements for conflict reduction. It then sets a framework for the discussion that will follow in subsequent chapters by identifying and comparing relevant issues raised by the theoretical and empirical approaches and then discusses the normative relevance of ethnic identity in politics by addressing the invention of identities and class arguments.

Chapter 2 presents a factual history of Nigeria and discusses the question of ethnic identity. It outlines the ethnic composition of Nigeria and examines the colonial policy of supporting and using ethnic groups for political governance. It also responds to the sociological argument that identity groups are socially constructed and therefore too illusory to be given political relevance.

Chapter 3 evaluates group claims and constitutional strategies for coping with diversity in the period from the immediate post-World War II era to 1958 when the Independence Constitutional Conference discussed the report of the Minorities Commission. It was during this period that the country put in place constitutional arrangements that recognized the three most numerous groups, but then denied the same recognition to other relevant minority groups. The chapter discusses the claims that were advanced in the 1949-50, 1953-54, 1957, and 1958 constitutional conferences and the arrangements that were negotiated in them. Finally, it evaluates these claims and considers what were the most feasible and best alternative arrangements at the time.

Chapter 4 evaluates opposing claims and strategies adopted during the period from independence to 1967 when a quota system was adopted and the Biafran secession prompted a redivision of the country into twelve states to recognize minority groups who were previously denied political recognition. It presents a descriptive account of the issues and makes a normative evaluation of them.

Chapter 5 is concerned with group demands and the constitutional strategy negotiated in the 1970s. It was during this decade that the country was divided into nineteen states and 301 local government units to further reflect ethnicity. In addition, a negotiated constitution required that appointments and recruitment reflect ethnic membership of states and local units. This chapter presents the government panel's 1975 assessment of the demands for more states. It also gives a narrative account of the opposing views of the constitutional negotiating team regarding the best way to accommodate ethnic diversity. It then conducts a critical assessment of the panel's recommendation for the creation of new states and considers possible alternatives. It further evaluates the constitutional agreement to determine if it was a desirable strategy for ensuring equity in government and what should have been done if it was not.

Chapter 6 looks at the claims and constitutional strategies adopted since the mid-1980s. This period saw the implementation of a revised federal character strategy from that of the 1970s and new claims emerged and were discussed at the 1994-95 Constitutional Conference. It was also a period of crisis for secularism as some states in northern Nigeria adopted the Muslim legal system as public law. Chapter 6 presents the revisions, the new claims that emerged, and the constitutional agreement for a more equitable arrangement and then evaluates them all.

Chapter 7 concludes the book by using the empirical Nigerian experience to revisit and evaluate the arguments of the normative political theorists.

Notes

1. Indeed, Alvin Rabushka and Kenneth Shepsle's (1972: 20) definition of a plural society, as one in which the overwhelming preponderance of political conflicts is along ethnic lines, still applies to the Nigeria of today as it did then.

2. I identify the insightful and excellent recent works by Crawford Young as belonging to the first and second categories while Donald Horowitz, Donald Rothchild, Arend Lijphart and Eric Nordlinger belong to the third. Crawford Young's *The Politics of Cultural Pluralism* (1976) is partly prescriptive and could be regarded as a different form of the third category.

3. This is true of most of the articles in African studies journals.

4. The exceptions here are some of the excellent articles in Peter Ekeh and Eghosa Osaghae's book *Federal Character and Federalism in Nigeria* (1989), especially the articles by Peter Bodunrin and Godwin Sogolo.

5. This is not to suggest that the prescriptions of political thinkers that serve as the basis for evaluating the Nigerian case are unjust. Rather the idea is to

show that theoretical prescriptions have to be practicable and should have minimal negative side effects. This, ultimately, is the test of their universal validity.

6. According to John Stremlau (1998: 1-2), only five of the ninety-six ongoing armed conflicts recorded between 1989 and 1996 were interstate wars; the rest were internal. In another study, Ted Gurr has shown that at the end of 1995 there were no less than forty peoples engaged in deadly ethnic conflicts, at least one of them in every region of the world, and in twenty-four instances the risks of escalation and repression were particularly high.

Chapter One

Normative and Empirical Approaches to Accommodating Ethnic Difference

One of the greatest challenges of the early twenty-first century is how to meet ethnic claims to equal treatment in the public sphere. In Eastern Europe, ethnic claims have led to the dissolution of states and, in the case of Yugoslavia, have resulted in the largest regional war the North Atlantic Treaty Organization (NATO) has fought since its formation in the middle of the twentieth century. In North America, ethnic claims have posed the greatest threat to the stability of Canada, forcing several constitutional negotiations each of which seemed to result in even more intense and threatening claims. In Africa in the 1960s, ethnic claims were the driving force behind secessionist movements in eighteen of the fifty-two states that gained independence during that decade (Young 1992: 29). They accounted for the state disintegration in Somalia, and challenged the authority and legitimacy of the state in Rwanda, Burundi, Ethiopia, Zaire, Chad, and Sudan (Ottaway 1999: 315). Ethnic claims also accounted for the reversal of democratic transitions in other countries during the 1990s. In light of this global history, this chapter asks what principles would be required to organize states to provide for equal treatment and also to avoid self-destructive conflict?

Until recently, liberal theory had no difficulty responding to problems related to this question. Starting with the principle that individuals are entitled to equal moral worth and respect, liberalism devised a model of society through which uniform rights were assigned. It proceeded by separating the public sphere from the private sphere—for example, the separation of state from religion—and everything particular was banished from the former. The public sphere provided a neutral ground for individuals to stand as equals in the distribution of rights and privileges without regard to their cultural or social background. Thus the project of ensuring justice for all required people to proceed from a neutral turf to put in place a difference-blind system of rights and liberties (Williams 1995: 67-91). We see this sort of project in the social contract doctrines that were developed in the early days of liberalism. In modern times, we see this model incorporated in John Rawls's "original position" which is premised on a "veil of ignorance" denying to individuals knowledge of their social background. We also see it in Bruce Ackerman's spacecraft journey or Ronald Dworkin's desert island with its insurance scheme. In all of these projects, a system of rights and liberties is derived without the influence of particularist ties and is therefore considered to be impartial and fair.

Recent strains and stresses in liberal democracy and, more especially, ethnic challenges to the state, have prompted greater philosophical inquiry into the ways to revise liberal principles to reconcile them with difference. This contemporary inquiry has yielded the argument that justice in the political community would require a constitutional order in which ethnic groups are considered in the assignment of rights. The general argument is that there is no necessary tension between liberalism's commitment to the principle of autonomy and differentiated citizenship along the lines of ethnic identities if those identities coincide with a discrete territorial space. Where tensions exist between individual autonomy and recognition of identities, especially those cultural identities whose survival is threatened, the latter must prevail.

Concurrent with the philosophical inquiry, empirical investigations conducted by political scientists have explored constitutional measures that would nurture democracy in African and Asian multiethnic societies. These investigations were prompted by the failure of liberal democracy to generate inclusive political regimes in those societies and by the deadly conflicts that resulted. These studies have determined that ethnically plural states must revise the Anglo-American model of democracy to enable political inclusion. They argue that the surest way of fostering injustice in such states is a wholesale adoption of the difference-blind system of rights that results in majoritarian rule. In what follows, I examine the philosophical and empirical arguments regarding group accommodation.

The Revision of Liberalism

In this section, I will examine the philosophical arguments made by Michael Walzer, Charles Taylor, and Will Kymlicka.

Michael Walzer

Michael Walzer attempts to revise liberal theory by confronting the Rawlsian argument that in the "original position," individuals who are denied knowledge of their social or cultural ties would adopt universal principles for the distribution of primary goods. He refutes Rawls by pointing out that the "original position" is imaginary and that, in reality, goods have different meanings in different societies and it is these meanings that determine their distribution. According to Walzer:

- goods do not "fall from space" but are made by people and have social meaning for those who make them;
- the social meaning of goods determines their movement and how they are distributed;
- justice is done if the values that govern distribution in one sphere of life (or a particular social good) are not used to govern distribution in another sphere life (or another social good). (Walzer 1983: 4-6, 8)

Because his arguments emphasize respect for values and meanings operational in other spheres of life, Walzer can be considered a relativist. Culture is deeply implicated in this form of value pluralism because different cultural communities would advance different values to govern distribution in different spheres of life. In a multiethnic country, Walzer's relativism would defend constitutional structures that recognize difference. He alludes to this when he makes the point about adjusting principles of justice operative in the political community to meet the requirements of historic communities (Walzer 1983: 28-29).

In his later book *Thick and Thin* (1994), the argument gravitates toward autonomy for groups. The moral understanding of a culture, according to Walzer, is thick and should not be overridden by external understandings. If a culture must be criticized, then criticism has to come from within and the standard that the critic appeals to has to be both internal and external. He calls this standard a "minimal universal moral standard," which I take to mean basic human rights.[1] This minimum universal moral standard is thin and is not thick enough to provide details about how life should be lived. Moral minimalism, therefore, cannot be the basis of political unity for diverse cultures. Rather, the minimum standard is conducive to the formation of a collective consciousness that stimulates people's mobilization to its defense whenever the standard is violated and, after which, people return to their rich, thickly constituted moral lives.

For Walzer, then, pluralism of values is the most meaningful aspect of cultural life and to supplant it with value unity would throw people into a moral wilderness.[2] Consequently, the most justifiable arrangement derives from, and is grounded on, thickly developed moral values. For this reason he endorses the right of cultural groups to self-determination. However, the chaos and anarchy that can result from the assertion of independence by one group after another causes him to conclude that self-determination does not provide the single best answer for all situations. The best alternative, he therefore thinks, is a confederal or federal arrangement where institutional checks will prevent the domination of some groups by others (Walzer 1987: 66-88, and 1992: 164-71).

Walzer's arguments have received much critical commentary that need not be repeated here.[3] What does need to be pointed out, as far as this book is concerned, is the false assumption that differentiated rights or internal autonomy for groups would foster political unity. His argument takes cultural groups as cast and fixed, not subject to self-multiplication in the event of goods being distributed on their terms. Goods such as rights, power, and opportunity are not ends in themselves but are means to further goods. Consider power, for example. Power could be a means to wealth, security, and even more rights and opportunities. Now if, according to Walzer's argument, values are used as criteria in the distribution of goods, what is the guarantee that cultural groups claiming different values would not increase their numbers in order to have a greater share? After all, elites encourage group differentiation in order to have access to power.

One of the attractions of difference-blind theories of justice is that the principles by which rights and privileges are assigned to individuals appear to be shielded from particular interests or claims. As a result, these principles provide an authoritative standard for regulating conduct in civil society. The principles appear to be disinterested in the sense that they are seemingly unaffected by particular social interests and this legitimizes their authority within the collectivity. Rawls makes a similar point when he speaks about how each of various religious and moral doctrines overlap to "accept this conception of justice as a reasonable basis for political and social cooperation" (Rawls: 1985: 248). Authoritative for their impartiality and disinterestedness, principles of justice are codified as the rule of law, made the object of public knowledge, and are legitimately enforced by the state. Thus, the rule of law defines a common standard for judgment. Cases are evaluated by following what is specified in a constitutional text (Williams 1995: 82-85). It is this emphasis on settled universal rules for governance that has won this position the name of "procedural liberalism" (Taylor 1991: 68-69).

Now, the elevation of cultural identity over universalist principles risks toppling the rule of law. The loss of publicly known laws could open a floodgate to particular claims. For example, a group of families could seek political recognition by claiming to be culturally different. Or, elites in search of power could mobilize members of a group of villages to claim difference. Without a common standard of judgment, the grounds for assessing such claims would be highly arbitrary. In any event, they would have to be recognized since cultural identity has become the criterion for the distribution of goods and, on Walzer's account, no culture ought to judge the other. The end result would be group proliferation, and political chaos, rather than stability, would prevail in the polity.

Charles Taylor

In his work, Charles Taylor (1994, 1991) argues for constitutional structures that give equal recognition to groups. He begins from the premise that the neutral turf from which universal rights are derived is actually permeated by the cultural values of a dominant group; he therefore views liberal universalism as exclusionary and unjust.

Taylor establishes a direct relationship between cultural membership and human agency. According to him, our identity comes from within us and is shaped by the recognition given to us by others. The denial of recognition—or mis-recognition—can inflict harm and can also constitute a form of oppression as in the case of colonial subjects who internalized a distorted image of themselves. In pre-modern times, Taylor suggests that identity and recognition were not issues because honor was intrinsically linked to social hierarchy (1994: 32). But, in the modern world, social hierarchies have collapsed and in place of hierarchical honor we have a universalism that emphasizes the equal dignity of all persons.

Equal dignity, according to Taylor, has come to mean two different things. On some peoples' understanding, it means that all human beings are worthy of equal respect by virtue of their capacity as rational agents. This perspective has given rise to a "politics of universalism" whose content incorporates the equalization of citizenship rights and entitlements. For others, equal dignity means equal respect by virtue of our capacity to form and define our own identity either as individuals or as cultural groups. This perspective has given birth to a "politics of difference" that demands equal respect for cultures (Taylor 1994: 38-42).

The politics of universalism fights for forms of nondiscrimination that are blind to the ways citizens differ, while the politics of difference redefines nondiscrimination to require that difference be recognized in the treatment of citizens. The first results in the proceduralist model of liberal society defended by Rawls, Ackerman, and Dworkin. The second produces a model of liberal society organized around collective goals. Taylor regards both models as mutually opposed, but he endorses the second, arguing that a society with collective goals can be liberal, "provided it is capable of respecting diversity" and provided it defends the fundamental rights recognized in the liberal tradition (1994: 59).

Taylor illustrates his point using the case of Canada where the province of Quebec is pressing for greater autonomy despite having language rights at the federal level, powerful positions held in the federal government by Quebeckers, and Quebec's de facto special status through its special immigration, income tax and pension systems. He shows that Quebec understands Canada as a pact between two nations—English Canada and French Canada—that embodies the idea that Canada exists to contribute to and guarantee the survival of both nations. For a long time, however, the French Canadian nation has not been given its due recognition as an equal partner. He notes that the recent transformation of the country into a multicultural mosaic has buoyed English-speaking Canada to build political unity around a Charter of Rights and Freedoms that accords some powers to collectives by entrenching linguistic rights and Aboriginal rights.

However, the Charter imposes a procedural model of liberalism by providing a set of individual rights and prohibiting discrimination on irrelevant grounds such as race. According to Taylor, the procedural norms enunciated in the Charter clash with and are perceived to have thwarted Quebeckers' aspiration to seek their common good: the survival and flourishing of *la nation canadienne française*. A proposed constitutional amendment—known as the Meech Lake Accord—sought to entrench a "distinct society" clause in the Charter but was defeated despite the de facto special status enjoyed by the province. Taylor regards the imposition of a procedural model of liberalism, where the state is necessarily uncommitted to a conception of the good, as diametrically opposed to what Quebeckers desire: namely, a liberal society organized around a definition of a good life that does not demean those who do not share in it. He speaks of multiculturalism—found in the ethnocultural rights embedded in the Charter—as a first level diversity that does not come close to what Quebeckers want. This first level diversity is hegemonic because, in substance, people are required to conform to procedural norms. For Quebeckers and Aboriginal peoples, he says, their sense of being rests on the survival of their national communities. There has to be a "a second level or deep diversity in which a plurality of ways of belonging would also be acknowledged and accepted" (1991: 75-76).

Group recognition, then, is not for profitable ends; rather, it has to do with the survival of a national community that is being denigrated, devalued, or threatened with extinction. But Taylor does not show how community goals can be reconciled with individual rights. He reproaches procedural liberalism for discriminating against those who do not belong to the dominant culture, but his arguments for a society organized around collective goals do not yield rules that tell us when to and when not to extend recognition to those who claim it. Nevertheless, his arguments boil down to internal autonomy for territorially concentrated groups and a regime of differentiated citizenship rights. However, the possibility of groups proliferating and undermining the stability of the arrangement still remains and Taylor's work does not address this problem.

Will Kymlicka

Will Kymlicka has tried to revise liberal theory in ways that would reconcile it with group rights. He argues that liberalism has enough theoretical room to incorporate special rights to protect endangered cultural identities, especially minority cultural groups residing within discrete territorial space.[4] Drawing on Immanuel Kant and J. S. Mill, he shows that the defining feature of liberalism lies in the concept of autonomy and the corresponding ability to make and revise personal choices. Drawing also on Ronald Dworkin, he argues that cultural membership provides the basis for individuals to understand, make, and remake meaningful life choices and that membership provides a secure sense of belonging and identity. Cultural membership is a primary good which the individual requires in order to live a good life.

However, Kymlicka sees the political process and the institutions of multicultural states as unintentionally reflecting the culture of the majority group. Worse still, the system of rights and liberties serves to assimilate minorities as they lose control of their land and resources. Kymlicka is then faced with the question of how best to redress "significant inequality . . . given the importance of cultural membership" (1995: 109). His solution is that "group differentiated rights—such as territorial autonomy, veto powers, guaranteed representation in central institutions, land claims and language rights—can help rectify these disadvantages" (1995: 109, chapters 2 and 3, and 139-44; 1989: chapters 7 and 9). He distinguishes between two types of multicultural claims: those made by immigrants and those made by national minorities. He shows that immigrants make claims for inclusion that enable them to participate in the mainstream society such as Sikhs' demand to wear a turban if they join the Royal Canadian Military Police and, in Britain, their successful revision of a law to enable them to carry ceremonial knives in public places. On the other hand, national minorities—people with historic ties to land—make claims to various levels of internal autonomy or self-government. Liberalism has to distinguish between these claims and process them accordingly. While self-government may present the danger of secession, Kymlicka thinks that secession is not an option for national minorities because they are usually not sufficiently self-reliant to form or sustain an independent state. Multination states, according to him, should promote unity not by denying differences but by respecting and nurturing them (1995: 189-91).

The model of society that emerges from Kymlicka's arguments is one that accommodates national minorities through subunits organized around their particular vision of a collective good. Kymlicka maintains that his prescriptions for minority groups should not lead to the violation of individual autonomy if an individual's choices are contrary to or destructive of the culture. But the logical validity of this argument remains in doubt. In chapter 9 of *Liberalism, Community and Culture* (1989), he tries to reconcile the autonomy of members with the community's good. Like Taylor, he does not show how the rights of those members who have different conceptions of the good can be defended.

There are other difficulties with Kymlicka's arguments that are well known and need not be recited here.[5] What needs to be discussed is his assumption about justice and stability in the political community. Like Walzer and Taylor whose arguments presuppose the immutability of groups, Kymlicka assumes that groups are discrete and immutable. Consequently, he thinks if they are accorded special resources or rights to pursue their conception of the good life, a just and stable normative order will obtain. It is understandable why he assumes that groups would not proliferate to take advantage of special rights. His argument presents special rights as creating conditions for equality and discounts the possibility of conceiving of them as benefits. But the reality is that they are not just formal rights. They are also tangible and entail internal self-government such as forming and filling the legislative and executive arms of government as well as requiring political representation at the center. The fact that these special rights are tangible and granted based on the criterion of ethnicity would likely generate new claims to minority status even from within the majority group and automatically create an opening for others to claim minority status in order to receive similar treatment. The general attitude would be: "You've had yours, we need ours because we are also a minority suffering domination." Kymlicka might counter this possibility by pointing to the use of political judgment in determining and rejecting spurious claims to recognition. This solution could be effective if groups are homogeneous, but if some groups consist of subgroups with different dialects and are attached to definite territorial homelands, then the problem remains.

The feasibility of Kymlicka's prescriptions becomes a real issue if a country is made up of one or two major groups and several minority groups. In this scenario, his prescriptions will require disentangling multiple minority groups to accord special recognition in separate subunits. This would trigger a slippery slope that may elevate the concern for stability over that of justice.

In sum, Walzer, Taylor, and Kymlicka make liberal arguments for constitutional arrangements that give recognition to group identities. The problem with their arguments lies in the fact that the structures they defend could give rise to elites' unrestrained use of identity as a means to power. The risk of demand overload in the political system, and of over-politicization of ethnicity, could, in turn, either cause regime breakdown or fuel constant institutional instability.

The problem of stability has been raised by some critics of multiculturalism in the United States who worry that group recognition might lead to state disintegration. Arthur Schlesinger Jr., for example, argues in a polemical work that the United States, like most countries, has been multiethnic from the start. But unlike most multiethnic countries it has cohered, endured, and achieved greatness because "individuals from all nations are melted into a new race of men" (Schlesinger Jr. 1998: 16). Although he thinks the American practice of citizenship lags behind the theory, he sees the latter as modifying the former through the ideal of assimilation without any contradiction. He therefore assails multiculturalism for encouraging "separate racial and ethnic communities" and advancing "the fragmentation of American life" (1998: 136, 151). In another polemic, Alvin Schmidt compares multiculturalists to soldiers seeking to conquer and destroy the American melting pot. Schmidt likens the introduction of bilingual education, and the revision of the curriculum of American colleges to reflect the concerns of diverse racial groups, to a Tower of Babel fostering ethnic separateness, disunity, and conflict (Schmidt 1997: chapter 8). Using Canada as an example, he shows that the foundations of the present secessionist tendency in the country were laid in the eighteenth and nineteenth centuries when the British colonial government rejected a melting pot philosophy by adopting bilingualism (1997: 116-18).

These criticisms emphasizing the danger of "balkanization" are similar to the ones I have made above, but they are also different in the sense that the empirical basis for the concern is less valid in the American context than in the African context. In fact, both Kymlicka and Taylor are conscious of the dangers of group proliferation in North America, for which reason they limit recognition to minority historical communities whose cultural survival is threatened and not to immigrant groups and cultures. Kymlicka (1995: 76) emphasizes that only those minority cultures having claims to definite territory as well as institutions that can provide the structure for freedom can qualify for special rights. Thus, groups covered by this limitation would be few and, perhaps, constitute only a small percentage of the population.[6] This narrowing of the category of cultural groups entitled to special protection rescues the arguments of the normative theorists regarding group claims and renders the instability argument less compelling. These arguments are attractive for my study of the Nigerian case because the concerns that motivate the theorists to argue for special rights for minorities in North America would also support the demands for political recognition of countless groups in Nigeria. However, unlike North America where the demands for recognition and problems of governability and stability may not be at odds, the tension exists in Nigeria and would need to be addressed in order to minimize it.

The Empirical Viewpoint

The empirical literature attempts to understand the actual relations among groups and the formal and informal rules regimes use to respond to demands for political inclusion. On the basis of such empirical observation, general rules are prescribed to reform liberal democracy. The empirical arguments I evaluate here are those of Sir Arthur Lewis, Eric Nordlinger, Arend Lijphart, Donald Horowitz, and Donald Rothchild.

Sir Arthur Lewis

Sir Arthur Lewis, the Nobel Prize-winning economist from St. Lucia, was the first to prescribe definite measures for reforming liberal democracies in West Africa. Between 1953 and 1965 he served as an adviser to various governments in the West African subregion, during which time he observed their democratic breakdowns firsthand. His empirical observations prompted his conclusion that ethnic pluralism was not the cause of democratic failures in the subregion; rather, the political institutions and philosophies inherited from Europe constituted the source.

He regarded Western democracy as giving license to the party that had obtained 51 percent of the electoral votes to exclude minority parties from government. He illustrated this point with the case of French West African countries where the party that won the most votes got all the seats in parliament, thereby absolutely excluding minority parties (Lewis 1965: 71). Lewis regarded the inherited democratic institutions as not democratic enough since they did not give adequate representation to minority parties. He observed that the geographic bases of parties were composed of particular ethnic groups, some rich in natural resources. Parties were therefore supported by or were representative of groups. To exclude several minority parties from government was to exclude the groups behind them from public decisions regarding taxation, employment, public spending, and so on. Lewis considered this exclusion to be a violation of the primary meaning of democracy, understood as the basic opportunity to be represented in decision making, and destructive for any prospects of building nations in which groups could live together in peace. He thought that liberal democracy could be made workable if three measures were adopted to reform it.

First, where a country is large and contains widely differing regions, a federal constitution would be required to enable regions to look after their own affairs and to prevent richer areas from contributing too heavily and subsidizing the rest of the country. Second, institutions guaranteeing all-group representation in decision making would have to be created. In this respect, the electoral system of proportional representation is the best and, within that system, the "single transferable vote" type is superior to the "list type." Third, the central government must be shared. This would require a coalition government in which parties are represented in proportion to their electoral performance but on the condition that they meet a certain percentage threshold, say 20 percent of the total vote (1965: 51-55, 66, 73-74, 79-83). Lewis did not label his prescriptions, but they add up to what Arend Lijphart would later and variously refer to as consociationalism, power-sharing, or consensus democracy.

Eric Nordlinger

In 1972, Eric Nordlinger published a monograph in which he surveyed the strategies used by open regimes in Austria, Belgium, the Netherlands, Switzerland, Malaysia, and Lebanon to bring intense conflict under control during various periods in the twentieth century. By open regimes, he meant the free functioning of interest groups and bargaining, rather than repression, as the principal means of conflict reduction. Drawing on the strategies used by the six countries, Nordlinger proposed six conflict-regulating measures: 1) a "stable governing coalition between . . . the major conflict organizations"; 2) the "principle of proportionality" where offices are distributed according to the relative size of societal "segments"; 3) a mutual veto requiring government decisions to be agreed upon by all "conflict organizations"; and, 4) "depoliticization," meaning that conflicting groups agree not to involve government in policy areas that might touch on segments' values. The two remaining measures are "compromise" or the mutual adjustment of interests, and "concession" by a stronger to a weaker group (Nordlinger 1972: 21-29). This list is similar to, but longer than Lewis's list.

According to Nordlinger, only the leaders of conflict groups are in a position to negotiate the above measures. Followers could accept or reject these measures, but he thought that leaders would be able to induce acceptance of them. Nordlinger excluded federalism from his strategies because he did not regard it as a conflict-regulating measure. From his perspective, drawing internal boundaries around groups could create new minorities with ties to another group from which they have been separated. Worse still, federalism's grant of internal self-government might encourage secession and civil war. For these reasons, Nordlinger (1972: 31-32) regarded federalism as a factor that only intensifies conflict. He also regarded then-conventional strategies, such as the creation of an integrative national identity and spatial isolation of conflict groups, as ineffectual and counterproductive.

While Nordlinger's six practices constitute a great contribution to strategies for conflict regulation, they seem to apply to a broad range of conflict. His use of concepts such as "conflict organizations," "conflict groups," and "segments" suggests that his study covers all forms of conflict, including class. Also, as Milton Esman has rightly argued, the restriction of Nordlinger's study to countries with "open" regimes, and in which two parties are in conflict, severely limits the relevance of his prescriptions to ethnically plural societies.

Arend Lijphart

The term consociation was first used by the German political theorist Johannes Althusius in 1603, but it was the eminently influential Arend Lijphart who engaged in a detailed analysis of the concept in the late 1960s when he undertook a comparative research project on a number of European countries. Lijphart posited four defining features of consociational democracy that overlap with the measures promoted by Lewis and Nordlinger. They are: 1) a grand coalition of leaders from all significant groups; 2) a mutual veto in decision making; 3) proportional distribution of offices and resources; and, 4) segmental autonomy expressed through federal arrangements (Lijphart 1977: 25-44).

Like Nordlinger, Lijphart derived these measures from the conflict-regulating techniques used by the six countries mentioned above. In recent times, Lijphart has prioritized these features by listing the sharing of executive power as the first and group autonomy as the second most important attributes. He refers to these two aspects as the "primary characteristics" of consociational democracy. Proportionality and mutual veto are listed third and fourth, respectively, and are referred to as "secondary characteristics" (1999: 3-4). On some occasions, Lijphart had labeled his prescriptions *power-sharing* because critics found *consociation* to be too much of a tongue twister while, on other occasions, he has switched to the term *consensus democracy* to describe the institutional characteristics of democracies that have governing coalitions (1998: 99-108).

Lijphart's prescriptive arguments have elicited several criticisms to which he has responded (1985: chapter 4). I wish to draw attention to some of the assumptions contained in his arguments. First, there is the assumption that ethnic groups are unitary actors, each having a set of united elites within a single party and who would rationally enter into coalitions with the others. Where internal group fissures and factional elites exist, as is always the case, a grand coalition would be difficult to establish. If formed, new groups would emerge protesting their exclusion from the arrangement, thus making for adversarial politics. Or, conversely, the autonomy and legitimacy of the elites would be undermined by the emergence of rival subgroup elites opposed to compromises. This latter phenomenon is known as "outflanking." Thus, elites of a particular ethnic community engaged in negotiating compromises are sure to be frustrated by rival elites emerging from the flanks to repudiate them on grounds that they do not represent the various subgroups or to denounce them as sell-outs. Lijphart argues that this criticism does not contradict his consociational theory because the theory does not claim that its "solutions will always work" (1985: 100). In the example he gives of Belgium, he shows that very few of the French-speaking minorities belong to the French parties that always participate in cabinet. And, in the case of Lebanon, several Maronite factions compete for the presidency but only one succeeds in winning it at any given time. So, in his view, groups are not assumed to be unitary and consociation does work even when factions are present.

Second, implicit in consociational strategies is the assumption that countries have few determinate groups that would easily be recognized in political subunits. This might not be true for countries with multiple ethnic groups where it would be difficult to recognize all of the groups at one time. If the subunits were created, the indeterminacy of some groups would result in the continuous emergence of new ones, producing an unstable political order. The limits of consociational measures were probably recognized by Lijphart when he noted that: "Actually, a society with relatively few segments, say three or four, constitutes a more favorable base for consociational democracy than one with a relatively many segments, and a much more favorable base than a fractionalized society" (1977: 5-7).

Donald Horowitz

Donald Horowitz, certainly one of the best known experts on ethnicity, takes a different approach to conflict reduction from the three empirical writers discussed above. He believes consociational measures are incapable of achieving the purpose for which they are prescribed. According to Horowitz, consociational prescriptions require political elites to share sovereign power with rival elites and this remains no more than a wish as those in control of power have no incentive to give a large fraction of it away. Even when leaders are inclined to compromise, extremists emerge from the flanks to undermine the process. More importantly he believes that the idea of a grand coalition does not acknowledge opposition as a vital and permanent feature of democracy. He thinks a grand coalition can hardly be negotiated because intraethnic competition makes it difficult to have a single party representing a particular group (Horowitz 1998: 5-7).

Moreover, Horowitz states that the electoral system of proportional representation (PR) does not produce conciliatory outcomes. Instead, where parties are ethnically based (as they often are), PR assures minority support for the minority and perfects majoritarian democracy that is compatible with political domination of some groups by others (1998: 6-8). For these reasons, he favors electoral systems that induce politicians and their followers to cooperate across group lines. The recommended electoral systems are the *alternative vote* system, which is best for a country where groups are mixed, and the *plurality plus distribution* system for countries in which groups have discrete territorial space.

The alternative vote method works by requiring voters to rank candidates in order of preference, and the candidate that receives an absolute majority is elected. If this does not occur, then the candidate with the least number of votes is eliminated and the second preferences in that candidate's ballots are counted among the remaining candidates, the one who receives a majority is elected. This type of scheme is supposed to encourage ethnic parties to reach across fault lines and pool votes in order to win, thereby producing moderate politicians, a leader who is pan-ethnic, and an inclusive political center.

The plurality plus distribution method requires a federal arrangement that fragments groups in states or provinces. Politicians are then expected to win majority votes in several states (at least 75 percent of the states) across the country. This electoral system is expected to reward politicians and parties with power if they incorporate the interests of voters from groups other than their own (1998: 9-18; 1991: chapter 5).[7] Horowitz thinks that the plurality plus distribution scheme possesses enough internal incentives to harness selfish calculations for interethnic cooperation. Therefore, there will be no need for minority rights as they would be superfluous.

Horowitz's prescriptions sound very attractive. The electoral mechanisms he prescribes seem to provide very good measures for inducing intergroup cooperation. In the late 1960s, Giovanni Sartori (1968: 261-98) saw electoral systems as the most effective tools for manipulating politics. Here, Horowitz presents them as the best levers for engineering harmony in multiethnic societies. Brilliant as they are, the systems are in essence majoritarian, first-past-the-post forms that may not generate an inclusive government or create peace and stability. The alternative vote system, for example, was entrenched in the Fijian constitution of 1997 (under Horowitz's influence) and was tested in the 1999 elections. This system led to the emergence of Mahendra Chaudhry, an ethnic Indian, as Fiji's prime minister—the first in the history of the country. The election of an Indian-Fijian generated resentment among some native Fijians and precipitated the subsequent coup by George Speight in May 2000. Similarly, Nigeria's adoption and use of the plurality plus distribution method in 1979 and again in 1999 has not made for an inclusive center or a peaceful coexistence. Ethnic conflict remains as it was in the 1960s. As David Welsh (1994: 226) has observed, Horowitz's scheme does not generate the kind of benign results he anticipates. Lijphart (1991: 91) in fact regards it as another form of a winner-take-all system.

Donald Rothchild

Donald Rothchild has made pragmatic and detailed prescriptive arguments for conflict-reduction in his book *Managing Ethnic Conflict in Africa* (1997). He presents ethnic groups as collectivities having consciousness of a common identity that may be socially constructed. They also have a corporate interest that leaders maximize by pressing demands on the state. Ethnic demands and state responses, according to him, are not fixed processes in which one side makes all the demands and the other side responds; rather, the policy choices of regimes could determine how group leaders frame their demands, and the nature and intensity of demands could determine the readiness of regimes to cooperate. It is a two-way process that is mutually reinforcing but, because regimes wield power and formulate policies for society in general, they have a significant impact on conflict management. Regime types are therefore critical in the determination of responses, and Rothchild presents three types: hegemonic, elite power-sharing, and polyarchic regimes.

Hegemonic regimes are authoritarian. They regard group leaders' claims as threatening to the political system, and they respond by imposing their preferences which range from subjection to ethnic cleansing. Elite power-sharing regimes are combinations of authoritarian and consociational democratic regimes. They come into being when elites in hegemonic regimes co-opt and strike bargains with powerful ethnoregional entrepreneurs in order to contain pressures from civil society. They treat demands in pragmatic terms, and their informal rules for coalitions and balanced representation in national institutions constitute responses to ethno-regional pressures. Polyarchic regimes are democratic and are characterized by extensive societal participation in governance and "low state control over the political process" (1997: 11). [8] By virtue of institutionalized electoral competition and accountability, they tend to have regularized public access to decisionmakers. [9]

According to Rothchild, both elite power-sharing and polyarchical regimes are more inclined to promote unity and stability by accepting the legitimacy of autonomous groups in civil society and by accommodating them politically. However, Rothchild qualifies this statement by noting the tendency for some authoritarian regimes to incorporate various ethnic elites into high governmental positions. This is when domination becomes terribly expensive either in monetary terms or in terms of intense conflict (for example, Nigeria in the early 1970s, Guinea under Sékou Touré, Kenya before the 1992 election, and Zaire under Mobutu Sese Seko) (1997: 43; 1993: 237-38). In any event, the readiness to respond, according to him, carries the positive effects of encouraging ethnic elites to frame demands in moderate terms and facilitating negotiation by creating opportunities for them to withdraw from inflexible positions without the loss of face. Polyarchic regimes, and to a lesser extent elite power systems, and to a still lesser extent hegemonic regimes, have the effect of providing incentives for cooperative relations.

Rothchild identifies four key incentives that encourage ethnic groups to engage in moderate and cooperative behavior: 1) intergroup equality as a primary rule in the allocation of offices and resources; 2) an electoral system that ensures the inclusion of various ethnic elites in decision making; 3) the representation of various ethnic and other interests in the ruling coalition (as in the Transitional Constitution of South Africa or the "federal character" principle in Nigeria); and, 4) a form of federalism designed to separate geographically concentrated groups into distinct subunits thereby dispersing power among a great array of actors. These measures can be seen as a combination of the prescriptions of Horowitz and the consociational writers.

In a tempered but optimistic tone, Rothchild cautions that his prescriptions might not necessarily produce regime stability because of elites' political ambitions and inclination toward corrupt behavior, demand overload, and resource scarcity. Nonetheless, he hopes that if political routines for inclusion are established and repeated over time, elites will become accustomed to norms of reciprocity and accommodative behavior. In his words, "the initial act of forging a constitution is not an end in itself but of a larger process of confidence building that leads to repeated interactions" (1997: 49). Compared to the writers discussed above, then, Rothchild is more circumspect. He recognizes that elite competition and corruption could undermine concrete attempts to achieve conciliatory politics, and he deals with this problem by insisting on perseverance.

The Theoretical and the Empirical

The philosophical and empirical arguments presented thus far shed some light on the principles that support the political recognition of ethnic groups and how this recognition should be carried out. The theoretical arguments show that liberalism is not opposed to group claims, and that an individual's freedom and self-respect actually rest on the identity that constitutes him or herself. It is on this point that Will Kymlicka and Charles Taylor separately argue for various forms of recognition for national minority groups who are dominated by majorities. Walzer is a bit different, for he rests his arguments on the existence of differential values that govern various spheres of life. In a multicultural country where groups have different values, each group would require a form of arrangement that protects its particular system of right and wrong, according to Walzer. What unites all three theorists, however, is the basic claim that group recognition is required for justice.

The empirical arguments, on the other hand, illustrate the fact that liberal democracy is "two-faced" in multiethnic societies: it is universal in its claims to equal respect and opportunities for persons but exclusionary in practice. The institutional reforms prescribed by the empirical thinkers aim to harmonize the practice of democracy with its theoretical claims. The principle of equality is therefore foundational to their prescriptions and the project of designing arrangements that would reduce conflict is one that rests on the demands of justice. In this respect, unity exists between the empirical and philosophical thinkers. From this standpoint, one could hypothesize the probable requirements of justice by unpacking the measures presented by both sets of thinkers.

The first requirement is a federalist constitution that provides some room for groups to govern themselves. Both sets of thinkers present a federalist constitution as a mechanism that institutionalizes pluralism by dividing political power between defined jurisdictions. Walzer prescribes it because its institutional checks enable minority groups to control their local political space. Kymlicka also finds it attractive because the provision for internal autonomy compensates minority groups for the unequal circumstances that put their members at a systemic disadvantage in the cultural marketplace (Kymlicka 1995: 113). The empirical thinkers, and the consociationalists in particular, take a similar position when they present federalism as a neutralizer of majority rule by permitting minority groups to rule themselves in issues exclusive to themselves and to be effectively represented in the central cabinet. Nordlinger, however, departs somewhat in his view that federalism should be excluded as an inclusive measure because it creates new sets of oppressed minorities requiring protection and also opens the door to political disunity. Horowitz, on the other hand, adopts a somewhat utilitarian view by presenting the political subunits as part of a structural package for inducing cross-ethnic alliances. With these federal subunits in place, ethnic elites can be induced through electoral mechanisms to reach out to various groups, take moderate positions on issues, and build a network of alliances with other group elites. The outcome would be a government built on complex cross-ethnic alliances. For this reason, Horowitz (1991: 99-100, 216-17) argues that boundaries need not enclose homogeneous groups since the incentive to accommodate would neutralize the control of government by majority groups.

The criterion for boundary drawing remains contentious. For Kymlicka (1995: 182-83), the boundaries of federal units could be blind to groups, but where there are national minority groups with ties to a definite territory, they should have their own units in order to exercise self-government rights that will shield them from the decisions of the majority.[10] Similarly, the arguments of Walzer and Taylor require that minority groups have their own federal units. The same goes for the consociationalists, while Rothchild is implicit about the homogeneity of units when he speaks about the devolution of power to territorially discrete groups. Nordlinger remains the only exception and here we see a remarkable departure, as he regards federal units as having the potential for creating new sets of oppressed minorities and inducing secession.

At one extreme, then, are those who regard federalism as a way of providing space for minorities to govern themselves and suggest that the criterion for boundary drawing should be ethnicity. Ivo Duchacek (1970: 293) calls this form of federalism, in which the constituent units coincide with ethnicity, *polyethnic federalism.* At the other extreme is Nordlinger, who thinks federalism is a recipe for the political breakup of a country, which is why he discounts it as a viable measure for accommodating groups. Horowitz is in the middle since he views polyethnic federalism as a conciliatory institution for neutralizing census-type politics; that is, it negates political processes whose outcomes are determined by pre-formed majorities and minorities.[11] We can see from these arguments that homogeneous units are neither the only nor the best way of mitigating zero-sum politics.

A second requirement is what Kymlicka refers to as minority group rights, including rights to internal self-government, special representation in central governmental bodies, and veto rights on issues that affect minority groups. Because he presents these rights as the minimum conditions required for members of minority groups to secure their culture and exercise autonomy as majority group members do, one could say that his project is all about security and freedom for minority group members. For Taylor (1994: 40n.16), national minority groups are equal political partners with the majority group and should be recognized as such. This entails different political units for them and a different set of citizenship rights that would guarantee group survival and equal membership in the state. Walzer does not say much about minority rights. Instead, he argues for the adjustment of principles that will fit circumstances on the ground and rejects arrangements that are determined in an a priori way (Walzer 1992: 167-70). Nonetheless, he argues that groups separated in federal units would need to be protected by constitutional checks and by the possible use of international sanctions if the majority violated minority rights.

The equivalent of all of these requirements for the empirical thinkers would be the consociational prescriptions whose main elements are:

- a grand coalition government;
- group autonomy through federal arrangements;
- an electoral system that ensures for proportional representation of groups; and,
- a mutual veto over government policy.

These measures do not apply exclusively to minority groups, but they are designed to enable them to participate equally in the making and execution of national decisions. They also do not constitute special rights for any particular national population; rather, they are inclusive measures to share the rewards and burdens of citizenship equally across groups. They therefore have the same underlying purpose as minority group rights.

Horowitz is strongly opposed to group rights and consociational measures such as proportional representation electoral system (PR) and veto powers. He regards special rights and veto powers as agreements based on constraints that the majority will readily violate if their interest so demands. He cites the case of Zimbabwe in which special representation rights for Whites in the legislature, provided for in the country's 1980 constitution, were expeditiously abolished in 1987 by the government of Robert Mugabe. Horowitz regards group rights as "providing illusory security, easily pierced." This weakness informs his scathing remark about international lawyers who "with little knowledge of ethnic relations . . . have been creating a whole new set of understandings about group rights" (Horowitz 1991: 136). His problem with PR is well known: it gives minority seats to minority groups and perpetually locks them out of the executive—the real seat of government. In place of these measures, he prescribes electoral systems that induce politics of moderation and alliance. He prefers the plurality *plus* distribution or the alternative vote method that is majoritarian. Either of them works by requiring parties to reach across to groups to obtain electoral support. Thus, politicians have to reach out and accommodate not because they are benevolent but because their self-interest requires them to do so. As bridges are built, so group interests become intertwined over time to produce conciliatory institutions (Horowitz 1991: 150 and chapter 5; 1998: 10). This incentive approach, according to Horowitz, must apply to all elected officials in order for it to be effective.

The third requirement is a readiness to bargain, without which the institutional measures discussed above will not be easily accepted by all parties. Readiness to negotiate is implicit in Nordlinger's concession and compromise principles. It is explicit in Rothchild's discussion of how conflicting parties can come to the negotiation table. And, according to Walzer's argument, unity within a federal framework rests on agreement between groups. Walzer's cultural relativism locates authoritative moral values within groups, which makes political union conditional upon the convergence of values. Without common values, the federal sphere of unity would be left without a moral foundation, in which case it would have to be derived from an agreement based on the immediate interests of each party. On this point, Kymlicka is not so different. He explicitly states that if minority and majority groups do not share basic principles in common and one group cannot be persuaded to adopt the other's principles, then they would have to accommodate each other on the basis of a modus vivendi (Kymlicka 1995: 168).

Horowitz rejects constitutional arrangements grounded solely on self-interest because they are transient. Citing constitutional arrangements like the Lebanese National Pact of 1943, the Malaysian Constitutional Bargain of 1956, the Indian Punjabi Regional Formula of 1956, and the B-C Pact in Sri Lanka, Horowitz (1991: 149; 1985: 581) says that:

> they are all "bargains", "pacts", "contracts." They are treaties between semi-sovereign peoples based on reciprocity, and they have all the characteristic problems all contracts have: the preferences of the parties change over time; conditions also change; the returns to the parties from the deal are uneven. . . . If incommensurables are traded—X in return for Y—and if X proves more valuable over the long term, the party that received Y may nurse a grievance. Unless provision is made for amendment contract alone is not a lasting basis for accommodation. Inter-group contracts tend to be their own undoing.

To achieve unity, he presents a design for living together premised on incentives for accommodative behavior without sacrificing immediate group interest. This design, drawn from the constitutional arrangements of Nigeria and Sri Lanka in the mid-1970s, is the agreement on electoral systems that induce politicians to a politics of moderation and conciliation discussed earlier (1991: 184-86).

Horowitz regards an agreement on electoral systems, which place a high premium on accommodative behavior, as similar to the Rawlsian "original position." The original position is a device that can function as a model for parties who want to enter into social cooperation. It is characterized by a "veil of ignorance" in which parties are ignorant of both their class positions and social circumstances and do not know who will be placed at the top or lower scale of the social ladder in the society they are trying to form. So situated, they will agree on principles that are fair and just for all involved (Rawls 1993: 304-5; 1971: 136-42).

Horowitz follows Rawls in his suggestion that an electoral law requiring multiethnic support in the election of officials will induce parties to reach across the table to build alliances to pool votes because the cost of not reaching out is electoral defeat. Horowitz (1991: 151) regards this arrangement as "not merely reflect[ing] transient interests but [are] a design for living together premised on incentives for accommodative behavior transcending group interests at the moment of enactment." However, he acknowledges that in Nigeria and Sri Lanka, upon which he draws his models, the electoral arrangements were not enough to produce enduring unity. They failed—especially in Nigeria—because of politicians' ambitions and the intense competition between them. Despite the failure of the Nigerian experiment to prevent conflicts, Horowitz thinks that it will produce the much-desired stability if this type of electoral system is continually refined. Rothchild (1997: 49) takes a similar position when he argues that the incentives for cooperative behavior, if built upon and nurtured, would predispose politicians to learn and become acculturated to the politics of reciprocity.

These three measures for political inclusion and conflict reduction help to set the framework for discussing the principles required for resolving competing claims to recognition. They set the framework, not in the sense of providing models for dealing with problems on the ground but in providing a departure point for discussing ethnically based claims in Nigeria and the types of responses to them. However, a modern sociological view of ethnicity as a modern invention and the neo-Marxist view of ethnicity as a vehicle for class privilege might challenge their potential relevance. It will therefore be necessary to consider these objections briefly.

Possible Objections to the Prescriptive Arguments

The social science community has increasingly accepted the contemporary idea that ethnicity is a social construction. Its origin is closely associated with Benedict Anderson's idea of the nation as an "imagined community," which he first developed in 1983. According to Anderson (1990: chapter 7), the emergence of the printed word in Europe made it possible for anonymous individuals who inhabited the same homogeneous space to imagine sovereign communities with which they could identify.

The arguments of Anderson have inspired a growing body of literature seeking to elaborate the idea of identities as social inventions. There are two versions of this idea. One holds that modern tribal groups expanded from kinship corporations that had been formed as security networks during the age of slavery and state-sponsored terrorism. Another version presents contemporary ethnic groups as coterminous with the development of colonialism. It argues that the determinations of colonial administrators defined what they thought were traditional African communities and, despite attempts by local chiefs and literate members to stake their own claims in the new colonial political economy, resulted in the invention or the making of custom and tradition (Charnock 1985; Ranger 1983 and 1993). The immediate utility of the contemporary understanding is that it compels recognition of groups as dynamic, fluid, and prone to unending differentiation.

The idea that identity groups are colonial creations is implicit in colonial history, which proves that ethnic differences were *fostered* by administrative policies adopted by the colonizers. After the partitions and wars of conquest, the small crop of administrators recruited from the metropolis could not make colonial government acceptable. A solution was found in the policy of governing through local intermediaries, but this required the drawing of internal administrative boundaries around people who were "believed" to have similar cultures and whose affinities were based on co-residence on a contiguous stretch of land. Such political compartmentalization enhanced ethnic consciousness among those so enclosed without necessarily transforming members into fully integrated unitary groups. Other policies discouraged horizontal interactions (government policies against national political parties in Nigeria and the Gold Coast in the early 1920s and in Kenya in the 1950s, for example), widened cleavages, and enhanced internal awareness. Thus, a sense of solidarity was fostered and groups were created that probably had little in common initially. Within groups, then, were constellations of subgroups. The consequence was the emergence, at the group level, of elites who organized and negotiated common positions within the group in order to compete at the wider state level. Sometimes intense rivalry or competition among subgroups could generate conflict or prompt leaders of one subgroup to ally with leaders of a rival ethnic group as when the Yoruba-speaking people of Ibadan joined forces with Igbo elites against other Yoruba in Nigeria during the 1950s and 1960s.

The positive aspect of the discourse of social constructionism is that it draws attention to the salience of ethnicity during colonial rule. It helps us understand that governance within the colonial framework was not possible without its use and that ethnicity, as a principle in governance, became entrenched during colonialism. In fact, ethnicity as a principle of governance emerged concurrently with the modern state system in Africa and both have marched hand-in-hand ever since. This discourse also helps us to see that some groups did not emerge as coherent unitary actors and are therefore prone to splintering or redefinition. So, the salience of ethnicity in governance is contradicted by the definitional fluidity of ethnic groups and their members.

The above contradiction could be reinforced by class interests. In Africa, as in most postcolonial societies, the dominant class does not have its material base in industrial economic production, and this is largely a legacy of the colonial political economy. During colonialism, the state transformed the economy by monetizing the economy, introducing cash crops and enforcing their production, opening mines and recruiting labor to work in them, and adopting policies that favored the operation of monopoly firms. Like the true entrepreneur that it was, the state was directly immersed in the economy and, together with monopoly firms, dominated it.[12] This domination blocked the path of the colonized seeking upward social mobility, especially for the trading class whose transition into industrial entrepreneurship was constrained by monopoly firms, and the educated class who were denied positions in the colonial system (Ake 1996: chapter 1; Ekekwe 1986: chapter 7; Joseph 1987: 55; Sklar 1965: 203-5). Thus, the indigenous educated and trading classes regarded political power as the chief medium for economic betterment and one that had to be captured from foreign rulers by all means necessary.

The importance of political power for a fragile class of elites determined to improve their material well-being may intersect with group fluidity thereby opening a large gap in the prescriptive arguments discussed above. But one has to be cautious here. Groups aspire to have their elites in power regardless of the elites' agendas—this is in fact how they are able to advance their interests in the larger society. Elites might initially be motivated by personal gain but they become overwhelmed by group pressures as they go deeper into the business of politics. The interests of elites and their groups converge to some extent and power is used for both personal and group gains. Today in Africa, for example, a public official might occupy an office but the powers of that office are actually exercised by his or her kin group. A known official would head a ministry or an organization, but chiefs in the official's ethnic community would determine its actual operation. Fred Riggs refers to this phenomenon as the "sala bureaucracy" and Claude Ake sees it as contradictory to the form and content of the state. According to Ake (1996:14):

> the person who holds office may not exercise its powers, the person who exercises the powers of a given office may not be its holder, informal relations often override formal relations, the formal hierarchies of bureaucratic structure and power are

not always the clue to decision making power. Positions that seem to be held by persons are in fact held by kinship groups; at one point the public is privatized and at another the private is "publicized."

Elites are not so single-minded in their quest for and use of power as some would like to think. This is not intended to suggest that corruption is a necessary part of political ethics; rather, the presupposition here is that public institutions ought to be functionally responsive to diverse groups within the polity.

Summary

On the whole, this chapter raises two key questions for my work.[13] One is normative and the other is empirical and they are interrelated. The normative question is: Under what circumstances should recognition of in-group interests be displaced by the concern for political and social stability? The empirical question is: Under what circumstances are constitutional structures expressive of ethnic difference more likely to increase political and social stability than constitutional structures that deny difference? The answer to the normative question is that where recognition has the prospect of generating intense social and political conflict, the concern for stability must supplant the moral claims of groups. The answer to the empirical question is that where the expression of difference promises greater stability than its denial, justice would require some form of recognition. In this case, no grave tension exists between the moral claims of groups and the concern for stability or, for that matter, between justice and stability. What is needed is a form of recognition that will not prejudice stability.

Notes

1. In his discussion of the Spanish intervention in Mexico to stop the cultural practice of human sacrifice by the Aztecs, Walzer (1987: 45) makes the point that the local understanding of sacrifice was not commonly shared by all Aztecs, that it was contrary to the conscience of some, and that traces of human rights could be seen within the local culture. In his words:

> they [the Spaniards] had, to be sure, a Catholic understanding of natural law, but they may still have been right to oppose human sacrifice, for example, not because it

was contrary to orthodox Christian doctrine, but because it was 'against nature.' The Aztecs probably did not understand, and yet the argument did not have the same degree of externality as did arguments about the blood and body of Christ, Christian communion, and so on (and it may well have been connected with the feelings, if not the convictions, of the sacrificial victims).

Conclusively, the moral minimum is basic human rights that are a part of, and not a substitute for, local meanings that are thickly constituted.

2. Walzer's theory is opposed to the domination of one cultural lifeworld by another. To judge people solely by an external moral standard amounts to imperialism, rather like an imperial judge in a colony who uses principles derived from the mother country to bring the natives to justice (Walzer 1987: 38).

3. For a critical discussion of Walzer's arguments see Carens (1995: 137-59); Kymlicka (1995: chapter 11); Miller and Walzer (1995).

4. The two texts I rely on here are *Liberalism, Community and Culture* and *Multicultural Citizenship*

5. For criticisms of Kymlicka see Kukathas (1992: 105-39) and Williams (1994: 35-65).

6. In one of his later works, Nathan Glazer (1997: 14-15) endorses the limits set by multiculturalists for equal recognition. However, he argues that "even after one has confined the beneficiaries of multiculturalism to the oppressed . . . one discovers that, even among victims of the oppressed, not all groups are entitled to . . . attention."

7. These prescriptions are revisions of the ones Horowitz made in *Ethnic Groups in Conflict* (1985). There, he recommended the following: the creation of lower level political units with a view to proliferating points of power and taking the heat off the center; an electoral system that places high premium on multiethnic support in the election of state officials; the adoption of policies that encourage alignments based on interest other than ethnicity; and, affirmative action programs to reduce disparities between groups (1985: 597-99).

8. It is not clear if Rothchild draws on Robert Dahl's definition of polyarchy. If he does, the problem of permanent minorities would arise, but the two paragraphs that follow address the issue somewhat.

9. In an earlier article written with Victor Olorunsola, Rothchild presented two models of state responses to ethnic claims: the hegemonic and the bargaining models (Rothchild and Olorunsola 1993: 233-49). Certainly the views expressed in Rothchild's 1997 book are revised versions.

10. Kymlicka's position is even more explicit in statements like this:

So what is a fair way to recognize languages, draw boundaries, and distribute powers? And the answer I think is that we should aim at ensuring that all national groups should have the opportunity to maintain themselves as a distinct culture, if they so choose. This ensures that the good of cultural membership is equally protected for the members of all national groups. In a democratic society, the majority nation will always have its language and societal culture supported, and will have the legislative power to protect its interest in culture affecting decisions. The question is whether fairness requires that the same benefits and opportunities should be given to national minorities. The answer, I think, is clearly yes. (Kymlicka 1995: 113).

11. In census politics, minorities know their fate in advance of elections (Horowitz 1991).

12. An example of state domination was the setting up of marketing boards to purchase export crops from peasant farmers at stabilized prices for sale in Europe. The difference between the market-determined international price and the stabilized domestic price produced huge profits for government (Sklar 1965).

13. I owe the framing of the content in this section to Melissa Williams.

Chapter Two

Ethnicity in Nigeria

Do ethnic identities matter in Nigerian politics? This chapter will attempt to answer the question by exploring some of the most enduring aspects of colonialism, such as the use of ethnic identities in political governance and the emergence of a nationalist movement fractured along ethnic lines. This discussion will create a base upon which I will respond to sociological claims about identities as socially constructed and therefore too illusory to be accommodated in the design of political institutions.

Ethnicity and Colonialism

Ethnic Composition

Geographically, Nigeria is divided into the north, east, and west by the Niger and Benue Rivers that merge into one at a point below the center and then flow southward into the Atlantic Ocean. The North occupies the entire northern portion of the country and therefore is geographically referred to as the "North," while the East and West occupy the southern portion of the country and are collectively referred to as the "South."

Each of the three geographic regions—the North, East, and West— houses a numerically dominant ethnic group as well as a significant number of minority groups. The North consists of majority Islamic Hausa-Fulani and several minority groups most of whom are non-Islamic and live largely in the northeastern, southeastern, and southwestern parts of the region. The Hausa-Fulani were formerly two different groups but are currently considered one due to the near fusion caused by inter-marriages, political conquest of the region by the Fulani during the nineteenth century, the common use of the Hausa language, and the common Islamic religion.

The eastern geographic region houses the majority Igbo and several other minority groups, including the Efik and Ijaw, who both exercised power over their neighbors before the advent of colonial rule. The West

41

consists of the numerically dominant Yoruba and several minority groups, including the Edo, whose monarchs were the suzerains of Lagos and other Yoruba towns and were also recorded as having exchanged diplomatic missions with Portugal during the sixteenth century.

Exact figures on the total number of groups in Nigeria do not exist but they are conservatively put at around 350. Most, especially the larger groups, are not entirely homogeneous since they are internally divided by linguistic and communal cleavages.[1] However, collective group loyalty often exists vis-à-vis other groups when it comes to crucial political, social, and economic issues (Glickman 1995: 314). Of the over 350 groups, none is large enough to claim a majority: the Hausa-Fulani comprise no more than 30 percent, the Igbo about 17 percent, and the Yoruba 20 percent. The remaining 33 percent is shared unequally among a variety of minority groups, ranging from the relatively large Islamic Kanuri in the extreme northeast, who constitute 4 percent, to the very small Ogoni in the East, who have 0.04 percent (Nigeria 1979: 173-74; Sklar 1999: 8; Udogu 1990: 174). It must be emphasized that all of these figures are only approximations and both individual membership and group boundaries are sometimes contested.

Internal Political Boundaries and Ethnic Groups

As a political entity, Nigeria owes its emergence to British traders who occupied the coastal regions in the 1860s and 1870s where exports in slaves had just been supplanted by the palm oil business. Trade in industrial raw materials triggered the occupation of the entire South with the active assistance of Catholic and Protestant missionaries who taught Western moral virtues to the indigenous people. In contrast, anxiety prompted the British to occupy the North as, at that time, a greater part of the region was under the political rule of Islamic crusaders and was economically and culturally oriented toward Arab civilization. British traders raced to establish their presence in the region with the principal objective of overtaking the French, who were closing in during the general "scramble for Africa." Because of this situation, the United African Company, a British trading firm, obtained a royal charter in 1886 and set up an army, declared sovereign power over the huge region, and began routine political administration. The Colonial Office took over in 1899 thereby beginning formal colonial rule.

An issue that has always received comments in Nigerian political history is the decision to govern northern and southern Nigeria as two separate territories. The possessions began as separate colonies: the Protectorate of Northern Nigeria and the Protectorate of Southern Nigeria. To shift the cost of administering the North from British taxpayers to the economically solvent South, the British appointed Lord Lugard as governor general in 1912 with the express purpose of uniting the two territories.[2] Muslim rulers were opposed to the proposed amalgamation, preferring the North to remain separate from the South. They were persuaded to accept amalgamation by Lugard's promise to: 1) keep separate northern administration from that of the South; 2) ensure the continuous functioning of the emirate system of rule in the North;[3] and, 3) shield the North from proselytizing by Christian missionaries.[4] The British kept their promise and, after amalgamation was effected in 1914, the two units continued to be administered as two different territories. Each had its own civil service and lingua franca—English in the South and Hausa in the North.

The real challenge to the British was making foreign rule legitimate and acceptable. First, the North-South political boundary that roughly coincided with, but in some places went beyond, the territorial limits of the Sokoto caliphate was retained[5] on grounds that the two units had been under different sets of laws and government and that it would be politically safe to have two political subunits. However, the boundaries were adjusted to unify groups that were divided when the Northern Protectorate was declared in 1900.[6] Margery Perham, Lugard's official biographer, later declared that this move was "a frank recognition of differences, some inherent, some due to divergences in our administration, between the two parts" (Perham 1962: 64).

Second, the country was divided into twenty-one provinces—twelve in the North and nine in the South—and British residents were appointed to administer them. The boundaries were drawn for administrative convenience, but attempts were made to avoid splitting homogeneous groups into different provinces. According to Lugard (1968: 243), the boundaries "follow[ed] tribal limits as far as possible," though there were cases where homogeneous groups were split between separate provinces. The provinces were further divided into districts, and district officers were posted to each.

With the above divisions in place, an indirect rule policy was adopted, which involved governing the people through their customary political institutions. Chiefs who had been subdued were reinstated and given executive authority to govern, not as independent rulers but as salaried agents accountable to district officers. In areas where the institution of chieftaincy was weak, it was shored up, and, where it was non-existent, individuals were randomly chosen and given warrants or certificates to preside over native courts that were created for purposes of dispensing justice.[7]

The policy of indirect rule was based both on the mistaken assumption that chieftaincy institutions existed in all parts of the country and on the mistaken premise that traditional political institutions in all parts of the country were centralized and hierarchical like the emirate system. In northern Nigeria, the policy ignored the fact that the region contained sizable non-Islamic areas whose inhabitants had resisted Sokoto jihadists and had maintained their independence until the British conquest. In some of these areas where the institution of chieftaincy existed, people were divided into districts that were merged with emirates to form provinces and then unknowingly delivered to the political rule of emirs, something the emirs could not achieve by holy war. In other areas where the family and lineage system prevailed and boundaries were open, the people were federated at successively higher stages to form districts. Chiefs, some of whom were Hausa agents of the British, were then appointed as integrative symbols (Meek 1931: 2b).

In southern Nigeria, the policy of indirect rule was generalized without accounting for differences in political organization. For example, chiefs of Yoruba towns who were traditionally accountable to, and could be removed by a council of, titled chiefs, acquired executive authority that became anathema to the people. In the Niger Delta and in the East, there were no chiefs; instead, decisions emerged by consensus at the village assembly. In these areas, the British federated clans and appointed warrant chiefs to preside over courts whose jurisdictional areas had no affinity with ethnic groups.

Between 1919 and 1920 tensions and restiveness among some non-Islamic groups in the North emerged over the introduction of indirect rule. In addition, between 1921 and 1930 uprisings occurred in the South.[8] In reaction, the secretary of state for the colonies criticized the colonial government in Nigeria for not having adequate knowledge of social groups and their institutions. These developments prompted the recruitment of anthropologists, including the well-known Dr. Charles Kingsley Meek, to carry out surveys of ethnic groups.[9] These surveys provided the relevant information required to adjust provincial and divisional boundaries and to remove non-Islamic peoples of the North from emirate rule. Information gathered from the ethnic surveys was also used to reform indirect rule to suit the cultural peculiarities of different groups. It must be stated that the resulting recognition of group difference in the readjustment of administrative boundaries happened completely within the limits of the knowledge provided by colonial anthropologists, most of whom were amateurs.

James Coleman has discussed the internal ethnic integration that resulted from indirect rule (Coleman 1958: 52-53). According to him, the policy encouraged both the fragmentation and integration of groups who had either failed to achieve unity or were disintegrating on account of wars. He cites the example of the Yoruba who were locked in self-consuming wars before the British conquest.[10] Yoruba subgroups, according to Coleman, were split into a number of administrative units and chiefs were appointed to each. This facilitated the fragmentation that had been taking place since 1780 but, at the same time, a pan-Yoruba consciousness was fostered by bringing first-class chiefs (that is, the hereditary monarchs of precolonial kingdoms) together to participate in annual conferences.

Ethnic integration, Coleman writes, was also enhanced among those who were organized in lineage and clans and whose boundaries were undefined. Federation into compact units of native administration resulted in some sense of a defined boundary and also fostered a common consciousness. He concludes that the policy of indirect rule centered public life in traditional communities and complicated the task of welding diverse groups into one Nigeria.

The Role of Ethnicity in Colonial Constitutional Policy

Constitutional policy in colonial Nigeria developed with some regard to ethnic differences. Apart from the North and the South having separate administrations after their political formation, northern emirs were encouraged to have conferences (known as the Conference of Emirs) which first met in 1912 and more frequently thereafter in the early 1930s. Chiefs of the non-Muslim northern areas were also encouraged to, and some did, attend these gatherings. In the gatherings, emirs and chiefs met to discuss common issues concerning administration, advise their British superiors, and vent their resentment against rules affecting their religions and customs.[11] These annual gatherings helped create an integrated northern political elite having common political commitments despite their religious and ethnic differences.

Unlike the North, the South with its laissez-faire mentality did not have an annual gathering of its chiefs. Instead, a Nigeria-wide advisory body called the Nigerian Council was established in 1913.[12] This was abolished in 1922 and replaced with a legislative council that theoretically held jurisdiction over the South, but actually legislated for the North too.[13] This council had four African-elected members but the North was not represented. This gave the South an edge over the North in terms of constitutional development.

Separate constitutional development was maintained until the 1930s when colonial governors who were posted to Nigeria decided to treat the country unreservedly as one polity. They felt that it would be wise to take a holistic approach to Nigerian politics because at this stage of the country's evolution, no part of it, for geographic and economic reasons, would "likely be a separate, self contained political and economic unit" in the future (Kirk-Greene 1965: 195-96). To ensure the development of the country as one polity, Bernard Bourdillon, the colonial governor who assumed office in 1935, produced a memorandum in which he developed the idea of regional legislative councils for the northern, eastern, and western parts of the country. Membership in each jurisdictional area would be drawn from the emirs and chiefs of the Native Authorities (for the North) or the chiefs of the Native Councils (for the east and the west). In addition, there would be a central legislative council whose membership would be drawn from the three regional legislative councils.

Both emirs and British political administrators in the North opposed Bourdillon's memorandum, which they felt amounted to a unitary state with three regions. British administrators in the North tried to kill it by emphasizing that regionalism would encourage separatist tendencies. Bourdillon accepted the view that regional councils might foster separatist tendencies, but he argued that such tendencies could be averted if the councils' deliberations were properly guided. According to him: "A certain measure of regional thinking is not only inevitable but even desirable" (Kirk-Greene 1965: 4).

Preliminary steps to implement the proposal for regional legislative councils were taken in 1939 when the country was divided into three administrative units by splitting the South into the east and the west. With this division, the North comprised more than twice the combined area of both east and west and more than equaled them in size of population. Sir Arthur Richards, the successor to Bourdillon, introduced a unitary constitution in 1946 recognizing the three units as political regions, and he also instituted the legislative bodies that were proposed by Bourdillon. The creation of the three political regions was ultimately defended in terms of recognizing the fundamental cultural differences between the

Hausa-Fulani, the Igbo, and the Yoruba. In the words of Richards: "Socially and politically, there are deep differences between the major tribal groups. They do not speak the same language and they have highly divergent customs and ways of life and they represent different stages of culture" (Akinyemi 1979: 97).

Differential Responses to British Rule

In its origin, the colonial state in Nigeria was a trading company. Its economic role, however, did not fundamentally change throughout the colonial period. The state continued to play a leading role in the socio-economic transformation of the country by setting up centers of research into the cultivation of export crops, constructing roads, railways, and ports for crop export, and introducing money and compelling people to sell their labor power.

These steps taken by the state accelerated the emergence of modern social differentiation—wage workers, transporters, and middlemen supplying export companies with commodity crops. The changes were most remarkable in the South, which offered no resistance to laissez-faire economics. The North, with the exception of its non-Islamic areas, remained impervious to change because of the policy of preserving the region from Western influences. Workers and traders employed in the natural resources sectors such as mining, as well as other modern sectors that opened in the region, were drawn primarily from temporary residents who came from the South, and most of those from Igbo land. In accordance with the policy of preventing Western influence in the region, resident southerners were made to live in special quarters (*Sabongaris)* outside the city gates where they remained segregated from Muslims.

In contrast to the North, the reception of a laissez-faire mentality in the South led to the proliferation of schools and the emergence of the Western-educated. Many were Yoruba, mainly because intensive missionary contact first began in the west, and also because liberated slaves returned to Yorubaland with a Western outlook and soon constituted an emergent middle class in the Lagos-Egba axis. By the 1930s, the Igbo had equaled them and a rivalry ensued between the two over educational progress. The Yoruba lost ground, and a latent hostility developed.[14]

While there was competition between the Igbo and Yoruba over educational progress, the North remained the same. The policy of preserving the region in its Islamic character inhibited the emergence of a Western-educated class. For example, the region did not have a university gradu-

ate until 1951. This had two consequences. One was that lower administrative positions in the region were filled by southerners, especially Igbos
and Yorubas. The other was that the educated men and women who led
the opposition to continued British rule were mostly southerners. They
were all self-employed journalists because colonial policy forbade the
employment of Africans at the higher levels of political administration.
They asked to be accommodated at the higher levels of the colonial political superstructure, especially in the legislative branch, but their demands were rebuffed. In response, they asked the British to surrender
power, and then they used the press to mobilize the masses to make colonial rule unworkable. The North remained aloof from these developments especially since there were few educated people in the region who
spoke the language of popular politics.

When the Richards's Constitution was introduced in 1946, the educated class in the South vehemently denounced it as "one rotten fruit of
imperialism" (Coleman 1958: 280). More specifically, the constitution
was rejected because of the innovations it contained. It was criticized on
the basis that membership in the regional and central legislatures was
undemocratic.[15] The tri-regional structure—the most notable innovation—was also criticized. Some argued that the three regions were created without regard to ethnological factors. In a letter to the colonial
governor, Obafemi Awolowo, an educated Yoruba elite, argued for the
creation of thirty or forty states for the diverse groups in the country so
that each could maintain its own cultural tradition and develop at its own
pace (Awolowo 1960: 173-75; 1947: chapter 5). Nnamdi Azikiwe, an
educated elite of Igbo origin, argued for a quasi-federation of eight units,
some of which would coincide with ethnic groupings. These criticisms
were joined by protests from some minority groups over inadequate representation in the central legislative council that was introduced through
the constitution.

In response to these criticisms and also to preempt revolutionary uprisings that were already sweeping across colonial territories, the Labour
government in Britain took steps to entrench a liberal democracy. Sir
John Macpherson, a newly appointed governor under the Labour government, began the process of decolonization by inviting Nigerians to
hold a conference during which they would decide on the political arrangements they most desired. A number of questions were formulated to
serve as a guide. Two of these questions were:

1. Do we wish to see a fully centralized system with all legislative and executive power concentrated at the center, or do we wish to develop a federal system under which each region would exercise a measure of internal autonomy?
2. If we favor a federal system, should we retain the existing regions with some modification of existing regional boundaries, or should we form regions on some new basis such as the many linguistic groups that exist in Nigeria? (Awolowo 1960: 173)

Conferences were held from which recommendations were made to the colonial government. The recommendations resulted in the Macpherson Constitution introduced in 1951.

In sum, the British colonial power respected ethnic differences and reinforced them in some respects, but the colonial rulers also ignored them and undermined them in others. For the most part, the reinforcing and reconstructing tendencies were strongest.

Should Ethnic Difference Have Political Salience?

From the historical narrative related above, it can be queried whether one should regard ethnic identities in Nigeria as genuine or mere fictions. If they exist (as illusions or as realities), do they matter? I will attempt to answer these questions below.

The Question of the Reality of Ethnic Identities

Recent sociological and historical studies have heightened awareness about identities as nongivens (Young 1994). These studies have revealed that ethnic groups are created and constantly reformed, a view that supplants the earlier, and now thought false, conception that identities are primordial. Studies focusing on Africa illustrate the socially constructed nature of identities during both the precolonial past and the colonial era, although those constructed during the latter period were fundamentally different. There are various versions of this argument, which I synthesize below.

The sociological and historical arguments regard ethnicity in Africa as the outcome of a continuous but conflict-ridden interaction between political and cultural forces (Berman 1998: 310). Peter Ekeh (1990: 673-83) argues that in the precolonial world, identities arose as defensive reactions to the violence and disruptions of slavery and to the whims of despotic rulers. People formed networks of alliances and defenses on the basis of unilinear descent as a kind of safety net from this violence. Thus, the taxonomy of groups was ordered along kinship ties. Crawford Young's work (1995: 232) shows that the vocabularies of classification were fluid, but recognition was given according to ancestral descent, ritual practice, political groupings, and language. In effect, the ethnic groups of the twentieth century such as the Yoruba had no definite institutional existence, but there were several culturally similar kinship groups who would later be "imagined" as one community called "Yoruba."

The sociological and historical studies show that the emergence of the colonial political order also marked a change in identity. Identity became a product of the hegemony of the colonial state and the responses of the local population. According to this argument, the colonial state constructed its hegemony by mapping the local population into "tribal" units for political rule. Creating the tribe was essentially an expansion and classification of kinship groups who were believed to be linguistically related or who lived in the same discrete territorial space and were believed to look similar in physical features. According to Bruce Berman (1998: 316-18), the incorporation of the ethnically mapped-out administrative units involved alliances with local "Big Men" (chiefs and headmen) who could link the state with, and enforce state mandates in, the networks of society. As the principal agents of the state and the linkage with the people below, the Big Men became the most powerful figures in the local society networks. They determined and enforced codes of behavior with the backing of state power, for which reason they emerged as the embodiment of custom. Terence Ranger (1993: 84-87) explains how both the local chiefs (who could no longer carve out conquest polities for themselves) and the young literate elites gave moral content to what the state had invented. They gave moral content to the empty boxes of "tribes" by imagining a common history, common language, and common descent; in other words, by inventing custom.

But Mahmood Mamdani (1996: 118) argues that substantive custom was neither a "fabrication, arbitrarily manufactured without regard to any historical backdrop" nor "a kind a historical residue carried by groups resistant to modernization." On the contrary, as the change from an old regime of force and a commodity market dependent on slaves (that is, the legal slavery of the precolonial era) to colonial markets in a wage-labor economy fueled by export crops occurred, people with and without interest in the old order sought to make claims in the new one. Every claim presented itself as customary and no neutral arbiter existed to determine their validity. In this context characterized by contradictory claims, those without access to colonial authority could not press their views. The chiefs, who were the makers and executors of the law, were also the prosecutors, adjudicators, and jailers enabling them to decisively shape the substance of custom.

The dialectic unfolded as Africans selected ethnic identity as a weapon for autonomous action to be used either as security against state oppression or for welfare purposes (Ekeh 1990: 685). Young (1995: 234) argues that uneven penetration and transformation of the economy by the forces of modernity reinforced the dialectic. People living in areas where capitalism had greater presence gloated in their "advanced" stereotype and mobilized to seize what opportunities could be had in the colonial economy. On the other hand, people in areas where capitalism had relatively little impact were pejoratively stereotyped as "backward" and they mobilized to reverse this negative status. Thus, ethnicity was a form colonial rule took that also made for a form of politics among migrants in urban areas who organized ethnic associations as a protective shield in their new habitats and as a link with their rural homes (Mamdani 1996: 192-93).

I accept the argument that contemporary ethnic groups are socially constructed, not dating beyond the colonial period. What I now want to address is whether invented groups qualify for recognition according to the arguments advanced by Walzer, Taylor, and Kymlicka.

Should Socially Constructed Groups Have Political Recognition?

Should ethnic identities matter in politics if they are socially constructed? Some invention theorists hold that identity groups should not be given political relevance because they lack cohesion and are highly fluid and dynamic (Bayart 1993: 49). There are some who argue that groups should be given political recognition because they were constructed for the purposes of governance and have served as the medium for national citizenship (Ekeh 1990: 683-85). These arguments will not be evaluated here; instead, I will attempt to situate the political importance of groups within the arguments of the normative writers.

One point that emerges from the social constructionist theory is that ethnicity emerged from two interconnected processes. One, and a primary one, was the colonial rulers' (mis)perception of traditional African community and the attempt to give political salience to what they perceived to be African custom (Chabal 1994: 60). The other was the attempt by the colonized to find cultural and political defenses against the disruptions of modernity (Berman 1998: 340). Both processes produced networks of kinship alliances, loyalty, patronage, clientelism, and reciprocal obligations, all of which could be regarded as the real civil society overlapping both the public and the private spheres in Africa.[16] These networks, which constructionist theory regards as constituting African ethnicity, produced what Patrick Chabal (1994: 204) calls the "communal individual," meaning the interest of the individual is tied to that of her family and her village. What follows from these views is that the importance of ethnicity has to be understood in terms of the conception of citizenship held in postcolonial Africa.

In Africa, two levels of citizenship exist: the national and the ethnic (or subnational). Ethnic citizenship comprises a community that has the same language, culture, territory, and is believed to have a common origin and history. The ethnic individual participates in an immediate community that is exclusive and functions beside the wider national inclusive level (Ake 1987; Ekeh 1990; 1975; Ndegwa 1996). Membership is conferred by birth into a family known to share in the community's culture and history, and requires active participation in the defense of the community and in the preservation of its members. In return, individuals gain rights and security—physical, economic, and emotional. Thus, in the individualist and cold surroundings of the civic state, ethnic membership provides a starting point for dealing with the problems of collective existence. As a member, the individual receives respect as a person. Ethnic groups are, therefore, invisible governments that cater to the interests of their members.

This form of citizenship does not reject citizenship at the national level. In dominant liberalism, the view is that the nation-state is the arena of citizen formation. Everyone is expected to identify with the state because "personhood" and primary political identity are drawn from it (Carens 1996-97: 113; Janoski 1998: 11). In this view, to be stateless is to be a person without a political identity or legal recognition, which is the most dreadful political fate that can befall anyone (Shklar 1991: 4).

In sub-Saharan Africa, as elsewhere, universal citizenship does not work because the identity of the individual is primarily tied to that of her ethnic community. The individual is born into the community and is socialized within it. Her membership in it and exclusion from others last forever. As Kearney (1967: 6) has noted, "virtually every permanent member of a plural society identifies himself and is identified by others as belonging to one and only one community." To give up this identification for a commitment to the larger civic order is to be made "rootless." In the words of Clifford Geertz (1963: 108-9), it would mean a loss of identity "through absorption into a culturally differentiated mass or, what is even worse, through domination by some other rival ethnic, racial, or linguistic community that is able to imbue that order with the temper of its own personality." For this reason, most people would prefer to die than be absorbed by another group. Contrary to the views of dominant liberalism, then, it is from ethnic communities that primary identity is drawn. Rupert Emerson refers to them as terminal communities, meaning they are "the largest community that, when the chips are down, effectively commands men's loyalty (Rabushka and Shepsle 1972: 63). Here, identity formation combines with the discourse of rights and obligations to make this level the most meaningful sphere of citizenship for the individual.

Ivo Duchacek acknowledged the importance of the subnational sphere to the individual when he discussed the individual and collective aspects of rights and freedom. According to Duchacek, identification with and valuation of one's own group is universal, and human beings consider the satisfaction of group interests as a precondition for the fulfillment of their individual goals and liberties. He notes that the right to promote the interest of a subnational group belongs to the standard list of fundamental individual rights (Duchacek 1970: 97-98).

The above argument about subnational citizenship helps to shed some light on the close linkages between African political incumbents and their communities. The interests of officials and those of their communities are fused together, making it hard to differentiate one from the other. As in most relationships of reciprocal obligation, both are obliged to service each other's interests. For example, an African American appointed to the Supreme Court in the United States might have no obligations to her community. She might even use her position to strike down affirmative action programs without any qualms; in Africa, not so. Upon appointment to an office, a Supreme Court justice would have to attract social amenities, infrastructure, and educational and developmental projects to her community. Nonperformance provokes a range of informal sanctions, including forced disengagement from the community's activities, rather like the way clients would abandon a patron or partner if the latter fails in her obligations to them. Chabal (1994: 205) highlights the point about the individual's interest being fused with that of her community when he notes:

> No one disputes the connection between individual and communal self-interest. Houphouët-Biogny's fantastic extravagance in the development of his "village," Yamassoukro, is objectionable not because the President is lavishing millions on his "village" but because he is lavishing too many millions. The same applies to Mobutu's "village," which includes a private runway to accommodate the Concorde hired for his foreign travels.

Some, like Berman, regard the connection between the individual's interest and that of her community as the root of political clientelism, prebendalism, and corruption in Africa. Others, like Mamdani, see the communal connection positively because it contains the possibility of democracy and stability. Here, I endorse Mamdani's views by arguing that subnational citizenship provides the medium for rights at the national sphere. Thus, subnational citizenship has to be foundational for a meaningful national citizenship and will entail recognizing subnational communities as political communities with a right to autonomy in Nigeria. Where there are several groups, two levels of political community must obtain: the subnational or ethnic level with which its members have a stronger identification and which provides a foundation for the exercise of rights and duties in the overarching national level.

Notes

1. The Yoruba are highly fractured while the Igbo are equally divided within. It is generally acknowledged that the Yoruba were already in the process of fission and that the process was stalled by the nineteenth-century British conquest, which put an end to civil wars among various factions.

2. Southern Nigeria had been financially self-sufficient right from the start of British occupation in the late nineteenth century, to the point of financing the costs of its own occupation. Its prosperity hinged on its economic relations with European merchants, more specifically on the export of agricultural produce and from custom duties on imports. On the other hand, the cost of administering the North was offset by grants from the South and by money voted by the British Parliament. The official mind-set was that the economic burden on British taxpayers could be removed if the two territories had a common source of revenue (Lugard, 1968: 6; Orr 1969: 77–78; Perham 1962: 61–62).

3. *Emirate* refers to the provinces that were formerly territories conquered by nineteenth-century Fulani crusaders in the holy war (jihad) and subsequently divided and administered. The ruler of each emirate or province was known as emir, meaning a representative of the *caliph*. Caliph was the title adopted by the leader of the holy war and meant "Successor of the Prophet Mohammed." The title was corrupted by European explorers who instead used the term *sultan*. The sultan or caliph was therefore the supreme leader of the Sokoto caliphate and all emirs owed him political and spiritual allegiance for which they paid him periodic visits to his headquarters in Sokoto.

4. This is not to suggest that the British did not subdue the emirs militarily. They were, except that after the British military conquest the emirs promised obedience on the condition that their religion would not be desecrated. For example, when Aliyu Babba, emir of Kano, was subdued in 1913, Wambai Abbas, who was appointed to replace him, promised "in the name of Allah and Mohammed his Prophet" that he would "serve well his Majesty King Edward VII and his representative the High Commissioner . . . provided they are not contrary to my religion" (Ibrahim 1991: 128).

5. *Caliphate*, meaning Muslim territory, designated the territorial area conquered by the jihadists whose headquarters were established in Sokoto. The caliphate was held together by the values of Islam that were embodied in Islamic laws written by the caliph. It was also held together by the appointment of the caliph's followers as emirs and by the practice of having an annual gathering of all emirs known as the Manya Sarakuna, or meeting of big chiefs, in Sokoto. In addition, the machinery of caliphate government placed a premium on the obedience and subordination of emirs to the "Leader of the Faithful" while making room for the emirs to enjoy independence in their own emirates.

6. The adjustment did not unify the Yoruba of Ilorin and Kabba in the North with their kin groups in the South. The Yoruba of Ilorin and Kabba were conquered by the Sokoto jihadists during the nineteenth century and became an emirate within the caliphate. Like groups in other parts of the caliphate, they became Islamic and looked toward Sokoto as their spiritual capital. There was therefore some attention to cultural history in the decision to retain the boundary separating the two units (Lugard 1968: 63).

7. Indirect rule was an adaptation of the emirate administrative system characterized by patron-client relationships, the existence of Islamic courts presided over by Muslim judges who administered Islamic laws purged of their canonical aspects, and a fiscal system where taxes were collected directly from the people. The British liked the emirate system because it made for a neat and ordered administration, shielded the British from the masses, and made colonial rule appear as self-rule (Lugard 1968: 182, 296-300, and 312).

8. According to Charles K. Meek (1937: ix):

> the manner in which the riots had been conducted had
> made it evident that there were other predisposing causes

of discontent, and chief among these was the widespread hatred of the system of Native Administration conducted through the artificial channel of Native Courts. . . . Had there been a genuine system of Native Administrations based on the institutions of the people and giving full freedom of expression, the riots, if they had occurred at all, could not have attained the dimensions they did.

9. As a matter of policy, all divisional officers were required to carry out an anthropological survey of the groups in their units. They were therefore required to study and acquire knowledge of the indigenous languages within their political subunits and it was these political officers who doubled as amateur anthropologists.

10. History records that the Yoruba country was beset by warfare during the whole of the nineteenth century. Chiefs were desperate for peace but could not bring themselves to negotiate it because of mutual hostility and distrust. According to Ayandele (1979: 19-20 and 30-33), a Yoruba historian, a universal appeal had to be made by Yoruba rulers to the British, who had annexed Lagos, to put an end to their wars. This was how the British entered Yoruba hinterland and made several treaties, agreements, and proclamations of protection.

11. Perham points out that the emirs' conference established some bond among the rulers who, in 1900, could not even unite against an infidel (Perham 1962: 126-31).

12. Its members were appointed chiefs but no northern emir sat on it; instead, it was British residents who attended on their behalf.

13. A legislative council had existed in Lagos since 1861 when it was conquered and made a crown colony by the British. As part of the British policy for all crown colonies, Lagos was given a legislative council when it was annexed. However, the council acted as an advisory body to the governor in making laws for the colony. In 1922 it was expanded to serve both the colony and the South

14. This rivalry gave birth to community self-help projects. Not to be outdone in the race for Western education, communities began to establish their own secondary schools and, in turn, successful graduates built schools for their communities.

15. The bodies were composed of British officials and chiefs. Members of the regional legislative councils were chiefs appointed from Native Authorities/Native Councils, and members of the central legislative council were chiefs drawn from the three regional legislatures.

16. According to Hegel, civil society is that sphere of life between the private sphere of the family and the public sphere of the state. It is where individuals seek their interests and satisfy their needs by addressing those of others in exchange relationships. Thus, civil society is where we have specialized occupations that give birth to associations and unions that seek the welfare of members. In these associations and unions, members receive respect as persons. For Hegel,

this is a higher level of civil society and is a threshold to the state—the sphere of complete universality. Whereas Hegel regards civil society as an intermediate sphere between the private and the state, Louis Althusser regards it as overlapping with the state. Consequently, he presents civil society as different from but also part of the state. My idea of civil society in Africa is a combination of Hegel's and Althusser's conceptions. Hegel's notion of civil society presupposes a developed capitalist society in which commodity relations are generalized and entrenched. Instead of market-derived autonomous associations, I present ethnic and cultural associations as occupying the sphere between the private realm and the state. They are different from, but also overlap with, the state.

Chapter Three

The First Political Strategy for Coping with Difference

Over the years, Nigeria has adopted no fewer than four different approaches to cope with ethnic difference and minimize conflict. The first approach, beginning from the immediate post-World War II period to 1958, involved recognition of the three most numerous groups in the political arrangements of the country, but denied equal recognition to several minority groups who had asked for similar treatment. A product of hard constitutional negotiations, this approach was adopted in response to competing claims by group elites during several constitutional conferences that were held in 1949-50, 1953-54, 1957, and 1958. This chapter will attempt to evaluate the claims and the important agreements that were negotiated during these conferences. It will begin by spelling out the claims and later proceed with a normative evaluation of them.

Competing Group Claims during the Preindependence Constitutional Conferences

Preindependence claims by group elites were not made at random. Rather, they were channeled through constitutional conferences that required representation of the three regions and political parties operating in them. While representation was not on the basis of ethnicity per se, the process was dominated by elites from the majority group in each region.[1] Thus, claims advanced in the constitutional conferences were mostly those that reflected the views of the majority ethnic groups, and they were presented in a manner that Donald Rothchild (1997: 31) would regard as non-negotiable. That is, representatives took positions on which they were not ready to compromise, and they did not wish to make concessions that would be interpreted by their opponents as signs of weakness. Claims and counter-claims, mostly on issues concerning political arrangements, political representation, and revenue allocation were therefore repeated in one conference after another and with greater intensity in every succeeding one. In this respect, Eric Nordlinger's (1972: 40) argument that conflict group leaders alone are capable of negotiating agreements on behalf of those they represent could be regarded as valid, for representatives to the conferences were not prepared to engage in conciliatory behavior on the issues mentioned above. It was the British mediators who used their position as sovereign rulers to influence the leaders of the three large ethnic groups to adopt a modus vivendi entailing the retention of the tri-regional structure and sharing of national assets.

When the elites of some of the ethnic minority groups realized the oppressive content within the constitutional agreements, they formed opposition parties or allied with the ruling parties in other regions. This gave them access to the Resumed Lagos Conference of 1954 and the 1957 conference for the review of the Lyttelton Constitution in which they voiced demands for political separation. In response, the Willink Commission was struck and was mandated to examine these fears and look for ways to allay them. In what follows, I lay out the competing claims voiced during this period and I begin with those pertaining to the political system.

The Political System

The type of political system adopted during the decolonization period was particularly important because it would structure power relations and determine who would become the politically dominant ethnoregional group. The issue of power was important not only because it was a means to an end but also because group honor had become a big issue in the 1940s. During this time, local newspapers either highlighted stories about Igbo accomplishments in education or about some other ethnic groups producing yet "another" medical or law graduate from Cambridge or Oxford with first-class honors.[2] Such irritating measures of group worth, which was also a subtle way of deprecating other groups, instilled sensitivity regarding the form of political arrangement and who would be at the top. It was in this context that the leaders of the Western and Northern Regions espoused forms of arrangement that respected difference.

In the General Conference of 1950, the Western Region's representatives advanced claims for a retention of the tri-regional structure within a federal framework, but with adjusted boundaries to acknowledge ethnicity. They used the ethnic principle to ask for a redrawing of the Northern boundary of the West in order to enclose the Yoruba-speaking people of Ilorin and Kabba Provinces of the North, and of the southern boundary to enclose Lagos and its colony. They combined this request with demands for an indirect system of election so that Igbos would be locked out of the region's political positions.[3] The quest for territorial expansion, which was also a quest for national political power, was justified on grounds that people in the affected areas had been clamoring for reunion with their kin-groups who had been separated by colonial administrative boundaries. On the other hand, demands for indirect election were defended on the ground that over 90 percent of people in the region were illiterate. The idea behind the illiteracy justification was that people had no knowledge of national political issues, could not make informed leadership choices, and did not even know how to cast a ballot.

At the London Conference of 1953, the Action Group (AG), which was the dominant party of Yoruba elite and also the governing party in the West from 1951 onward, argued for the recognition of the fundamentally federal character of Nigeria. This federal character emerged out of the presence of territorially contiguous ethnic groups having different political and social institutions, different educational and general development, and yet desiring to unite. The AG identified ten main ethnic groups in the country—five in the North, two in the west, and three in the east—and called for the grouping of each into a state (Nigeria 1953: 6-13). Meeting this demand would have made the Western Region, minus its minorities, one of the largest units in terms of size and population.

The Eastern Region, like the west, argued for a political federation of three regions during the 1950 General Conference, but objected to arguments both for the redrawing of internal boundaries to reflect ethnicity and for the indirect electoral system. By the commencement of the 1953 conference, the National Council of Nigeria and the Cameroons (NCNC), the key party for Igbo elites, had backed away from the federalist position to argue for a unitary system (Coleman 1958: 324-25). The leadership argued that a political federation would undermine unity in the country, while a unitary constitution with a strong center would create political cohesion. They referred to the regional structure as the "Pakistanization" of Nigeria—a reference to the separation of Pakistan from India. Their position, according to Udo Udoma, was informed by the dominant influence of the Ibo State Union in the party after 1950, which required that the latter respond to the needs of migrant Igbos for equal political rights.[4]

Like the easterners, northern leaders endorsed a federal system during the General Conference of 1950. Suspicions about the relative educational advancement of the two southern regions translating into political dominance influenced them to opt for retention of the three regions so that each could advance at its own pace toward self-government. They opposed any boundary adjustment that would transfer their territory to the west, arguing that the area conquered by the Sokoto jihadists in the 19th nineteenth extended far into the east and west, but had already been reduced at the time when the British imposed regional boundaries. Furthermore, they argued, at the northern fringes of their region were groups that were split by the international boundary drawn by the French and British. A revision of boundaries to unite groups would therefore inaugurate a slippery slope. If the Yoruba of Ilorin and Kabba Provinces had genuine grievances, which northerners believed was not really the case, there could be better ways to address them. However, if the West insisted on its position, then the affected people should migrate while the territory remained intact (Nigeria 1950: 109-19, 130 and 150).

The northern position changed in 1953 when the AG sponsored a motion in the central legislature calling for Nigerian self-government in 1956. The Northern People's Congress (NPC), the dominant party of northern elites, but especially Hausa-Fulani, went to the London Conference with an Eight Point Plan demanding a political confederation in which the three regions would enjoy complete autonomy. This idea hinged on the assumption that if the southern regions were bent on political domination by virtue of their relative educational advancement, then each region should go its own way.

The competing claims elaborated above were clearly not reconcilable and, unless each of the three parties was prepared to make some concessions, a compromise would remain elusive. The British colonial office, whose officials presided over the constitutional conferences, had decided after the 1953 self-government motion crisis that a loose federal association of the three regions was the best way to keep Nigeria together. It was this objective that the colonial office had in mind when the London Conference was convened and, in fact, the colonial secretary had announced the policy in the House of Commons in May 1953. Oliver Lyttelton (Chandos 1962: 409) (later known as Lord Viscount Chandos), the colonial governor during the period, made this point when he wrote that:

> the only cement which kept the rickety structure of Nigeria together was the British. . . What was the present Conference

for? It had been convened by us to keep the diverse elements in Nigeria together: left to themselves they would clearly fall apart in a few months. . . . It was clear that Nigeria, if it was to be a nation, must be a federation, with as few subjects reserved for the Central Government as would preserve national unity. (Chandos 1962: 409)

Perhaps the commitment of the British to forge an agreement that would keep the country together influenced the AG, the NCNC, and the NPC to compromise. For example, the AG dropped its demand for a reconstruction of internal boundaries along ethnic lines while the NCNC shifted from its unitary position to accept a federation of three regions (Nigeria 1953: 172; Udoma 1994: 147-48). In turn, the NPC backed away from its confederation demand to settle for a loose federation in which the center retained an enumerated and limited list of powers while the three regions controlled an unspecified list of subjects (known as a residual list of powers). This compromise agreement technically accorded semisovereign status to the regions and, together with a promise in 1956 from the British government that any region desiring self-government could have it, subsequently fueled political demands by minority elites for recognition in separate states.

Political Representation

In a Westminster-style parliamentary system, the party with the majority of seats in parliament forms the executive cabinet. Under this system, elections acquire greater importance because they produce both the lawmakers and rulers. Elections, then, have higher stakes attached to them in multiethnic societies because dominant parties acquire the identity of the majority groups and are able to control the majority of the votes within their ethnic area. Elections are no more than what Horowitz has referred to as "census elections," meaning their outcomes are determined in advance by ethnic numbers. The criteria used for political representation in the legislature could, therefore, determine in advance the party that would form the executive cabinet or the ethno-regional group that would produce the chief political ruler. For this reason, the basis of political representation becomes a big issue—a situation that has actually been proved true in Nigeria.

Territorially the Northern Region more than doubled the East and West combined, and also had a population larger than the other two regions combined. To avoid northern political dominance, eastern and western representatives took a common position in the General Conference of 1950 by demanding equal regional representation. They grounded their claim on arguments about the constituent regions of a federation being equals and about the legislature being a body that deals with issues of common interest to all the units. However, they softened their claim to recognize the population of the North and asked, in return, for an acceptance of the membership ratio of 30:22:22 for the North, East, and West respectively (Nigeria 1950).

Northern representatives, on the other hand, demanded acceptance of the population principle in representation and considered any figure not commensurate with the numerical size of the region to be arbitrary. Democracy, according to them, meant government by the people and if the people were to be properly represented, it would be on the basis of numerical size. They initially demanded that 59 percent of the legislative seats reflect the real weight of their region, but compromised by reducing the figure to 50 percent in response to the voiced fear that the southern regions would unite together to dominate if equal regional representation was conceded (Nigeria 1950).

Whereas in 1950, deadlock emerged on the issue of political representation and it was left for the legislative council to impose its own ratio, in 1953 compromise was achieved regarding fifty-fifty representation between the North and the South. The 1953 compromise represents one of the mutual concessions made to avert the political break-up of the country.[5] The 1957 conference for the review of the practical operation of the 1953 agreements resulted in the reconfiguration of the country into 312 equal constituencies, each consisting of 100,000 inhabitants. This gave 174 seats (about 55 percent of the total) to the North, thus paving the way for the NPC-controlled central government during independence. However, an upper chamber chosen on the basis of regional equality was established to temper the effects of majority power.

Revenue Allocation

The importance of revenue need not be stated. Revenue is income, it is money, call it wealth. Governments need money to discharge their functions, and the viability of political units is very much determined by the wealth that they generate and control. Like political representation in the legislature, the sharing of national revenue became an important and fiercely contested issue.

Recall that until 1946 the North was governed as a separate territory and had no representation in the legislative council that had been operating in Lagos since 1913. Its representatives to the 1950 General Conference claimed that people in the region were not aware of revenue allocation to the regions until 1946 when they achieved representation in the legislative council instituted by Arthur Richards. It was not until 1946, then that they first became aware the government had been distributing national revenue on the basis of the national interest. Instead, they argued for the use of the population principle in the distribution of wealth. Consequently, an expert body, called the Sydney Phillipson Commission, produced an allocation formula based on derivation, meaning each region received revenues in proportion to its contribution to the central fund. The commission produced figures that indicated the North contributed 42 percent to central revenues, the East 31 percent, and the West 27 percent. Still, Northern leaders considered the derivation principle to be unsatisfactory because the share accorded to each region, when divided by its population, gave the East the highest revenue per capita, followed by the West, while the North had the least. Moreover, they argued that taxation per head was inversely related because the North had the highest, followed by the West, while the East had the lowest. In effect, they argued that they had not been receiving their fair share in revenue allocation. What should have gone to their region was being used to develop the southern regions. For the North, then, the principle for allocating revenue had to be population (Nigeria 1950: 64-66, 132-33).

Eastern and western representatives collectively objected to the population principle. According to them, regional revenues in recent years had been derived from four different sources, namely: taxation, revenue generated exclusively by the regions, block grants, and grants from a ten-year development fund. Northern representative had limited their argument to only the first two. With respect to the two remaining sources, the North had always received the highest, followed by the East, and the West had received the least. The real problem for the North, they argued, was not the lack of funds but the ardent desire of its rulers to close the region to Western influences. They pointed out that money allocated to the region to build schools and train doctors and engineers had instead been left in the bank at the behest of regional leaders to generate interest money for the region.

In theory and practice, representatives negotiating a social contract are expected to make mutual concessions in order to reach common ground. This did not describe regional representatives during the 1950

General Conference. Indeed, it was the colonial governor who appointed a commission, chaired solely by British economist Professor Louis Hicks, to devise the criteria for revenue allocation. Hicks produced a system that based revenue sharing on the principles of derivation, need, and national interest. The principle of derivation has been explained above and need not be repeated here. The need principle entailed allocating money to a region in accordance with its needs and without regard to the revenue that region generates. The principle of national interest meant that the cost of certain public services, such as education and police, should, in the interest of the nation, be borne by the central government.

The Hicks Commission's formula was abandoned in 1953 when a loose federation of three regions was adopted. Instead, another commission, the Louis Chick Commission, was appointed to produce a formula that would be compatible with the increased responsibilities of the regions. The Chick Commission devised an allocation system in which 40 percent of total revenues went to the center and the remaining revenues were shared among the regions according to the derivation principle, including mineral royalties from the North. Commodity Marketing Boards, established for the purchase and sale of the country's export crops, were regionalized and their liquid assets shared on the basis of derivation. Although some aspects of the allocation system were criticized by the AG during the Resumed Lagos Conference of 1954 that met to examine the Chick Commission's recommendations, the adoption of the allocation system dispensed with the principles of need and national interest that were featured in the 1951 constitution.[6] Thus, the derivation-based formula completed the near liquidation of the center and returned the country back to the colonial policy of separate development. Richard Sklar (1971: 46) has referred to the compromise agreement as the "principle of regional security," meaning "the full regionalization of all political organizations capped by an agreement . . . to respect the political status quo and share the fruits thereof on an equitable basis." In this agreement, the East was the loser because unitarianism lost out and the region had to make do with whatever revenue it could generate from its apparently not well-endowed territory. All of this occurred before the discovery of oil resources in the East.

Minorities' Claims to Separation

Minorities' claims for recognition in new states were driven by what Richard Sklar has referred to as the "big tribe chauvinism within the major political parties" and by fears arising from the 1953-54 agreements that guaranteed regional power and security for the three largest groups. It is worth noting that some minority groups were not relatively backward in terms of education and social provision. For example, non-Muslim minorities in the North were more exposed to Western education through the missionary schools, had more trained personnel in the region's civil service, and were dominant in the army compared to the Hausa-Fulani. The NPC's adoption of an Eight-Point Plan in 1953, a plan that amounted to northern secession, drove some of them, especially the Tiv, to express their separate identity by demanding a separate state.

Similarly, in the Eastern Region the NCNC was assembled and led by elites of the minority Ibibio and Efik ethnic groups. The first NCNC government in the region was led by Professor Eyo Ita, an urbane, polished, articulate, principled, and American-trained teacher of the minority Efik group. When Ita was expelled from his post to make way for an Igbo leader, minorities in the region followed him en masse to form an opposition party—the National Independence Party (NIP)—to spearhead their demands for separation. In light of this historical experience, Ted Gurr's relevant thesis regarding autonomy claims needs some modification. Gurr's thesis states that ecological stress and cultural difference, not political or economic discrimination, drive group demands for autonomy.[7] In contrast, the preindependence Nigerian reality shows that fear of permanent political domination and its economic consequences can give rise to separatist claims.

Minorities' fears of permanent political exclusion were heightened by the 1953-54 constitutional agreement that divided the country between the three largest ethnic groups. Fear was first driven into them, however, during the 1949-50 nationwide three-stage conference when the demands of some minority provinces of the Northern and Western Regions for political recognition in separate states were suppressed at their respective regional conferences.[8]

The forceful removal of ethnic minority elites from leadership positions in the government of the Eastern Region further heightened fears. Having lost leadership positions because of their identity, they had to attend the 1953 conference as delegates of the official minority opposition party in the region. They demanded a strong center as a safeguard against majority dominance in their regions. They were rebuffed and forced to withdraw from the conference. At the Resumed Lagos Conference of 1954 (the conference that evaluated Louis Chick's revenue allocation report) these fears could no longer be contained. Elites of some minority groups in the East and West submitted memoranda asking for recognition in Benin-Delta State and Calabar-Ogoja-Rivers (COR) State, respectively. Some northern non-Muslim minority groups followed suit by demanding a Middle Belt State. The demands were based partly on fears concerning leaving "minority groups . . . entirely at the mercy of the majority groups" (Nigeria 1954: 271-72 and 285).

Strategic interests dictated the response of the dominant parties. In the Eastern Region, the NCNC's strategic interest was to break the political dominance of the Northern Region and reduce the size of the West by creating several states. It therefore advocated the division of the country into seventeen smaller and weaker states linked by a strong center (Rothchild 1964: 44-45). This required that, in principle, the regional government agree to separation demands. The NCNC actively backed demands in other regions but tried, at the same time, to open a schism among its own dissenting minorities by secretly sponsoring or encouraging rival state movements in the Ogoja and Rivers Provinces. Demands for Rivers and Cross Rivers States emerged to compete with the COR demand.

In the West, the AG's arguments for ethnic states required that it support separation demands. However, it initially opposed the Benin-Delta State (or a the Midwest State) because the area it would cover was controlled by the NCNC, and also because it did not wish to narrow its territory to the advantage of its rivals. The AG queried: "Why should we gratuitously widen the area of our opponents' influence by offering them another state practically on a platter?" (Awolowo 1960: 183). When the AG became a patron to the COR State Movement in the East, and thus gained a foothold in that region, it argued that the creation of COR State should be a condition for the creation of Midwest State, or that the two be created simultaneously.

In the North, the demand for a Middle Belt State was supported by the AG who felt that the "time had come when the North should be broken into at least two separate states" (Awolowo 1960: 184). The NPC, in dead opposition to this proposal, threatened "trouble" if the territorial boundaries of the region were tampered with. By the start of the 1957 London Conference, the conference held to evaluate the difficulties that may have arisen from the practical workings of the 1953-54 constitutional agreements and for the granting of self-government to the regions; separation claims and the positions of each ruling party were already set. Conference members agreed to the appointment of a commission to examine the fears of minorities and recommend ways of allaying them.

In each region the Minorities Commission (as it was popularly known) heard separation demands that were based on arguments concerning political exclusion, cultural domination, and discrimination in the provision of social services and infrastructure (Nigeria 1958: 28, 38-46 and 57-70). In its report, the commission noted that minorities' allegations of domination and discrimination were exaggerated but that, when the latter was discounted, there still "remained a body of genuine fears and . . . the future was regarded with apprehension" (Nigeria 1958: 88). However, it did not regard state creation as a remedy for these fears and apprehensions. It stated two reasons. First, in each region the area of the proposed state was made up of several groups, some of whom preferred to be excluded from the new state. It was therefore difficult to draw a clean boundary that would not create a fresh minority with new demands. For example, the Middle Belt State that would be carved from the North had no definite boundary (Nigeria 1958: 71). The same applied in the Eastern Region where the area for the proposed COR State covered that of the Rivers and Cross Rivers States (Nigeria 1958: 32-33 and 51).[9]

Second, the commission stated that, until the last few years, modernization—and especially the development of education—had blurred ethnic differences in the country. Growing indifference to ethnic difference was reversed when the prospect of independence became real. Regardless, this tendency would not likely continue, especially in a few years time when Nigeria would face the outside world as an independent nation and would find within herself forces working for unity. For this reason, the Minorities' Commission stated that "we do not accept in its entirety the principle of ethnic grouping, that is, the principle that a recognizable ethnic group should wherever possible form a political unit" (Nigeria 1958: 88). The commission felt that it was more important to find means of allaying fears, and, therefore, some constitutional safeguards were recommended, including: the incorporation of fundamental human rights into the constitution; a single Nigerian police force serving both federal and regional purposes but controlled by the federal government; the creation of a Special Area in the Niger Delta to be developed by the federal government and the governments of the East and West under the auspices of a board; and the formation of parts of the Western and Eastern Regions into Minority Areas for purposes of fostering cultural advancement and social and economic development (Nigeria 1958: 14).

Leaders of the state creation movements were not satisfied. They attended the Resumed Conference of 1958 that met to put final touches on the transfer of power from the British with the slogan of "no states, no independence." The British decided that political independence for the country would be postponed in order to conduct a referendum among the affected minority groups with the aim of testing the popularity of the demands. This would then be followed with other rounds of constitutional negotiations. The idea that the country's freedom from colonial rule would be compromised prompted the leaders of the three major parties to opt for the commission's report. Clauses for boundary adjustments and a state-creation procedure in the future were inserted in the report and also incorporated into the constitution adopted at independence. Minorities entered independence with their demands unrealized and became more assertive and violent.

Evaluation of the Competing Group Claims

If one big problem emerges from the lengthy narrative presented above, it is the issue of the political system that would best accommodate multiple groups in the country. Federalism triumphed over unitarianism but the question remained as to whether it should be used to accommodate minority groups. This larger issue structured claims and counter-claims regarding revenue allocation, political representation, and the agreements that were reached. I want to evaluate these issues and I begin with claims regarding the political system.

The Political System and Difference

Three positions must be considered here: the first position is that polyethnic federalism was the best option; the second is that federalism based on the three regional structure was the most desirable option; and the third position considered a unitary system as the ideal solution. Some minorities, in fact, endorsed polyethnic federalism since it entailed their equal recognition in separate regions. Each of these positions could be interpreted as rationalizations by group elites who sought to maximize power for themselves and on behalf of those they were representing. However, it is not enough to look at them in strict ideological terms. These positions were also used as rationalizations because there was something good within each of them. To make a fair judgment about what arrangement was desirable and what was not, one has to examine the inherent qualities of these proposals and not simply dismiss them as ideologies.

I begin with the position of the Western Region. Here the assumption within the claim for polyethnic federalism was that the creation of a common civic bond in the new and emergent Nigeria would need decentralized political structures to enable identity groups to organize their lives according to their cultural requirements and needs. Political autonomy for groups, then, was presented as a prerequisite for political coherence and stability. The wisdom here was that ethnic loyalty would not be transcended with the passage of time and, without the grant of autonomy to identity groups, nation building would be futile (Kaltefleiter and Schumacher 1994: 112).

The above assumption was valid on two grounds. The strong attachment by a vast majority of the population to their ethnic communities constituted the first of these grounds. Studies conducted in the mid-1970s showed that people enclosed within the Nigerian boundary have always had stronger loyalties to their communities than to the state (Ekeh 1975). Commitments to the former overrode and displaced commitments to the latter. As we have seen, colonial rule made ethnic communities the relevant unit of political identification and conferred powers on their chiefs. It was the chiefs who collected taxes, mobilized labor, supervised the construction of roads, and dispensed justice in the courts. For the governed, the ethnic community was the state. This was dramatized during the decolonization period when the local educated elites organized interethnic football tournaments the way nations meet in international sporting events. The side that emerged victorious in the tournaments proclaimed their group as having a "manifest destiny" to lead the rest of the country. Whereas modernization theorists were pontificating that the education middle class would be the historical agents in the project of eliminating particularism and effecting change from tradition to modernity, the opposite proved to be true as the middle class became the real harbingers of ethnic loyalty in Nigerian politics (Pye 1966).

The existence of ethnic communities as units of concrete rights and privileges comprised the second valid ground. Ethnic communities guaranteed rights to factors of production (such as land) and met the social welfare and material needs of members. They formed dense networks of aid that provided for the emotional and security needs of their members. They more or less preempted the state in these functions, for which reason some theorists have referred to them as the "primordial public" as opposed to the modern public of market society (Ake 1994; Ekeh 1975). People directed their energies, resources, and loyalty for collective self-realization through community and not the state.

The above views about loyalty and citizenship in the "primordial public" would align with contemporary theoretical explanations for the desirability of federalism. Explanations supporting federalism center on identity and attachment and present community, defined by cultural characteristics such as language and ethnicity, as a "sense of collective identity" (Norrie, Simeon, and Krasnick 1986: 4). The community in which we live and play out our lives defines who and what we are. Accordingly, we have a powerful sense of attachment and loyalty to community. At the political level, federalism becomes desirable not because it is administratively convenient but because its structures of participation and authority are organized to reflect underlying forms of belonging (Carens 1996-97: 112-15). Hence, it is commonly seen as "a device designed to cope with the problem of how distinct communities can live a common life together without ceasing to be distinct communities" (Norrie, Simeon, and Krasnick 1986: 25). This explanation echoes the sociological view of federalism associated mostly with William Livingstone. This view presents federalism as a device for coping with diversity and understands a country as having federal qualities if it consists of heterogeneous groups. This would suggest that the claims for polyethnic federalism had merit and should have been taken seriously.

What would a commitment to polyethnic federalism have required? Implementing the Yoruba proposal was one way of meeting the commitment, but it was an unpersuasive proposal because it did not take the principle of respecting ethnicity very seriously as evidenced in the fact that only ten states would be created in a country with over 250 ethnic groups and by proposing boundaries that clearly served Yoruba interests. The proposal by some minority communities for more states was another and perhaps more persuasive and genuine way of meeting the commitment. This is what the Minorities Commission ought to have considered. But this proposal, as the Minorities Commission rightly observed, was not free of difficulties because there were too many groups, their sizes varied too much, groups were mixed in several territories, membership was unclear, and some groups preferred the existing tri-regional structure to polyethnic federalism.

Given these difficulties, taking claims about polyethnic federalism seriously would probably have entailed ignoring minorities' claims. In this case, the salience of group membership would have been ignored and the problem of political unity and stability would have remained unaddressed. This is what actually happened. The 1953-54 constitutional agreement compromised unity when it retained the three regions and shared power and assets among them.

Let us turn now to the claim for a unitary system advanced by leaders of the Eastern Region. This claim was put forward in the interest of Igbos who had migrated to all parts of the country on account of the thin soil and high population density in their homeland. However, one should stand back from this ideological position and assess the claim for its normative worth. The claim rested on a form of political community in which citizenship is a matter of treating individuals as having equal rights under standard universal laws. Unlike the claim for polyethnic federalism, which presupposed a background conception of differentiated citizenship, this claim required treating people as equals in the assignment of rights and in the distribution of social goods. In principle, this would permit everyone to participate equally in the political community and its system of opportunities.

From this perspective, polyethnic federalism would be too divisive (Porter 1979: 128). The creation of ethnic regions would encourage citizens to look inward and focus on their ethnic difference, thereby compromising attempts to forge political unity. Such a state structure would foster sensitivity to, and preoccupation with, the ethnic origins of citizens in the competition for public offices and the allocation of social goods. In this context, differentiated citizenship would cease to be integrative and would become a device for cultivating distrust and conflict (Glazer 1983: 227-8; Kukathas 1993: 156). So, instead of unifying people with a system of common rights and privileges, citizenship would become a force for disunity. Moreover, the creation of ethnic regions would encourage excessive differentiation. Leaders of new groups would emerge with perceptions of, and claims to, difference. As claims are met one after the other, chaos would replace order, and the hope of attaining stability would be lost (Glazer 1983: 227).

Part of the case made for unitarianism was that, in principle, the system would maintain a common standard of rule for judging the actions of both rulers and ruled. Rules are authoritative precisely because of their universality, and they continue to take hold and operate in the mind of citizens because they are settled objects of knowledge. They define the roles and expectations that make for stable and secure interaction. Without standard rules, what is known as the rule of law would be severely threatened as there would be no universally known principles for judging the decisions of office-bearers and the actions of ordinary citizens (Williams 1995: 82). Rulers could act arbitrarily and get away with it. Citizens could suffer rights violations without being able to appeal to an impartial judge. This is where a unitary system offers a great deal of comfort. Within it, every individual is regarded as a rights-bearer (even if only abstractly), for which reason its system of rules is in principle dissociated from particularist social interests and appears to transcend politics. So, freedom and equality (even if they are abstract) are secured.

What principled objections could be posed to such a unitary system of rights? One is that the formal equality of the system masks the ways in which the arrangements would benefit some groups and disadvantage others. Under such a system, the educational advantages of the Igbos would have enabled them to obtain key positions in the East and in the North. But, given the salience of ethnic identity, they would have occupied these positions not as individuals but as representatives of their kinship and ethnic groups. This underlying sociocultural reality meant that a unitary system based on individual rights would have functioned quite differently in the Nigeria of the 1950s than from the way it functioned in Europe and America during the same period. So, the objections from the Yorubas and others to the Igbo proposal had some validity at root.

T. H. Marshall, a Cambridge sociologist, analyzed the tension in universal citizenship by showing the disjuncture between its claims to political equality and the actual inability of the industrial working class to exercise political rights. Before him, R. H. Tawney had, in the early 1920s, warned that British society would fall apart if the extension of political equality was unaccompanied by the grant of social and economic rights to the economically disadvantaged (Heater 1990: 100). Marshall (1950: 25-26), writing after the 1920s, pinned the integration of British society on the extension of citizenship to the social sphere, that is, the grant of social and welfare rights to disadvantaged members.

The British case would confirm the real fears of the Yoruba that common citizenship rights, by themselves, do not promise equal inclusion in the political community, the sphere of the exercise of political rights. Whereas in the British case, it was the economically weak who were excluded despite their possession of common rights of citizenship, in the Nigeria case it was ethnic groups who feared exclusion. And, whereas in Britain the response to exclusion was the empowerment of the weak, in Nigeria the response took the form of calls for states to accommodate ethnic difference. Despite its attractive qualities, then, the unitary system was unjust and could not have fostered national unity in Nigeria.

Consider now northern claims for a loose federation of three regions, which later changed to a demand for political separation. Horowitz (1985: 148, 179) has argued that the juxtaposition of groups in a common political environment creates anxiety about possible domination by those regarded as more advanced in terms of being proportionately better educated and better represented in the professions and in the modern sectors of the economy. Horowitz's argument falls within the domain of psychology because fear, apprehension, or anxiety comprise the response of the human mind to perceived external stimulus. Reactions may be exaggerated if they are disproportionately out of tune with the perceived danger, or irrational if the perception is shown to be false. Some would regard the fear and anxiety expressed by northern leaders as an exaggerated and irrational reaction to a false perception. However, this insight is not strong enough to brush aside their case because the apprehension not only existed but also provided the context for their inflexibility and what one could regard to be the extremity of their demands.

Understandably, the decision of the British to decolonize raised the issue of who would exercise power and, among the Muslim leaders of the North, caused anxiety about the future of their Islamic culture. The connection between power and the preservation of Muslim culture has to be grasped in order to make a fair judgment about northern leaders' claims to a federation of three regions or political disintegration. Recall that northern Muslim leaders agreed to the 1914 political amalgamation on the condition that the region be shielded from Western influences and administered separately from the South. Cultural and religious survival were therefore tied to the exercise of political power or, better still, to governance. This connection made northern leaders perceive with trepidation a unified Nigeria in which southerners who were not Muslims would occupy the top policy-making positions in government. The need to secure cultural and religious identities partly explains the tenacity of demands for recognition of the North as a region that had to be, at most, in loose political partnership with the other regions.

I have discussed the argument that cultural identity provides the basis for normative claims in chapter 1. There, I noted that Will Kymlicka has persuasively argued that cultural identity is a prerequisite for the moral worth of individuals and their ability to make the kinds of moral claims liberalism cherishes and attempts to secure for all citizens. Taylor took a similar position when he argued that our identity is shaped by the recognition we receive from others. This nature of identity, then, engenders demands for equal recognition, requiring respect for different cultural identities. One influential theorist, whose ideas were not discussed in chapter 1, is Iris Marion Young. According to her, liberal democracy is committed to equality in the political community, and attempts to achieve substantive equality will require affirming difference. She provides two reasons for this perspective, but the important one for this discussion is that cultural groups who are excluded from the political process have distinctive needs that can only be met through differentiated policies (Young 1990: 175-83). These arguments about the normative value of cultural difference compel us to give weight to the sort of claims that were made by northern leaders. Giving weight to their claims would entail recognizing the region as being primarily composed of a single cultural group.

Although the North was made up of several ethnic groups, a greater part of it was unified by Islamic culture. It is true that some Islamic groups in the region either maintained their independence from, or were opposed to, emirate rule. But it is also true that Islam defined the value system and identity of such groups, especially the Kanuri in the northeastern part of the region and the Hausa of the Kano-Kaduna axis. Despite internal opposition, the values and symbols of Islam provided a common bond, thereby creating a corporate identity. In this respect, one could speak of a greater part of the region as having an Islamic *Weltanschauung*.[10] It was no surprise that northern leaders boasted of "Islamic brotherhood" being "stronger than blood" (Paden 1986: 285). Neither was it a surprise that coherence and a united front existed among the leaders when they appeared in the several constitutional conferences to make demands; at no time did dissension or disagreement within their ranks appear. In light of this, Ted Gurr and Barbara Harff (1994: 84) may have been justified when they argued that group cohesion is a key factor that makes people subordinate their personal preferences to those of their group.

Given the above arguments, a grant of autonomy to the region would have been one way of responding to the claims of northern leaders. The problem with this option is that it would have entailed treating non-Muslim ethnic minorities of the region as sharing the same aspiration as the numerically dominant Muslim groups. Inasmuch as the former were just as opposed to southern political dominance of the region as the latter, and both were united in calls for the exclusion of southerners from political and administrative positions in the region, this treatment would be valid. But this is where their common aspiration ended. The bonds had no depth and were too thin and fragile to serve as a basis for common political life. This is not to suggest that different groups cannot unite in a political unit if a sense of a shared future exists (Rothchild 1997: 31-32). The point is that if the basis for unity is indeed some kind of shared values, then what existed between the two sets of groups was not enough because culturally they were too different. Most of the non-Muslim minorities repelled political conquest and cultural assimilation during the nineteenth century and, during the colonial era, they resisted the imposition of both an Islamic legal system and Islamic cultural practices over their customary ways of living. Meeting claims for autonomy of the region would have threatened their political and cultural security. This, in turn, would have opened the door to separatist claims, as they later did emerge.

Another alternative would have been either to do nothing or to leave intact the three regions within a quasi-federal system in which each would have no autonomy. This alternative leans more toward unitarianism, to which northern leaders were opposed, and adopting it would have deepened conflict. In this case, the Eight-Point Declaration would have culminated in northern secession. Non-Muslim minorities in the region would have been carried along, perhaps against their will, and domination and further secessionist claims would have emerged in the new state.

What alternative was desirable? In short, what did justice require? The preceding arguments show that each claim made by the three regional elites had its own merits and weaknesses. A desirable alternative should not be blind to these assessments. The critical issue is: what alternative arrangement was desirable and feasible, given the merit and weakness of each claim?

An alternative arrangement would have been one that drew on a Rawlsian type of agreement.[11] In this model, the regional leaders would have had to leave behind all particular social interests of their "people," isolate the necessary primary goods, and negotiate impartial principles that would assign and guarantee them these goods. The agreement would, therefore, be in the interest of everyone in general and not any person or group in particular. Such a blind agreement, if it were ever possible, would have been contested by both northern leaders and leaders from the Western Region. This is because the "veil of ignorance" eliminated substantial differences among groups, thus establishing a universal standpoint of the type the Igbos desired. The list of primary goods derived from a universal condition guaranteeing the rights of abstract individuals that, in effect, amounted to the kind of universal citizenship rights northern leaders and leaders of the Western region were dead set against. So, the neutral Rawlsian contract delivers an arrangement in which members have universal rights, very much in accord with Igbo demand for unitarianism, and very much in tension with the commitment of the Muslim north to regional autonomy and the commitment of the Yoruba to a federation of ethnic regions. As argued above, this was not fair in the Nigerian context and would have intensified conflict.

A possible alternative arrangement would have been one that combined elements of all forms demanded by the three regional leaders; something akin to Aristotle's mixed constitution. Confronted with competing claims to monarchical, democratic, and aristocratic systems of government, and the prospect of each being perverse and unstable, Aristotle came up with a composite constitution as the most desirable solution. The idea involved mixing institutions, in whole or in part, from competing constitutions. According to him, the finer the mixture, the more equitable the constitution, and therefore the more durable (Aristotle 1964: bk. IV, chaps. 9-12).

Taking a middle course that balanced the interests of the three parties would have entailed extracting and blending parts of the institutional features of polyethnic federalism, a unitary system, and the confederal system promoted by the NPC. Such a composite arrangement would have been inclusive of, and fair to, the three parties, but unworkable. Extracting and fusing institutional features of the three constitutional systems is not something that can be done. It could, perhaps, be achieved if the parties making claims were represented and assigned specific roles in government, rather like the composite constitution of Cicero (1929: 151). But this would still have required an overarching framework—either unitarian, a federation of ethnic groups, or confederation of the three regions.

Apart from its practical difficulties, a mixed regime (assuming it was possible to have one) would have been in the exclusive interest of those whose claims it reflected. Ethnic minorities that had no place in the constitutional negotiation processes and whose voices were therefore not heard stood to be excluded from such a deal. In short, a composite regime would have been a regime benefiting the dominant groups due to the exclusion of ethnic minorities.

A third alternative might have been the softening of claims in order to reach a mutually acceptable compromise. Rothchild has argued that the potential for conflict resolution is greater when group leaders make negotiable demands or are willing to moderate their extreme claims (Rothchild 1997: 31-33). It is true that, for the leaders to reach a reasonable agreement, it was necessary that they soften their claims in order to bridge the gaps that separated them. Such tradeoffs were a pragmatic way of reaching agreement on mutually accommodative normative arrangements. Instead of advancing inflexible demands resulting in confrontation and intense conflict, the leaders dropped aspects of their demands that were mutually unacceptable. I call this the principle of mutual concession.[12] The cost of not acting by that principle is self-consuming conflict, the reward for following it is peace. The principle made for an arrangement that was neither unitarian, confederal, nor polyethnic federalism. The arrangement, therefore, had an element of neutrality and, at the same time, gave each of the three negotiating parties a self-governing right to its territory.

Pragmatic as it was, the arrangement achieved through mutual concession was imperfect because it rested on the mutual advantages of the regional leaders and the majority ethnic groups they were representing. It did not accommodate the interests and claims of some minority ethnic groups as enunciated by their elites. Although the 1957-58 Commission argued that this was not feasible, it would still be necessary to examine claims of minorities to determine if the agreement for a federation of three regions was the best possible alternative.

Should Minorities Have Been Recognized in Separate States?

Some have argued, and very strongly too, that separatist demands constituted a strategy used by elites to gain access to power and resources. In his book on class formation and state creation in Nigeria, for example, Eme Ekekwe has argued that no correlation existed between minority membership and demands for new states. He argued that the demands were made by elites who belonged to parties in opposition and had no patronage from the ruling government. This set of politicians, according to him, withdrew their demands when given some access to power. To buttress his point, he cited the case of the Western Region in which there were demands for Central Yoruba and Ondo States to be peopled by Yorubas, most of whom supported the NCNC, which was in opposition to the ruling AG party. He also referred to the Midwest State where:

> The Oba of Benin in 1953 clearly demonstrated this case.
> Upon being offered the position of "Minister without Portfolio" in 1956 by the AG Government, he accepted it ostensibly
> in "the best interest of his people." Thereafter he "ceased to be

connected with the Opposition and . . . to campaign for the
[Midwest State Movement]." (Ekekwe 1986: 133)

Ekekwe also gave a similar example with the demand for a Middle Belt
State from the North. In these arguments, he did not take into account the
fact that separatist demands dated back to the provincial and regional
conferences of 1949, well before the advent of competitive party politics.
He also failed to note that intense precolonial hostilities among Yoruba
subgroups were opened as the British began to decolonize and some factions tried to counter the others by seeking external alliances. The tenacity of these demands, despite defections by some of the leaders, is
enough to warrant looking beyond the narrow self-interest of elites as the
sole explanation. Separatist demands may have been used by some to
advance their private agendas, but what has to be questioned is their
normative value. The demands would not have been used as a mask if
they had no normative importance.

Ted Gurr (1993: chapter 10) has shown that autonomy demands are
associated with identity groups desiring security and protection, and that
the reluctance of public officials to accommodate them intensifies conflict and sometimes leads to open warfare. Demands by elites and their
groups, both majority and minority, were driven by the fear that they
would suffer political subjection and would not feel at home when the
British handed over power. Despite the conflicting nature of the demands, they were united by a common purpose, namely: to achieve a fair
and acceptable arrangement that would make for peaceful coexistence.
Hobbes's thesis about tacit consent, formulated in a different context,
could be modified and applied here. His thesis states that a group of persons tacitly consent to peace if, of their own free will, they decide to join
others who are assembling to renounce lawlessness (Hobbes 1968:
231).[13] In the context of ethnic relations, one could modify the Hobbe-
sian thesis by saying that groups whose leaders are making claims for a
normative political arrangement are implicitly asking for peace. Deny,
repress or close these outlets for the expression of demands and conflict
will erupt.

Indeed, it was precisely the exclusion of minorities from the constitutional negotiation process that intensified their demands for autonomy.
The several and periodic constitutional conferences were convened with
the express purpose of negotiating a common and workable framework
for political life. This required that diverse voices be heard and considered, which turned out not to be the case as majority group members

dominated the constitutional process and excluded minority views. The agreement for a political federation of three regions was, therefore, not reflective of the minority interests but better represented the interests of the dominant groups. For example, for the Muslim Northerners, the agreement offered protection from the Christian and educationally advanced southerners. For the Yoruba, it was a shield against the ambitious Igbo. Even for the Igbo, it at least guaranteed a political right to their region.[14] It was not for nothing that Richard Sklar (1971: 46) referred to the compromise agreement that produced the arrangement as the "principle of regional security." This argument merely shows that the political arrangement based on compromise was chiefly for the benefit of majority groups. The issue of how much normative weight minority demands should carry still has to be established.

Political inclusion was the chief objective of minority demands and, to this extent, one could say they were demanding equal political treatment. Equality in the political community is one of the chief attributes of liberal democracy and one would expect that the process of transition from colonial subjection to parliamentary democracy would offer hopes for this attribute to become a reality. However, the transition process proved early on that classical liberal democracy could not reconcile itself with equality and freedom. Why was this so?

The source of this disappointment can be found in the hidden assumption in liberal theory that people belonging to a homogeneous culture constitute a political society. We saw this in the social contract theories of Locke and Rousseau where atomized individuals sharing the same cultural life associate in a political society. It was even more explicit in the utilitarianism of Mill. In contemporary times, we see it in the political liberalism of Rawls whose principles of justice recognize, but do not take into account, the salience of difference. Universal liberal theory grew out of a cultural milieu specific to certain European societies and did not reflect the heterogeneity that prevailed elsewhere. In Nigeria, its promise of a free and responsive government emerging from open political competition has been contradicted by ethnic voting and the emergence of governments responsive to the groups who brought them into office. Impartial rules that were supposed to ensure fairness in the distribution of societal goods and privileges turned out to work unintentionally to the advantage of some groups. In some cases, it was openly partial and worked in self-contradictory manner. For example, the educated Igbo who moved to the North and other parts of the country as clerks argued for universal citizenship rights. Yet they retained very strong loyalty to their homeland and closed off positions in the public service by bringing in their kin groups to fill vacant spots. By the time groups in the North became conscious of what was going on, Igbos had monopolized civil service positions in the region (Lloyd 1971: 173). The partiality and contradictory working of liberal principles meant that they were not quite appropriate for Nigeria. The heterogeneous ethnic composition of the country required that liberal rules be adjusted to account for the reality of cultural specifics.

The need to redefine liberal rules of justice to make them more responsive to cultural difference was recognized by elites from both majority and minority ethnic groups. In fact, the solution to the problem of liberal equality and difference was initiated by elites from the majority ethnic groups when they made arguments for a federation in which groups would be free from political and cultural domination. Their arguments presupposed what Melissa Williams (1995: 69) would refer to as the "political solution to the problem of difference." That is, they sought to make for the explicit recognition of groups by asking for a redefinition of the rules of justice, not on an abstract philosophical plane, but in the very process of politics. It was their political arguments and solutions that set off the several constitutional negotiations, beginning in 1949. The majority elites initiated it all and minorities followed. Both felt that federation was good and so they all demanded it. In principle, both sets of groups ought to have been treated equally in terms of political recognition. If the compromise federal arrangement was good for the numerically strong because it promised them freedom from oppression, then it is clear that the numerically weak needed it the most. This was voiced by a representative to the 1950 General Conference when he noted: "If a Region as large as the North can have . . . ears it is understandable that minor tribes in Nigeria must be anxious that adequate and unmistakable provisions are made to safeguard their survival, and assurance of place for them in the new Nigeria" (Nigeria 1950: 62).

The Problem of Feasibility

I have argued in support of minorities' demands for equal political recognition. The problem that immediately arises is balancing the "ought to" with the "is," namely, the realities on the ground. A desirable prescription might not be practicable and, on the other hand, what is realistic might not be desirable. Between these poles, a middle way might be found.

Social circumstances seemed to make separation unfeasible. First, although the demands for separate states were identifiable with multiple minority groups contiguously located in each region, they did not originate from, and were not unanimously supported by, all. Some groups felt safer with the status quo because they thought it was more tolerable to be dominated by some distant groups than to be subjected to an immediate neighbor who would occupy a majority position in the new state.[15] For example, in the Western Region, some groups did not want to be part of a Midwest State in which they would be numerically inferior to, and dominated by, their next-door neighbor. This was true of the Itsekiri, whose elites exercised power over the numerically superior Urhobo and Ijaw (before the declaration of colonial rule), but who feared that in a Midwest State the use of majoritarian vote would reverse power. Their leaders reacted by claiming ethnic affiliation with the Yoruba, and by opting to be in the Western Region.

Similarly, in the Eastern Region, the demand for a Rivers State ran into difficulties because the Ikwerre and the Ogba regarded the Ijaw as likely to be the majority group if the Western Region Ijaw were included. Their leaders opposed the demand on this ground, but they were ready to support it if they were granted majority status by excluding the western Ijaw from the state. Thus, in the proposed new states, those who were to be a minority knew their fate in advance and were not prepared to deliver themselves up to the majority. Each new state that was demanded in effect contained potential new states if it were to be created. New minorities would emerge with accusations of being dominated and oppressed. The problem here was not simply one of drawing boundaries, but threats to stability in terms of both the "camel's nose theory" and the "domino theory." The camel's nose theory holds that if the nose is let inside the tent the whole beast will soon follow. Some Israelis use this to justify their rejection of autonomy demands made by Gaza and West Bank Palestinians. The domino theory concerns the threatening prospect that the grant of recognition poses for larger groups containing subgroups and for the stability of the country (Gurr 1993: 300). This could be illustrated with some inland Yoruba subgroups—the Ekiti and Ibadans—who demanded recognition in two separate states on account of their rivalry with sister subgroups. Minority demands were already influencing some subgroups within the major groups to make claims based on difference and for separation. At the international level, the domino theory could be illustrated by the threatening prospect multiple defections by the former Soviet republics posed for other heterogeneous states. The lesson learned by those defections was used by Russia to deny Chechnya's claims to autonomy.

Second, each of the three sets of regional elites perceived separation demands as threats to regional power and security and therefore resisted separation by all means, including the use of force. For example, northern leaders regarded the entire region as having been ruled by their "great-great-grandfather's family through their Lieutenants or by the great Shehus of Bornu." They wondered why "a long slice of country running along both sides of the Rivers Niger and Benue, with an extension to cover the Plateau and southern Zaria," would be hived off (Bello 1962: 215, 216). They invoked war to defend the region's territorial boundaries. Similarly, the NCNC leadership was strongly opposed to the division of the East, despite their argument for splitting the country into smaller regions to create a stronger center and a united country. While they declared that the region "cannot stand dismemberment" after the 1954 separation of the UN trust territory of Southern Cameroon, the Ibo State Union, a cultural organization of Igbos from all over the country, threatened war if Port Harcourt or any other Igbo land was separated (Rothchild 1964: 39). The position of the AG was already clear: it would not gratuitously maximize the interest of its opponents by agreeing to the dismemberment of the West. It agreed to state creation on the condition that it be carried out simultaneously in all three regions.

With all of these positions, acceding to minorities' demands could precipitate conflict at two levels: between a region's majority group and its breakaway minorities, and between rival regional elites approving the exit of the other's aggrieved minorities. In other words, doing what was right would have opened the gates to war and confusion.[16] The "ought," then, was contradicted by practical realities on the ground.

What option was both most desirable and most feasible? I cannot provide a definite answer to this question, but will spell out the dangers of privileging the "is" over the "ought." One of the dangers is the transfer of minority problems into political independence, together with the strategic power games of the regional elites. Political independence was expected to usher in liberal democracy, whose defining attributes are its concern for the moral equality of persons and opposition to injustice manifested as domination of some by others. Now, rejecting the claims of minority groups opened a gulf between democracy and justice, and aggrieved minorities entering independence demanded that justice be done.[17] Moreover, electoral politics, which promises the formation of government on majority vote, would prompt dominant regional elites to link up with and patronize aggrieved minorities of rival regions. In this context, there was no way political confrontation was going to be avoided. The British, while they were around, played the role of third-party mediators by responding to crises and convening conferences to broker deals among the dominant regional actors. But, with their departure, the field would be open for a free-for-all.

Another relevant danger was that, down the road, minority demands would have to be addressed and a showdown between the dominant regional actors would be inevitable. The 1957-58 conference agreed on, and inserted into the new constitution, specific procedures for state creation after independence. But, without the mediating role of the British, the three dominant parties were not going to reach a fair agreement on how many states should be created from each region. For example, during the 1957 conference, the NCNC insisted on the division of the Western Region into four states: the Lagos and Colony State, the Midwest State, Central Yoruba State, and the Kolanut and Cassava State (Awolowo 1960: 185). It initiated demands for two of these during the Minorities Commission, in addition to the Midwest, which it had already supported. On its part, the AG, other than being the senior ally of the movements for the separation of minority groups in the Eastern and Northern Regions, was as committed as ever to an adjustment of boundaries to bring the Yoruba of the North into the Western Region. The NPC, on the other hand, had consistently held its position to not consider any violation of the North's territorial boundaries. To postpone political separation until after independence was to postpone the inevitable—a violent confrontation between the regional powers. The best way of avoiding conflict would have been for the British colonial administrators to use their power to separate aggrieved minorities. After all, and following Hume, political power is instituted in societies to promote justice. That the British should have used this power to force elites from the major groups to accept an arrangement that aimed at enthroning justice, is therefore not an action that should give rise to debate.

The practical difficulty that remains to be resolved was the refusal of some minorities to be included in the states that were demanded. The difficulty could be presented in this way: should just claims to separation be denied if they do not win the express consent of some group—call them minorities within minorities—whose territory is within the separatist unit?

Reg Whitaker has examined a similar problem in Canada where French-speaking Quebec has made repeated attempts at asserting sovereigny. The province contains scattered Aboriginal bands who refuse to accept Quebec's claim to self-determination as binding on them. In dealing with the problem of whether Quebec's claim can be imposed on the Aboriginal people without their consent, Whitaker argues that there should be two levels of negotiation: the first between the rest of Canada and Quebec for the right of the latter to separate; and, the second between French Quebeckers and Aboriginal peoples for mutual recognition of rights in the new unit that would come into being. Without negotiations for the recognition of rights, one party may resort to means that would prepare the way for mutual self-destruction (Carens 1995: 206-18).

Whitaker's argument is similar to the argument I made earlier that Nigeria risked catastrophe if the minorities that were asking for political recognition equal to that of the majority groups were not separated into new states. The new aspect that emerges from analysis of the Canadian case is that subgroups of minority groups opposed to separation have moral claims that should be respected, and that a clash of rights could be avoided by having structured negotiations. The problem of some minorities being opposed to other minorities would not be an insurmountable one. The dissenting minorities in Nigeria were not as strongly opposed to separation as the dominant regional elites and those they were representing. Their opposition was more strategic than foundational, for they actively supported the demands when they were sure of commanding the most dominant and influential positions, but they changed their mind when it was clear they would be disadvantaged.

Consider the example of the demand for the Midwest State from the Western Region. The Igbo subgroup within it preferred to merge with the main Igbo of the Eastern Region, but they also did not mind being in the Midwest, as they were sure of commanding a large share of influential political positions. This latter preference bred fear among the Edo who would be the most numerically dominant group in the Midwest (Nigeria 1958: 32). The example of the demand for a Rivers State is also instructive. The Ikwerre and Ahoada peoples (who spoke varieties of Igbo dialect unintelligible to the hinterland Igbo) actively supported demands for the state, but they changed their position on account of proposals for the inclusion of the western Ijaw with the Rivers' Ijaw. Without the western Ijaw, they would have enjoyed numerical superiority, but with the latter's inclusion they would have played second fiddle to the enlarged Ijaw (Nigeria 1958: 51). These examples show that, despite mutual distrust and fear, minority groups were not fundamentally apart on the desire for states. The issue was which group members would rule and which would be ruled in the new states. Resolving this problem required rounds of constitutional conferences on power-sharing and institutional checks to prevent domination.

When the majority ethnic elites disagreed over membership in the political community, several constitutional conferences were held to negotiate an agreement. It was during the course of these negotiations that minorities' claims to equal membership arose. Logically, and to be fair, new sets of conferences involving minorities ought to have been held. Minority-focused conferences would have produced compromises on power-sharing and devised institutional checks to potential domination in the new states that were demanded.

In sum, an alternative political arrangement in which minority groups would receive political treatment equal to majority groups was desirable and feasible. In fact, the British reluctantly suggested a plebiscite and further constitutional negotiations to put such an arrangement in place, but the majority ethnic elites opted for a speedy route to independence instead.

Revenue Sharing and Political Representation

I have argued that the political framework adopted during the pre-independence period was an unjust one, and suggested what desirable and practicable alternative existed. Two other substantive issues have to be addressed: claims regarding political representation and revenue allocation. We have seen that the 1953-54 and 1957 constitutional agreements freed political representation at the center from the regions by dividing the country into several equal federal constituencies. These agreements succeeded in separating representation in the central legislature from the tri-regional framework that I criticized as being unjust to minority groups. This separation did not happen in the case of revenue sharing. Here, the structural political framework determined that the constitutional agreement be that of a derivation-based revenue allocation system. That is, the 1953-54 agreement for a near liquidation of the center, and for the grant of autonomy to the regions, spurred agreement on the sharing of assets and revenue to be based on derivation. To object to the structural political framework is to object to the revenue sharing agreement ab initio. It would, therefore, be unnecessary to conduct detailed arguments about the desirability of the latter. What I want to do in the pages that follow is: 1) make arguments for the framework that ought to guide revenue allocation, given population, derivation, and need-based claims; and, 2) evaluate the desirability of the political representation agreement, given competing claims that were made. I begin with the latter.

Desirability of the Agreement on Political Representation

The agreement for political representation must be evaluated in terms of the claims that were made. There were two dominant claims: one was the Northern Region's demand for representation on population basis, and the other was the Eastern and Western Regions' demand for representation on the basis of the equality of states. These claims overshadowed and silenced demands by some minorities for their fair representation at the center. The three-level conference of 1949-50 was convened partly in response to protest by some of these minorities over their inadequate representation in the Arthur Richards's Legislative Council. Population and equality-of-states-based claims by the dominant regional elites not only silenced demands by some minorities but also were dissociated from the issue of adequate representation of groups in the regions. In spite of the dissociation, the two dominant claims can still be assessed on their merits.

By definition, democracy is sovereignty of numbers and, in its original Athenian form, consisted of the direct participation by the *demos* or people. The issue of indirect representation arises when, due to a large population, direct participation becomes impossible.[18] In this case, the population is divided into a number of constituencies to elect representatives. Numbers, as the defining element of democracy, are the operative principle in dividing the population. The smaller a constituency is in terms of population, the more the deputy is closer to, and is theoretically representative of, the member. The larger it is, the more remote the deputy. If, for example, there were ten people in a constituency, each member would have one tenth of the representative's voice in the legislature. If there were one hundred people, each member would have one hundredth of his/her voice. A small constituency is ideal because it comes closest to direct participation.

In a legislative assembly, therefore, representation has to be proportional to the size of the population. To abandon the population principle would be a deliberate attempt to underrepresent areas with a large number of people. In such areas, the people/deputy ratio will be large and the people will have less influence in law making compared to districts where the ratio of population to representation is small. On the other hand, the people/deputy ratio will be small in areas with relatively low populations and the people in such areas will have more influence in the legislative procedure. In this respect, arguments made by the dominant Northern elites had merit.

However, it is not enough to make arguments in defense of the population principle. If seats are allocated on the basis of regional population, questions have to be raised on how each region would distribute its share to enable fair representation of its diverse internal groups. What is the guarantee that each region's share would not be distributed in favor of its majority group, or that the method of election would not produce deputies who are mostly members of the numerically dominant group? This problem of fair representation constituted the kernel of the claim made by some minority groups, a claim that was silenced by majority group elites who dominated the constitutional process. The silencing of this claim, or the inattention paid to it by the dominant elites as they made their arguments, supports the view that representation in the regions was inevitably going to be biased.

This should not entail that the equality of region argument has no weight. Certainly in a political federation, the constituent units are equal partners. It is as equals that they must cooperate to form a larger community that does not smother local identity and power. Each maintains its internal autonomy and, as such, none is subordinate to the other. Being equals, they all have the same voting rights and this means sitting as equals together in the central legislature. So, the equality of region principle has to be recognized in the distribution of House membership.

But, as with the population principle, it also raises the problem of fair representation of groups. When the northern and western regional representatives to the 1950 General Conference pressed for an indirect system of election, their goal was to use their regional legislatures as electoral colleges to select deputies to the center. They succeeded and the result was the establishment of exclusionary politics in those regions. This, in turn, triggered the removal of minority elites from the head of the Eastern Region's government. With precedents like this, there was no guarantee that House membership distributed on the basis of equality of states would not be monopolized by majority group elites. It was even more likely that they would regard their state's share as belonging to the government, not to the people per se, and would proceed to allocate the seats among themselves, just as the regional legislatures were used in 1951 to select representatives to the center.

In fact, the use of the regional equality principle as the basis for distributing membership in the federal legislature technically elevates the regions as the primary units to be represented. If what matters in the center is equal representation of political units, it becomes immaterial whether the various peoples in the regions are adequately represented or not. As might be expected, representatives sent to the center would be comprised mostly of the majority group who dominate the political process in each region. In Nigeria, then, the equality of region argument could not have made for fair representation.

Were the 1953-54 and 1957 constitutional agreements for dividing the country into equal constituencies desirable in the end? One consideration resulting from the delimitation was the dissociation of representation from the regions. With the agreement, it was no longer the regions that were to be allocated federal seats. Rather, the country was regarded as being inhabited by people who were now divided into several constituencies and were required to produce their own deputies. The boundaries may not have coincided with ethnicity, but they did not enclose a random collection of people. Rather, they followed the colonial divisional boundaries, which, in most cases, enclosed subethnic groups (within larger groups) and small groups. In effect, the agreements made it possible for groups to have fair representation in the central legislature. The dominant but rival regional elites may not have set out to achieve this purpose at the negotiation table given that they were mostly interested in ensuring that their rivals did not receive any undue concessions. Through the negotiation process, they all arrived at an agreement that at once freed representation from the ambit of the regions and focused it at the level of groups.

In countries like the United States, the drawing of constituency boundaries along ethnic lines to ensure adequate representation of African Americans has been contested on grounds that it violates individual equality and that it promotes racial segregation and conflict.[19] In the case of Nigeria, the drawing of federal constituencies to follow subethnic and ethnic lines closely enabled equal representation and helped to minimize conflict. In fact, the 1953-54 and 1957 agreements resolved once and for all the problem of representation in the central legislature as heretofore the issue has never been seriously contested in national politics. Although some boundary adjustments were later made on some occasions, they were redrawn within the framework of the agreement. The fairness of the representational arrangement led to its use in the mid-1970s as a model for delimiting the country into 301 uniform local government areas.

A Desirable Framework for Revenue Allocation

When considering the issue of sharing national revenue, the determination is which political body has jurisdiction over the territorially based society from which revenue is generated. In the modern world the state is generally assumed to be the body that has legitimate jurisdiction. When I speak of the state I mean the "commonwealth," the *res publica*. Kohn appropriately defines it as "the people legally united as an independent entity" (Otubanjo 1988: 83). This union brings forth a national political community having universal jurisdiction within its territorial boundaries, but it also creates an agent endowed with authority to exercise jurisdictional powers on its behalf. As an agent, government is accountable to the national community and the revenue it generates to carry out its business belongs to the people as a collectivity.

However, the essence of federalism is local sovereignty within a national community. Jurisdictional right is shared between the national and local community. Thus, the federal and regional levels of government each have their respective jurisdictional spheres. Each level generates revenue in its own sphere to carry out its administrative responsibilities. Very often, revenues are centrally collected by the federal government and shared among the regions for a variety of reasons: convenience to taxpayers and collectors, inability of some regions to generate revenue, the effects of one region's economy on the other, and equal tax rates for identical professions across regions.[20] But, if governance were to be reduced to pure economics, then the generation and sharing of revenue would be considered in strict economic terms and each unit of government would receive from the central fund a proportional equivalent of what it contributed. The allocation system would, therefore, be based on the derivation principle. In this scenario, the center would be playing the role of a contractor that collects and returns revenue, but keeps a part of the revenue as payment for the services it has rendered. The various units would act like corporations or other business entities, and relations among them would be rooted in purely contractual terms. All of this would presuppose the nonexistence of a national community.

It should be noted that, in a political federation, the sharing of jurisdictional authority does not dissolve the national community. On the contrary, power-sharing helps impart a sense of belonging to people who are associated in the national community, which defines people that are to be united who have a mutual interest, a common political bond, and a common political fate. Although the constituent federal units have local autonomy, they collectively constitute a national community in which the good of all matters. The very fact that a national community exists, requires attending to the general good. This is assumed in the leading role the central government plays in revenue collection. For example, the reasons given above for the central collection of revenue implicitly conceptualizes the national community as one in which there is concern for the general welfare and presupposes that the constituent units are not like sovereign states in the international system acting on the basis of self-interest. Rather, they comprise a larger community in which there is an obligation to the common good. Perhaps it is for this reason that states such as Canada have developed economic programs for managing the country as a community that shares revenue between regions.

What the preceding argument suggests is that national revenue ought not to be distributed strictly on the basis of what each region has contributed.[21] While it is fair to recognize those regions that contribute the most, the common good requires that market economics be transcended. A balanced and desirable formula will be one that combines several principles—derivation, need, population, and so on. In this respect, the allocation formula produced by the Hicks Commission of 1951 was the best.[22]

Summary

This chapter set out to evaluate competing claims for, and constitutional agreements regarding, a desirable structural political arrangement, a desirable political representation system, and a desirable revenue allocation system during the several constitutional conferences that preceded the formal grant of independence.

Regarding the structural political arrangement, the findings have held that conflicting claims for a political federation of ethnic groups, a unitary system blind to ethnic difference, and a loose political partnership of the three regions all had their strengths and weaknesses. A desirable arrangement had to be one that took into account the strengths and weaknesses of all the claims. In this respect, a political framework produced by a Rawlsian-type of agreement would have been inadequate because of its intrinsic bias. One option could have been an arrangement that combined institutional elements from all three political systems, but this was found not to be feasible.

A more realistic alternative was a compromise arrangement that required claimants to soften their claims and make mutual adjustments and concessions. In this respect, the 1953-54 compromise agreement that nearly liquidated the center and gave full autonomy to the three regions was a pragmatic one, but it was grounded on the self-interest of the three majority groups and their elites who dominated both the regions and the national arena. Its pragmatism was contradicted by the unjust refusal to extend equal political recognition to some minorities who demanded similar recognition through the creation of new states. Although there were practical difficulties regarding such political separation, these problems were not irresolvable. Evidence suggests that the British colonial rulers were prepared to convene further constitutional conferences to resolve what existent difficulties, if independence would be postponed. But, having secured constitutional agreements that grounded political arrangements in their interests and those of their groups, the majority group elites refused to delay the immediate transfer of power by the British.

If the structural arrangement that was put in place was unjust, the arrangement for representation in the central legislature was not. Claims for fair representation rested on two competing principles: claims for the use of the population principle and counter-claims for the use of equality principle in the distribution of seats among the three regions. But, the final agreement to divide the country into over 300 equal constituencies unintentionally endorsed the proportional representation of groups both large and small. The drawing of constituency boundaries around colonial local administrative units that, in most cases, enclosed subethnic groups and smaller groups generated this unintended outcome. The arrangement terminated arguments about representation in the legislature and served as a model for local government reforms in 1976.

The same cannot be said for the revenue allocation agreement that was negotiated. The adoption in 1953 of a loose federation in which the three regions had full autonomy also structured the agreement for the sharing of revenue on the basis of each unit's contribution. This agreement effectively treated the regions as if they did not constitute a national community and had nothing in common. Unlike the representation arrangement that was dissociated from the structural political framework—that is, the federation of three regions—the revenue allocation agreement was a consequence of the adoption of the latter, and was not freed from it. In a federation, a national community exists as does a commitment to the collective well-being. These aspects provide the foundation for the combination of several principles governing revenue allocation. The principle agreed to in 1954 depended too much on derivation and amounted to no more than a sharing of assets. Indifference to the collective good was later realized to be a shortcoming and a commission set up in 1958 led to the introduction of a Distributive Pool Account for tempering derivation by allocating some revenues on the basis of both population and equality of regions.

Notes

1. Even the three-phase conference of 1949-50 that was structured to capture a broad representation of views turned out to exclude minority voices at the higher stages because the regional and national conferences were dominated by elites from the majority ethnic group in the regions (Nigeria 1950: 60).

2. In his memoir, the Yoruba leader Awolowo dwelt extensively on what he regarded as the annoying publicity of Igbo achievements generated by their journalist-politicians who, in their arrogance, also propagated the notion that the "Ibo nation was created by God to lead the people of Africa from darkness to light" (Awolowo 1960: 137-39).

3. Yoruba political elites were apprehensive about Igbos because the latter's educational achievements and rapid rise in national politics were perceived to give them competitive advantage in mass elections.

4. Igbos had migrated to all parts of the country to take advantage of whatever the modern market economy could offer and also to make a living because their land was not fertile enough to support their numbers (Awolowo 1960: 180; Coleman 1958: 324-25, and 347-49; Udoma 1994: 146).

5. In this arrangement, every 170,000 inhabitants were to have one representative, with the North having no more than 50 percent. A second chamber legislature that would safeguard against abuses of power by a region with preponderant representation was considered, but disagreements over its distribution of membership led to its abandonment (Nigeria 1953: 72, 149, and 246).

6. With this allocation system, the Eastern Region would receive aid grants from the center. The amount, totaling five hundred thousand pounds in the first year of the constitution's operation, and two hundred and fifty thousand pounds in the second year, would give the region some breathing space until it could raise more revenue to make up for its deficit. The AG contested this recommendation. It argued that the use of need and national interest in the previous allocation system was biased against the West, and that money which should have gone to the region had been used to subsidize the development of the Northern and Eastern Regions. The Eastern Region, the AG argued, had lived too much on resources of others, and "it is high time a halt was called to this parasitic habit" (Nigeria 1954: 192-93).

The NCNC responded to the above criticism by the AG with a seven-page document questioning the AG's understanding of "federalism from its pure political sense." In federalism, the NCNC argued, regions are not indifferent to the well-being of one another. Excessive derivation claims would amount to sharing national assets and liquidating the country. To refute the claim that the East owed its development to financial subsidies from the West, the names of several secondary schools founded by communities, and of some leading politicians trained by their local communities, were presented. Finally, they concluded their refutation by showing that palm oil from the (former) Oil Rivers Protectorate was the country's major source of revenue long before cocoa was established in the West. Revenue so derived was used to finance the Moors Plantation at Ibadan, which, in turn, accelerated cocoa cultivation in the entire Western Region (Nigeria 1954: 19-25).

7. According to his thesis, political and economic discrimination gives rise to demands for political and economic rights, not to separatist demands (Gurr 1993: 79, 82).

8. Some northern minorities provinces and two western minorities provinces had responded to the question regarding the optimal form of political arrangement by recommending separation into a "Central Region" and "Warri-Benin State," respectively. These recommendations were rejected at the regional conference level dominated by representatives of majority groups who then proceeded to retain the three regional structure at the highest level of the three-stage conference (Nigeria 1950: 60). One of the questions asked at the provincial conferences in the North was: "should there be a centralized or federal system of government?" To this, the people of the Benue Province answered: "There should be a fourth Region, comprising Adamawa, Benue, Ilorin, Niger, and Plateau Provinces. It should be known as the "Central Region" (Northern Nigeria 1949: 3).

9. The above difficulties compelled the commission to consider the possibility of paring down the proposed state in each region to an area in which it enjoyed unanimous support. However, it noted that such states would be of "lesser status" than the older regions. The constitutional conference of 1957 did not completely rule out the creation of states with "lesser powers," but argued that they would be unfeasible because, in the words of the commission: "it is hard to picture the successful working of a federation in which there were first class and second class states. Nor will the latter be content with such a state. . . . This consideration, when combined with the difficulty of finding a clean boundary, was . . . decisive in recommending against separation" (Nigeria 1958: 32, 87).

10. Dissenting Muslim groups from Kano-Kaduna and the independent Muslim groups of Bornu preferred political reform of the Islamic *Weltanschauung* over arguments against its existence (Ilesanmi 1997: 140-41).

11. In this scheme, representatives of free and equal citizens negotiate fair terms regarding social cooperation from an "original position" in which no one has a advantage over the other in the bargaining process. The original position is created by eliminating contingencies of the social world—for example, historical circumstances, natural endowments, social positions, ethnicity, and moral doctrines of those represented. Thus, symmetrically situated behind a "veil of

ignorance," representatives of free citizens cannot deem who would occupy the top or lower positions of the society being created. These representatives, however, remain rational and would try as much as possible to advance the good of those they are representing even though the 'veil of ignorance' makes it impossible to determine what their representative good is. This problem is resolved by singling out five primary goods (or things that are generally thought to be necessary social conditions and means for the pursuit of good life) and adopting principles guaranteeing them. The five, in order of priority, are: a) basic liberties such as freedom of thought and of conscience; b) freedom of movement and free choice of occupation against a background of diverse opportunities; c) powers and prerogatives of offices and positions of responsibility; d) income and wealth as means to achieve a wide range of ends, and; e) the social bases of self-respect.

The principles adopted to guarantee and assign priority to these primary goods specifically regulate political, social, and economic institutions that constitute the basic structure of society. Also, they are derived from behind a veil of ignorance, without reference to any of the diverse moral doctrines in society. Therefore, they stand independently and command overlapping consensus concerning their fairness in society (Rawls 1993: 3-46, 133-172, 289-371; 1971: chapter 3).

12. This argument follows Nordlinger, who presented compromise and concession as two of six strategies to reduce conflict. Recall that Northern Regional leaders dropped their claim for confederation and, instead, agreed for a federal union. Eastern leaders also made concessions by dropping their unitary demand for a federation of the existing three regions. In turn, leaders of the Western Region backed away from their demand for a regrouping of the country along ethnic lines in order to agree on retaining the three regions.

13. He went on to say that people consent if they submit to a conqueror. This part of his thesis could be used to argue that people could achieve peace by giving up their just claims, but the idea that people tacitly consent when they submit to a conqueror is one that has been refuted by both Locke and Rousseau.

14. The agreement made it possible for each region to close its elective and civil service positions to citizens whose ethnic origin was not traceable to the region, thus violating individual rights.

15. A contemporary form of the aversion to subjection by an immediate neighbor is the demand by suspected perpetrators of ethnic genocide (such as war crime suspects in Rwanda) that judges from foreign countries should try them and, if convicted, other countries should provide jails for them. The idea here is that they would rather endure punishment from a distant and unknown power than from an immediate rival.

16. The British used this to deny demands. In the words of James Robertson, then colonial governor: "I believed strongly that with Independence near, it would cause a great deal of confusion and possibly trouble to create new states in 1958; I felt that this would be setting Nigeria off its new independent future in

very uncertain and disturbed conditions. I told Sir Henry Willink that in my view any new state should be recommended only in the most imperative circumstances" (Robertson 1974: 217).

17. For a discussion of the convergence between democracy and justice see Ian Shapiro (1996: chapter 4).

18. The ideas in the lines that follow are an adoption of Rousseau's argument about the relation between the subject and the sovereign (Rousseau 1968: bk. III, chap. 1).

19. A recent case was the creation in North Carolina of a 160-mile snakelike constituency that was less than one mile wide. This was aimed at rectifying the underrepresentation of African Americans but was nullified by a recent U.S. Supreme Court ruling (Kymlicka 1995: 135-36).

20. Let me explain each of the factors I have just listed.

Convenience to Taxpayers and Collectors: It is more convenient for both the payers—individuals and companies—and the levels of government if certain revenues like taxes and import/export duties are collected by one bureaucracy. Several bureaucracies and different tax forms will be required if the constituent units (regions here) and the center collect their taxes separately. To avoid the problem of individuals and companies filling two or more tax forms each year, and of multiple bureaucracies competing for returns, one government collects all revenues and then returns moneys to the regions.

Inability of Some Regions to Generate Revenue: Some regions might not be able to raise enough funds to carry out their responsibilities, while others might generate in excess of what they require. Unconditional transfers of surplus to those in deficit is possible if the center is collecting revenues. What are generally known as federal grants are a consequence of the inability to generate revenue to match responsibilities.

Effects of One Region's Economic Activities on the Other: If the goods and services of a region do not coincide with its geographic boundaries, they might spill over to, and have positive or negative effects on, residents in other jurisdictions. Where goods and services trade across regions, as they always do, the taxation and expenditure policy of one government will implicate the other's economy. For example, investments in higher education, medical health, highways, and canals affect the economic decisions of people in other regions (for instance, regarding investments, trade, or labor migration). In this case, the benefits of fiscal decisions are externally enjoyed, but the government cannot claim political rewards from the electorate who happens to be in the other jurisdiction. On the other hand, the fiscal policy could have an adverse external effect, in which case the cost is exported and the government cannot be held accountable.

The solution to spillover is to expand the jurisdictional boundaries of political authorities to coincide with the geographic span of public goods—which is impossible in practice. Since the center has national jurisdiction, it automatically exercises political authority over the territorial area of public goods. It addresses the problem of spillover by using grants to match the actions of regions whose fiscal policies affect others. By assuming the major role in revenue collection, it can either compensate regions that receive the burdens of others or subsidize those whose expenditure benefits others.

Harmonious Tax Rates: If the tax system were left completely with the regions, rates and expenditure would vary for identical people across jurisdictions. A teacher in one region will pay more income tax than another teacher who has the same income but resides in another region. Unemployment benefits will vary in like manner. The concept of a national community requires that there should be horizontal equity. That is, citizens of like incomes residing in different regions should be treated equally. It is therefore up to the center to define the tax base and the applicable rates, collect these taxes, and turn part of the revenue back to the regions from which the taxes are imposed and collected.

To obtain the best tax treatment, a worker will rationally migrate to a low wage area if she finds that it contains a package of public sector benefits—such as free education, free medicare, and subsidized housing—to be gained in return for some sacrifice in income. At the macroeconomic level, this movement of labor from high-wage to low-wage area is wrong because labor migrates from low productivity employment to one of high productivity. There is a loss in societal output which is not regained. To avoid a situation in which social interests will be sacrificed for narrow private interests, a harmonized tax system has to prevail across the board. For a discussion on a harmonized tax system in a federal state, see Richard Simeon and Mark Krasnick (1986: chapter 9).

21. Igbos and several minorities in the East were constrained by the derivation system that was put in place because agricultural exports were mostly from the North and East. This did not immediately generate conflict because the center was practically liquidated and, as a result, no basis existed to complain about neglect or the uneven allocation of funds. The derivation system nevertheless showed indifference and lack of unity. This sort of indifference to the well-being of the other could trigger exit. Some have argued that it was a change of fortune in the East following the discovery and emergence of crude oil that prompted Igbos to take the region out of the country. In other words, the rationale was that since people in the region were left alone to take care of themselves during their period of economic adversity, they might as well exit now that their fortune changed for the good.

22. My objective, as I stated earlier on, is to argue for a framework for revenue allocation. I will, therefore, not go into practical details concerning in what proportion the principles ought to be mixed.

Chapter Four

The Second Political Strategy

Independence in 1960 marked the beginning of the second political strategy to cope with ethnic difference and reduce conflict. This strategy was characterized by the adoption of a quota system for appointment into strategic institutions such as the military, and by the redivision of the country into twelve states to take into account smaller groups who were previously denied political recognition. This chapter will assess the quota system and the recognition of minorities in separate states.

The Quota System

The quota system had its origin in the "Nigerianization" policy adopted in the 1950s as the country moved closer to political independence. Through this policy, Nigeria's political achievement in terms of participation in the legislative and executive spheres of government would be matched in the administrative sphere where expatriates dominated the civil service. The policy required the withdrawal of Europeans from both the federal and regional civil service and the appointment of Nigerians to fill those vacated positions. Since the two regions in the South already had skilled personnel, they easily filled available positions in their regional and federal services. A large number of people from the two regions moved to the Northern Region to fill positions in its regional service and in the federal institutions located there. Because of this labor influx from the Eastern and Western Regions, the Northern Regional Government developed the policy of closing its public service to people who did not belong to the region by basing appointment on "nativity." Nativity was measured by the ethnicity of one's parents and it was managed by hiring people from the two southern regions on contract if they were appointed. At the federal level, the Northern Regional Government succeeded in negotiating a lower entry qualification for northern applicants seeking to fill positions in the civil service (Ekeh and Osaghae 1989: 173-75).

99

Restrictions regarding appointments into the regional service, and the lowering of entry qualifications to federal civil service for natives of some regions, were not provided for by the Independence Constitution. In fact, northern representatives to the Independence Constitutional Conference tried but failed to secure an agreement for the use of federal public service quotas. Moreover, the 1963 Republican Constitution, while forbidding discrimination "against a particular community, tribe, place of origin, religion or political opinion," permitted any region to implement policies protecting the rights of its members to employment (Bach 1997: 338). Balanced and representative appointment into the bureaucracy was therefore not formalized at the national level.

Balance was first created among the three regions in the military. From the mid-1950s to independence, when British disengagement was on course, merit was the criterion for recruiting Nigerians, and a greater number of applicants came from the Eastern Region. Between 1955 and 1961, about two-thirds of the officer ranks that were recruited came from the east, while 80 percent of the other ranks came from the north (and two-thirds of these were from minority areas in that region). Fearing that one section of the country might use the army to dominate the others, the NPC-controlled federal government introduced a policy for balanced recruitment into the officer ranks in 1962. It adopted a recruitment formula in which 50 percent of military cadets would originate from the north and the other 50 percent would be equally shared between the east and west. This 50:25:25 formula was intended to reflect the distribution of the national population among the regions. The then minister for army affairs defended the quota system in the Senate saying:

> We introduced the quota system in the Army . . . thus preventing the possible fear that the army would sometime become unreliable. If any part of the country is not represented in the army, we harbor, some fear that a particular section will begin to feel it is being dominated. But now . . . the country's safety is assured. (Dudley 1973: 96)

One consequence of the quota recruitment was that the North's share of officers commissioned in 1963-64 rose to 42 percent from 21 percent in 1960. By 1966, the upper crust of the military was still dominated by easterners (mainly Igbos), but the use of quotas for appointment and promotion blocked the rise of middle-ranking officers—such as captains and majors—from the East and West (Dudley 1973: 92)[1] and this grievance partly contributed to the majors' coup of January 1966, which violently terminated the First Republic.

Another consequence of the quota system entailed the reproduction of societal cleavages and conflict in the military. The coherence and command structure of the military was weakened as ethno-regional identification and attachment displaced loyalty to superiors. Noncommissioned officers openly flouted military norms by refusing to take orders from superiors who were not from the same geo-ethnic region as them. A northern sergeant, for example, told a brigadier of western origin, and who was also the most senior officer in the army in July 1966, that "I do not take orders from you until my captain comes" (Ademoyega 1981: 119).

The fear that "regional armies" would emerge within the military, and the need to have a combat-ready, esprit de corps army to defeat secession, led to the abandonment of the quota system in 1966.[2] In its place, recruitment was based on individual merit and fitness irrespective of regional and ethnic origin. After the civil war in 1970, the quota system was thought to have been abandoned forever as some high-ranking military officers publicly declared that there were no plans to introduce ethnic balancing in the post-civil war political rehabilitation (Ekeh and Osaghae 1989: 237). However, various segments in Nigerian society made demands for the use of quotas for admission into federal institutions, including universities and military schools. By 1975, the quota system was back, this time, however, not only in the military but also in civil institutions including, the civil service. It was later formalized by the "federal character" constitution drafted in 1976.

The Separation of Minorities

The separation of ethnic minorities into new states in the 1960s was not a conscious effort; rather, it represented more the unexpected outcome of power struggles among the dominant parties. The 1959 federal elections saw the NPC winning the greatest number of votes, but not an absolute majority. To form a government, the NPC leadership invited its two major rivals, the AG and the NCNC, to join in a three-way coalition. The NPC needed one of the two parties to form a government and pass its bills in Parliament. However, it also believed that the inherited form of Western government and opposition politics was unsuitable for Nigeria because of its multiethnic composition. The NCNC leadership accepted the invitation, whereas the AG leadership turned it down and went on to form the opposition, much to the consternation of a faction of its leaders who thought that joining the coalition would bring public service jobs and positions in government boards to Yorubas. The refusal split the AG into two factions in 1962, setting off a crisis within the party.

The NPC-NCNC coalition soon ran into difficulties. As discussed above, the introduction of the quota system for recruitment into the army worked against easterners, especially Igbos. Even though the NCNC thought the coalition yielded more benefits to the NPC in terms of government jobs, patronage, and the siting of projects,[3] it did not separate. Instead, it sought to wrest power from the NPC, its senior ally, and to do so it had to shore up its strength in the federal legislature. The AG crisis provided the opportunity for calling on the coalition government to divide the Western Region with the expectation that the new units that emerged would fall under its control.

The NPC, on the other hand, saw the crisis within the AG, and the consequent breakdown of law and order in the Western Region, as an opportunity to eliminate the AG, which had been performing its opposition role in the federal legislature in a confrontational and embarrassing manner. The NPC also saw this as an opportunity to show the NCNC what it could expect if it were not the pliable and submissive junior ally it should be (Ige 1995: 196). Under these circumstances, the coalition government used constitutional means to carve the Midwest out of the Western Region in 1963. The Midwest immediately fell under the political control of the NCNC, thus increasing that party's bargaining power.

Ethnic fighting within the military (such as the coup and counter-coups from January to July 1966) prompted the calling of an Ad Hoc Constitutional Conference in September 1966, whose purpose was to debate and recommend the most suitable constitutional arrangements available for Nigeria. Debates shifted from claims concerning political confederation to arguments for the creation of new states from the existing regions. The killing of Igbos residing in the North, however, abruptly terminated the conference. At the same time, the military government of the Eastern Region convened a consultative assembly of easterners to decide on secession. To preempt the declaration of secession from Biafra, the federal military government divided the country into a total of twelve states, six of which were controlled by minorities. The goal was to separate eastern minorities into new states so that they would challenge Biafran secession.[4] As in the case of the Midwest, strategic considerations prompted the creation of twelve states, which separated ethnic minority groups from the three major groups. In both the 1963 and 1967 cases, strategic needs intersected with the preindependence claims of minorities to achieve recognition in separate states.

The Public Good and Fairness

This section assesses the quota policy and the 1963 and 1967 political separation of minorities in order to determine if the policy and the political exercise of creating the Midwest State from the Western Region, and the subsequent creation of twelve states, was morally right. The analysis that follows rests on two assumptions: that political subunits (or states) and employment positions in national institutions are goods that are generally desirable and that these goods are relatively scarce in society. These two assumptions entail that social justice becomes an issue. If there were no moral norms regarding things that are desirable and reprehensible, and if things were in absolute scarcity or in abundant supply, issues of social justice would not arise in human interactions. It is because these conditions are not universal that we have morality and laws to regulate our interactions and resolve any conflicts that might arise. This section, therefore, regards morality and laws as means to an end, the end being a well-ordered and stable society.

The Quota System and Fairness

Two conceptions of justice are generally operative in the distribution of social goods. The first is meritocratic and maintains that people should be treated according to their ability. Achievement is the chief criterion for determining the distribution of social goods. Those who have achieved the most receive the most while those who have achieved the least receive the least. The emphasis here is on formal equality and competition in the public domain. Unequals are only formally regarded as equals and are subject to seemingly impartial universal rules.

This conception of justice is blind to the historical background of society's members and is intolerant of preferential treatment for or temporary reservation of goods for the weak. Preferential treatment and/or reservation of goods are regarded as violations of state neutrality and considered deviations from fairness. By reserving positions for the weak, the state, which is supposedly public and neutral, is perceived to be siding with or adopting the particular good of certain members as the public good. Thus, a quota system or affirmative action offends the meritocratic conception of justice by violating the principle of equal treatment of citizens. Also, the reservation of positions for the weak is believed to work against organizational goals. Public institutions and offices are established to discharge particular social functions, the effective realization of which requires that only those with relevant qualifications be appointed. To hire people who do not have the required skills would undermine these social ends (Gutman and Thompson 1996: 311).

Meritocracy in itself might be a good principle for distributing goods, but it has some difficulties. First, it has been argued that hiring on the basis of skills is just if competence in producing specified outcomes can be measured objectively, or if technical skills translate directly into excellent performance, or if performance could be judged individually. These conditions can hardly be met because: a) most jobs are too complex to allow for a value-free measurement of individual performance; b) production is generally done by team work, which makes it difficult to determine the contribution of each worker; and, c) in the modern world where the production process is automated, workers contribute little to actual production and, at the management level, work entails the use of discretion (Gutman and Thompson 1996: 311-12; Young 1990: 201-5).

Second, the merit principle wrongly assumes that people have equal opportunities and therefore judges them strictly by achievement. Implicitly, it upholds underlying social inequalities and fails to consider the social circumstances that produce inequality. In the Nigerian case, the principle is incapable of offering a satisfactory moral account of why people from the Northern Region should be responsible for their "backwardness" especially since it was not the people who closed the region to Western civilization but, rather, their leaders. It is not clear why they should be responsible for what they did not do. Accepting the merit principle would entail nothing more than holding the people accountable for their leaders' actions.

The above argument could be illustrated by authoritarianism in some African states. The predatory action of some leaders in Africa may or may not be acceptable to the people—the ruled. It is likely that they object to it because no society exists whose moral norms uphold oppression and looting. The people would be bewildered if they were to be held accountable for the unjust acts their leaders committed. Obviously countries of the First World impose sanctions on political leaders of some states. At the same time they take appropriate measures to address the difficulties such sanctions might have on the people because they recognize that the latter should not be punished for the deeds of their rulers.

One could counter this position by presuming that leaders are the legitimate representatives of the people and therefore the latter are fully accountable for what is done on their behalf. For example, if state officials contract foreign loans, the citizens have an obligation to pay through their tax money. If the very leaders that contracted the loan cease to be in office on account of death or expiration of tenure, the citizens are obliged to honor the debt.

With respect to the case at hand, one could counter the counterargument by accounting for Nigeria's significant differences. The closure of the Northern Region to Western influences was done in the context of resistance to foreign conquest and domination. In itself, political conquest was not a desirable thing because it brought both the loss of freedom and the lack of self-respect. The most denigrating and pernicious aspect of colonialism was the loss of self-worth caused by the replacement of the indigenous culture with a foreign culture. Within the Nigerian territory, resistance to both the political and the cultural aspects of colonialism was universal. The difference was that the Muslim northerners mounted cultural resistance more effectively than the non-Muslim people of the South. The relative backwardness of the North should be understood, then, as the result of its successful resistance to the cultural aspects of colonialism, while southern progress was the result of its ineffectual resistance. Therefore, the South cannot be praised for putting up a weak resistance to the assault on self-respect and the North blamed for mounting a successful resistance; indeed, it is the North that deserves respect. Seen in this manner, the relatively educationally and economically backward North had every moral justification to demand preferential treatment if it suffered on account of its successful resistance to colonialism. Moral explanations like these remain elusive to merit-based conceptions of distributive justice.

The other conception of distributive justice is welfarist. Drawing on stoicism and natural law theory, it holds that people are equal by nature and, as natural equals, each person has the same right to the satisfaction of their basic needs. From this perspective, therefore, it is the responsibility of society to provide everyone with an equal opportunity for the realization of that right and this entails the provision of compensatory treatment for those who are historically disadvantaged. With respect to Nigeria, the welfarist conception of justice would view the quota system implemented by the NPC government not as a violation of equality but as a way of mitigating historically rooted inequalities. Using ethnic balancing to moderate the weaknesses of the merit principle would necessarily accommodate the historically disadvantaged people of the North and function as a necessary component to achieve the goal of long-term substantive equality. The assumption here is that the state's subscription to formal equality in constitutional texts would not really produce substantive equality of opportunity unless concrete measures were adopted to advance weaker members of society. In fact, some democratic equality theorists argue that state institutions have social responsibilities in the environment in which they are situated, and that these responsibilities include the representation of diverse social interests as a way to ensure that services are delivered to, and can be accessed by, all members in a diverse polity (Gutman and Thompson 1996: chapters 4 and 5).

Two problems can be found in welfarist notions of justice. First, social justice does not arise among people who are perfectly equal (as in a pre-social state), but among those who interact and influence one another in a civil state (Hume 1948: "Treatise of Human Nature," bk. 3, part 2(2); "Enquiry Concerning Principles of Morality," §3(2)). Equality of opportunity derived from the idea of human equality is only practical in a nonhuman society, such as Rousseau's savage state of nature where no one is subject to the influence of the other. Insofar as people interact and influence one another, inequality is bound to arise and, for precisely this reason, human communities have need of justice. Still, a well-devised system of justice ought to reduce inequality and, in fact, the system is unfair if it fails in reducing inequality.[5] I will speak more on this in a moment.

Second, equal treatment of people irrespective of their historical circumstances has the danger of rewarding those who are responsible for their misfortune. As already discussed, however, the people of the Northern Region could not be held responsible for their educational backwardness and so this particular criticism would not easily apply in the Nigerian context.

What emerges from this discussion is that equality is the substantive goal of social justice and that it could not have been met by the sole use of either the merit or welfare principles as the standard for recruitment into national institutions such as the military. By itself, the merit principle was unjust because it did not promote the good of all sections of the country. And yet, the interests of those sections that this principle reflected should not be discounted. So, a system of justice that takes into account the interests of all sections ought to balance merit with welfare. Balancing both would depend on the goals of the community and the choices the people have made about the type of country they want to live in. Let me explain this.

The existence of morality or moral discourse within any given society presupposes some desired ends; if not, what is right and what is wrong would hardly become issues (Ekeh and Osaghae 1989: 319-20). A society that agrees on justice as one of its goals, and one should think that every society would agree on this, would also agree that it is desirable to promote the general good instead of the good of some individuals or groups. This society would agree that it is desirable to adopt measures that improve the general quality of life rather than those that increase and widely distribute the conditions and effects of poverty. The Nigerian people could not have been against these ends, for the Independence Constitution of 1960 had social justice as one of its fundamental objectives. If these ends were desirable (and agreed upon either tacitly or explicitly), and if justice requires that people ought to be treated equally, then there was enough moral ground to use principles other than merit for including northerners in national institutions. Ethnic balancing was required to promote their interest as merit was used to promote the interests of people in the two southern regions. The use of the quota system, then, was not morally reprehensible. Although it worked to the disadvantage of the more qualified, its use was justified by an overriding moral consideration.

Some might argue that the Nigerian Independence and Republican Constitutions enshrined equal rights and opportunities before the law, and that the administration of justice should entail appealing to the laws of the land and as such not to morality. From this perspective, a policy, such as the quota system, would be seen as illegal and unjust if it were found not to be in accordance with promulgated and perspicuous laws. To deal with this objection, one might note that laws are not independent of morality but, rather, are derived from and seek to realize some moral principles. For example, the legal equality of citizens as enshrined in liberal constitutions has its foundation in Christian morality. But even if equality is a designated moral value, this does not mean that laws and morality always coincide. What is legal might not be morally right, just as the morally right might be illegal. An impartial judge who follows the judicial process and dispenses justice according to the law can be said to have acted within the bounds of legality. She is legally right if she nullifies a quota-based appointment on ground that it violates prescribed laws. However, the laws could be unjust if they violate or deviate considerably from moral principles. A judge might then be reluctant to nullify the quota-derived appointment if the universal law is unjust. She might heed the voice of morality by either revising legal precedent to uphold the appointment or by resigning from office on account of the injustice brought about by the merit-based law. In other words, moral considerations can override legal claims, as in the case of Socrates' madman and the borrower of his weapons, or Hegel's economically distressed debtor whose right to life takes priority over his creditor's legal claims. A morally acceptable greater good for society can justify revision of the existing laws to make them less morally repugnant. Injustice rules if legality is not brought in tune with morality.

Were the 1963 and 1967 State-Creation Exercises Morally Justifiable?

I have just argued in defense of the quota system. I will now examine the creation of the Midwest State and the twelve states.

Political events between 1960 and 1963 indicate that the creation of the Midwest State resulted from a power struggle between the NPC and the NCNC, its junior ally. Each wanted exclusive control of federal power and, to achieve that objective, each tried to increase its strength in the federal legislature by annexing part of the Western Region. Out of these circumstances, the AG- or opposition-controlled Western Region became a victim in 1963. The strategic needs of both the NPC and NCNC to fragment the West intersected with long-standing minority claims for separation of the region into a Midwest State. Now, a puzzle arises: if claims to separation made by western minorities have normative weight, as argued previously, were they met by the 1963 exercise that was driven by considerations of power? Before answering this question, it will be necessary to raise another related puzzle.

Debate in the 1966 Ad Hoc Conference shifted between issues of confederation and of creation of new states from the existing regions. As noted earlier, the conference was inconclusive and, as a result, no agreement was reached. The federal military government, led by a northern minority, tried to preempt the Biafran declaration of secession in 1967 by: 1) separating eastern minorities into new states so that they would assume the primary role of resisting Biafran secession; and, 2) meeting the preindependence aspirations of some northern minorities for political separation as a way of countering Igbo charges about northern domination of the federation. As in the case of the Midwest, the need to defeat Biafran secession through state creation converged with the decade old claims of minority groups for separation. The puzzle here is: if minority claims to separate states were morally justified, were they met by the 1967 military strategy? In his memoir, Udo Udoma (1994: 257) notes that "to those who for years had crusaded . . . their dreams had come true by the grace of Lieutenant Colonel Yakubu Gowon. There were rejoicings. . . ." If this is true, was the exercise not praiseworthy?

The two puzzles are the same, for they concern the morality behind the 1963 and 1967 projects of state creation. To address these puzzles, it is helpful to recall John Stuart Mill's (1972: 19) distinction between *intention* and *motive*. According to Mill, intention is "what [an] agent wills to do" while motive is "the feeling which makes him will so to do." The former suggests what the agent aims to achieve in a particular act while the latter indicates the mental qualities that produce the act. Thus, the morality of an action depends on the agent's aim, that is, what she wills to do. The mental quality from which the act emanates makes no difference to, and has nothing to do with, its moral estimate. Ethically, an act is not judged reprehensible or praiseworthy because it is done by a humble person, a rude person, an honest person, or a dubious person. These considerations only count in the estimation of the person's moral worth. No one is judged in a court of law by the qualities of her character—what counts is the person's intention. It is common for us to think that motive matters, but Mill's distinction shows us that we should be speaking of intention and that it would be a misunderstanding of the concept of motive if we use it in our judgments.

An application of the above distinction would lead one to comprehend the 1963 and 1967 state-creation exercises strictly in terms of their aims. One would then regard these exercises as having been driven by strategic considerations regarding power and military success, not by more fundamental considerations for local self-determination and equal recognition on which the claims of minorities were rooted. The distinction would prompt the judgment that minority claims provided rationalizations for state creation and helped mask the real agenda. Following this line of thought, the 1967 creation of two minority states out of the Eastern Region would be seen as an attempt to place the territorial areas covered by the two states under the control of their indigenous inhabitants, who would then position themselves against Biafran secession. Irrespective of its outcome, the exercise would be regarded as a crime because it was used merely as a pretense for normative claims while actually sending the claimants to war. Pretending to meet normative claims and using this pretense to send the claimants to war is a crime, even if the end is to rescue the larger state.[6]

Despite the utility of and inspiration brought by Mill's moral interpretation, it is narrow because it does not account for the outcome of the state-creation exercises overall. Preindependence claims of minorities were ostensibly used to mask a hidden agenda but the moral importance of the rationalizations remains unexplained. Mill's account of what constitutes a moral act does not provide an adequate tool for understanding the issue under discussion. Instead, Hegel provides us with a better method for comprehension. Hegel's distinction differentiated between *intention* and *purpose,* which enables us to understand what makes people morally responsible for their actions. According to Hegel, intention is the knowledge of the anticipated consequences of an action as, for example, applying a match to papers in order to burn them. Purpose is the relation between an action and its overall outcome, both intended and unintended, as when the application of match not only burns the papers but also sets the house on fire. The relation between the physical act of applying a match and the house going up in flames makes one morally responsible for arson (Hegel: 1952: 115-20).[7]

Now, the act of breaking the country into twelve states produced a sequence of events. First, minority states came under the rulership of their indigenous inhabitants. Then, to be masters of their new units, it became imperative for indigencs of minority states in the East to expel Igbos and seize their property.[8] In response to these actions, a deadly battle occurred in Rivers State. Secession was defeated, a peace agreement was signed, and the country was saved. Here, a relationship existed between the act of separating minorities and the sequence of events that followed. The act produced internal self-determination for minorities, thereby meeting their preindependence demands for equal political recognition, and it saved the country from disintegration. Overall, then, the act was morally praiseworthy since separation was desired, not for the evil intention of sending minorities to war, but for the larger purpose of freeing them and saving the country from disaster. In other words, state stability was found in a normative arrangement in which subunits were created to adequately recognize groups.

The moral weight of the 1963 and 1967 exercises can be better appreciated if one considers that the dominant parties of the pre-independence and independence era were opposed to any arrangement that would divide their regions. They were determined not to let their ethnic minorities go, and only force could bring about that desired arrangement in which minorities would be well accommodated. In order for the Midwest State to be created in 1963, the Western Region had to be placed under a state of emergency and its key AG leaders imprisoned on charges of plotting to overthrow the federal government. In other words, those who had opposed the creation of the Midwest all along, and were in the position of power to continue with such opposition, had to be disposed of forcefully. This was done in the context of a power struggle between the NPC and the NCNC. Similarly, force had to be used in the division of the Eastern Region. This was done under contingencies of secession and war, the very contingencies that also made for the disuniting of the North in order to free and win the support of its ethnic minorities. Conditions on the ground required the use of force if the three regions were to be divided, and both the 1963 power struggle and the 1967 secession provided exactly these opportunities. The exercises were morally justified, regardless of the intentions behind them.

Summary

This chapter aimed to evaluate the quota policy for appointment into, and promotion within, the Nigerian military, and the 1963 and 1967 separation of ethnic minorities into new political units. The quota system greatly disadvantaged people in the Western and Eastern Regions, more especially the Eastern, as it reduced the positions they would have filled under the merit system and slowed their upward mobility into the top hierarchy. Although grievances about this contributed to the first military coup by young Igbo officers in 1966, evaluation of the policy shows that the historically rooted educational backwardness of the Muslim North required the use of a distributive principle other than merit for a just allocation of positions. Educational backwardness was the result of resistance to the cultural aspect of colonialism, and the people ought not to be excluded from national institutions through an exclusive merit principle for their resistance to the most denigrating aspect of colonialism. To insist on merit is to insist on punishing people in the predominantly Muslim North for securing their culture against Western values, and to reward people in the South for their failure to do so. The historical roots of educational backwardness of the North, then, would justify the adoption of quota policy.

This justification is further strengthened by the Nigerian state's adherence to the constitutional norms of justice and equality. Adopting these as fundamental state objectives presupposed a desire to promote the common good. It presupposed a desire for the general well-being, not the well-being of some. Meeting the common good required a set of distributive principles that would take into account the circumstances and interests of each section of the country. The merit principle reflected the circumstances and interests of the southern regions, while reservation of positions through a quota system addressed the circumstances and interests of the north. One can conclude that a combination of both principles was reasonable and fair.

Regarding the 1963 and 1967 political separations, they were done in a context of a power struggle and imminent secession by the Eastern Region. The context could prompt one to argue that the separation exercises were purely strategic and that they were not actually meant to address minority claims for internal self-determination. But this argument is narrow and unsatisfactory because it does not account for the normative and political importance of the arrangements that were produced by the separation of minorities. Though strategic considerations lay behind the state-creation exercises, what also emerges as true is the existence of clear knowledge that the exercises would meet the preindependence claims of minorities and enable an arrangement that would adequately accommodate difference. No doubt there were some dubious intentions, but, overall, it can be determined that the larger purpose was an arrangement that was fair to both majority and minority groups.

Notes

1. The Eastern Region's share of the upper echelon of the military stood at 60 percent in 1966 (Ademoyega 1981: 111).

2. This response came too late. The army was already divided on ethno-regional lines and, by 1966, in-fighting had erupted in the form of coups and counter-coups, all of which resulted in the declaration of secession by the eastern faction led by Colonel Ojukwu.

3. By 1964, the NCNC had accumulated a list of grievances. An official document was released in that year detailing northern gains:

> Take a look at what they [i.e., the NPC] have done with the little power we surrendered to them to preserve a unity which does not exist: Kainji Dam Project—about 150 million pounds of our money when completed—all in the North; Bornu Railway Extension—about 75 million pounds of our money when completed—all in the North. Spending over 50 million pounds on the Northern Nige-

rian Army in the name of the Federal Republic. Military training and all ammunition factories and installations are based in the North, thereby using your money to train Northerners to fight Southerners. Building of a road to link the dam site and the Sokoto cement works—7 million pounds when completed—all in the North. Total on all these four projects about 262 million pounds. Now, they have refused to allow the building of an iron and steel industry in the East and [have] paid experts to produce a distorted report. (Mackintosh 1966: 557-78)

4. It turned out not to be fortuitous that those appointed to govern the new states were indigenes.

5. The relationship between inequality and justice was the subject of Rousseau's "Discourse on the Origin of Inequality." He tied justice to the emergence of inequality, just as Hume (1948: 60-64) did when he presented human interaction and relative scarcity of goods as the origin of justice.

6. Mill (1972: 19) makes a moral judgment about a related but different issue when he discusses the difference between intention and motive. According to him, anyone who saves someone from drowning does a morally right act, whatever the motive might be. But anyone betraying a friend who trusts him, is guilty of a crime, even if the aim is to serve another friend in danger.

7. Because lunatics have a defective mental capacity, they are not held morally responsible for their actions. Similarly, children have an unformed and weak mental capacity for which reason they are not held morally accountable for what they do.

8. Recall Rousseau's argument that the easiest way to subject a people is to occupy their land. Igbos had taken up residence in the minority regions of the East, especially in the Rivers Province where they owned significant landed property in the city of Port Harcourt and had emerged as the rulers. To control their new political unit, the peoples of Rivers State had to first expel the Igbos and confiscate their property.

Chapter Five

The Federal Character Approach

The inadequacies of the Nigerian political arrangements of the 1960s and the resultant three-year civil war prompted the search for a new strategy that would better accommodate diversity. Thereafter, constitution-makers drawn from various sections of the country negotiated an arrangement that would facilitate the broad inclusion of ethnic elites and also ensure stability. One aspect of the new arrangement was the restructuring of the federation into nineteen states reflecting Nigeria's ethnic composition, and then the division of the states into local government areas to further reflect subethnic differences. Another element was the adoption of a policy requiring that membership in federal institutions reflect the constituent states, which meant that membership in state-level institutions would reflect the constituent local governments. This chapter critically evaluates this constitutional strategy in order to determine its desirability. It begins with a contextual description.

The Background

Nigeria emerged from its three-year civil war with a new approach to governance. Its military rulers tried to promote intergroup equity by resorting to the use of what Rothchild (1997: 51, 66) has called the *informal proportionality principle* to guide appointments into high offices of state and the civil service as well as the allocation of resources. A reconstruction program, designed to rebuild infrastructure destroyed during the war, was initiated through the proportional allocation of projects—ranging from highways and airports to housing projects and to university campuses—to various geo-ethnic sections of the country. The adoption of the ad hoc proportionality principle coincided with the emergence of petroleum exports as the major source of national revenue. To apply the principle, this profitable natural resource was brought under the firm control of the central government through various decrees, and most of its revenues were claimed for the Distributive Pool Account established

115

by the Raisman Commission of 1959.[1] The use of proportionality in the allocation of revenue reduced to 20 percent the share of mineral rent and royalties going back to states from which they were derived. According to Akin Olaloku, the near-elimination of the derivation formula gave a considerable boost to the resources of the federal pool, which benefited the non-oil-producing states (Akinyemi et al. 1979: 119).

The central government's pooling of resources for redistribution to states and its postwar reconstruction projects triggered competition for patronage. States became clients of the central government while groups and individuals also competed for patronage at both levels of government. According to Richard Joseph (1987: 73) government. as the key decider of who gets what is being distributed and how, was subjected to real pressures for the conversion of what was being dispensed into "means of individual and group appropriation." These pressures included memoranda "demanding separate states to bring government nearer to the people" (Ekekwe 1986: 137).[2] An avalanche of demands for new states hit the federal government from all parts of the country, the intensity of which was reported to have reached a crisis point in 1973 (Nigeria 1976a: 8). The new demands emerged mostly from states dominated by the majority groups (the east-central and western states), not the minority states as the 1957 Minorities' Commission had earlier anticipated.

In response to these demands, a panel was commissioned in August 1975 to examine the possibility of creating new states.[3] Requests for internal self-determination made before the panel were all based on the need to: a) make government more democratic by bringing it nearer to the people; b) quicken the pace of development by localizing state capitals; c) assuage fears of new minorities; and, d) guarantee a balanced federation (Nigeria 1976a: 10).

In its report, the panel noted that during its tour of the country, groups regarded its mission of ascertaining the nature of these demands as being more about the distribution of political and economic goods; in other words, more of a "booty sharing exercise" (Nigeria 1976a: 10). This made the panel view state-creation exercises somewhat pessimistically. The panel felt that more states would neither accelerate economic development nor solve the problem of new minorities. Instead, increasing the number of states would lead to a degree of proliferation in which each town or village would be a state (Nigeria 1976a: 9). Yet, it went on to recommend the creation of eight new states, seven of which were accepted by government and distributed among various groups in the country.[4]

During its public hearings, the panel observed "the strength of ethnic loyalty, mutual suspicion and even hatred among the diverse peoples which make up Nigeria" and was convinced that "political stability cannot be guaranteed" if states were not created (Nigeria 1976a: 9, 110). It held the view that more states would foster "greater participatory democracy" and "produce . . . balanced and stable federation" (Nigeria 1976a: 9, 10). It was on this basis that the panel changed its perspective to make positive recommendations. Both the panel and government verbally rejected ethnic difference as a criterion for the drawing of boundaries, but both still took it into account in practice. Redrawing boundaries along ethnic lines permitted several minority groups in the North to be clearly separated in a number of states from the majority Hausa-Fulani. In turn, the country was divided into 301 local government units of uniform population range. Their boundaries closely followed colonial local administrative units that had enclosed subgroups of larger groups and smaller groups. Each of the nineteen states came to comprise local governments whose boundaries were drawn to accommodate diversity at the lower level.[5] Thus, Nigeria adopted what Duchacek has referred to as polyethnic federalism.

The creation of states and local governments turned out to be one of the two structural elements in a constitutional design for democratic inclusion. The other element was the drafting of a constitution that would require the origins of members in governmental bodies to represent the nineteen states (which themselves were assumed to reflect their internal ethnic composition). Inaugurated in September 1975, a Constitution Drafting Committee (CDC) of forty-nine members was instructed by General Murtala Mohammed, the then military ruler, to "eliminate over centralization of power in a few hands" by requiring that recruitment into public offices reflect the *federal character* of the country (Nigeria 1976b Vol. 1: xliii).[6]

The CDC took its task seriously, but it refused to mindlessly follow General Mohammed's instructions. It argued over competing alternatives for political inclusion as presented by its own internal factional groups. One faction promoted the belief that ethnic identity should be considered irrelevant in the determination of a person's human qualities and should therefore not be used as a basis for recruitment into elected and appointed positions. This reflected the dominant mainstream thought handed down by classical liberals and currently espoused by contemporaries such as Rawls and Ackerman. Another faction of the CDC advanced a second alternative, that the principle of equality would be met if power were dispersed to groups through the creation of new political units. The exercise undertaken in 1976 had done just that, which meant that it would be unnecessary to make constitutional provision for ethnic membership as the basis for participation in government. In effect, this suggestion is no different from the first option, for it is part of the liberal moral ontology recognizing individuals as rights claimants while canceling any competing claims made by the communities to which they belong. A third alternative pressed by still another faction argued that ethnic dominance had occurred at various levels in the past and that, to effectively guard against it, political inclusion should be deepened beyond the federal level to the state and local government levels as well as to government agencies (Nigeria 1976b Vol. 2: 54). This would reflect the arguments of both the theoretical and empirical thinkers discussed in chapter 1.

The CDC opted for the third proposition by formalizing the proportionality principle that had been in use since the end of the war. In effect, General Mohammed's instructions were followed and the phrase "federal character principle" was used to capture the new approach to democratic inclusion. According to the CDC, the principle required that:

> The composition of the Federal Government or any of its agencies and the conduct of its affairs shall be carried out in such manner as to reflect the federal character of Nigeria and the need to promote national unity, and also to command national loyalty. Accordingly, the predominance in that Government or in its agencies of persons from a few states, or from a few ethnic groups or other sectional groups shall be avoided. The composition of a government other than the Federal Government or any of the agencies of such government and the conduct of their affairs shall be carried out in such manner as to recognize the nature and character of the peoples within their area of authority and the need to promote a sense of belonging and loyalty among all such peoples. (Nigeria 1976b Vol. 1: ix-x)

Membership in the constituent states of the federation was defined along biological terms. According to the CDC, to "[b]elong to . . . when used with reference to a person in a state refers to person who either of whose parents or any of whose grandparents was a member of a community indigenous to that state" (Nigeria 1976b Vol. 1: §321(1)). With this clarification, federal character was applied to the highest office, which was to consist of a single chief executive known as president. He or she was expected to derive his or her authority directly from the people, for which purpose the entire country was to be regarded as one single constituency. Almost a decade earlier, Giovanni Sartori (1968: 272-75) had argued that electoral systems were the most powerful instruments of political engineering; here we see the CDC charting that same course. A majoritarian plurality *plus* distribution electoral method was devised by which presidential candidates were required to secure the highest number of voter support in a widespread geographic area in order to be elected. Constitutionally, this translated into not less than 25 percent of the vote in at least 75 percent of the states (Nigeria 1976b Vol. 1: xxix-xxx). The assumption made here was that presidential candidates would appeal across ethnic fault lines, build multiethnic alliances, and that the victor would therefore emerge as a pan-ethnic figure. This electoral inducement was also applied to the states and local governments.

Arend Lijphart (1985: 80) presented the rotation of the executive office as part of his consociational arrangements for South Africa. Ten years before Lijphart made his prescriptions, Nigerian constitutional engineers raised, debated, and abandoned the idea of dividing the country into four geographic zones for the purpose of rotating the offices of the president and vice president. Instead, attention was focused on political parties that would produce candidates for the elective and appointive offices such that two-thirds of the members of a party executive had to be drawn from at least two-thirds of the states that made up the federation. This was a way of requiring parties to be the chief instruments of multiethnic alliance formation. This constitutional device was topped with a provision making it difficult to further multiply the number of state units.

Evaluation of the Federal Character Approach

What emerges from the historical narrative presented above is the definite commitment by a post-civil war Nigeria to adopt a constitutional strategy that would make democracy live up to its promise of equal access to decision making and opportunities. The creation of seven new states and the adoption of a federal character principle were two interrelated elements that defined the strategy. I will now turn to a critical assessment of the federal character strategy.

Demands for More States: Based on Justice or Economics?

The government panel in 1975 viewed the demand for more states as purely economic, which, if met, would lead to state proliferation and the destruction of the principle of federation. These were considered highly undesirable effects. On the other hand, going by what it observed during its national tour concerning the strength of ethnic loyalty and suspicion, the panel thought that meeting these demands would also further distribute power and guarantee political stability. Ultimately, it considered the political factor to have greater weight than the economic factor. The critical issue here is the conflict between the economic and political considerations and which one should take priority.

To begin with the economic, neo-Marxist-inspired views would regard the demands as class demands not meriting attention. The class aspect might be true, but it is also necessary to go beyond narrow selfish motives to consider the intersection of interests between elites and the groups to which they belong. Like all human beings, elites have their personal interests to satisfy, but as members of groups having a common consciousness and purpose, they may also promote the salient interests of their groups. They claim the legitimacy of group leadership not through elections but by advancing group interests in the state arena. They authoritatively advance meaningful claims by holding consultations and negotiating common positions within the group. They can move back and forth between the state arena and the group, continually negotiating salient interests within the latter and continually making demands on the former. Hence, in the public sphere, elites enjoy considerable support from their ethnic members and are able to mobilize them for action when the need arises.

The demand for states was therefore not necessarily made solely to achieve the ambition of power-seekers. Rather, a unity of purpose existed between elites and their groups, which the government panel identified to be a share of national wealth. This unity of interest could be discerned in the following findings of the panel:

> the agitation is mainly led by old disreputed, disgruntled, and tainted politicians whose motive is to create little empires for themselves . . . the panel's firm belief is that the basic motivation in the demand . . . is rapid economic development. All other reasons are . . . to a large extent mere rationalizations to achieve the basic purpose of development. (Nigeria 1976a: 9, 10)

The relevant issue that must be addressed, then, is whether ethnically based demands driven by the desire for public resources had any merit. Drawing on Aristotle's judgments concerning competing claims to justice, one could argue that competition for national wealth should not translate into claims to internal self-determination.[7] Wealth is temporary, not something that lasts forever. A country that witnesses a good turn in its economic fortunes might grant economically based demands for internal self-determination, but it might also choose not to. If self-determination is granted on account of good fortune, the units will be sustained while the wealth lasts. But it is also probable that economic decline would occur at some point in time in which case the internally self-governing units would either collapse or ask to be reunited. Wealth is too transient to justify claims to internal self-government.

On the other hand, the demand for more states could be regarded as having been driven by the need for justice. This line of reasoning requires an understanding of the state structure that emerged from the 1967 state-creation exercise as unbalanced and working to the disadvantage of groups that did not have their proportionate share of states. In this position, demands have to be regarded as political claims made to redress injustice. For example, the 1967 state-creation exercise grouped Igbos into one state while Yorubas and the Hausa-Fulani had three each. By having only one state, Igbos and their elites were not treated as equally as the Yorubas despite being almost equal to them in population size. The panel's observation about the presence of "mutual ethnic suspicion" and demands "made in bitterness" should not be taken at face value because underneath these negative expressions were perceived injustices in the state structure which served to disadvantage some in the distributional sphere. So, while political claims were not justified by competition for economic goods, the need for equity was also very compelling.

What, then, did justice require given the two competing options? One possible response would have been to uphold the economic argument. Instead of endorsing wealth-based claims that could result in the endless fragmentation of dependent units, those in power might have ensured stability just as well by retaining the twelve-state structure already in place. This might have been a desirable option, but it would have been unrealistic given conditions on the ground. Facts about some groups, such as Igbos, being grouped in one state, and of others such as the Yoruba, being in three, would have rendered such a decision highly biased and politically imprudent. More important, attempts at building legitimate governance and winning the confidence of groups through the use of the proportionality principle would have been undermined. Equity would have been vitiated, for government would have been perceived as dispensing social goods unequally among groups and their elites. In this case, those vanquished during the civil war would have considered themselves targets of political domination.

The other option was to uphold the justice-based argument and risk the proliferation of unviable states. This option would have dispensed justice by accommodating groups proportionately in accordance with their demographics or geographic distribution. The state would have freed itself from charges of domination by elites from a few groups, and a framework for mutual trust and conciliatory politics would have been established. On this score, the decision of the panel to meet the demands was justified, despite the potential risk.

Federal Character and Justice

I want to discuss the desirability or undesirability of "federal character" as a strategy for ensuring equity in the composition of government. Recall that the constitutional engineers were split between two broad strategies. One considered state creation to have adequately accommodated difference and viewed ethnic membership as irrelevant in appointment and recruitment. The other emphasized the use of ethnic identity for appointments at all levels of government as a means of preventing domination by elites from a few ethnic groups. What normative importance did each of these strategies have and what alternative options were available?

The first of the two strategies reflects the Kantian-derived liberal principle that each person deserves respect because human beings are rational agents capable of directing their own lives. Individuals are regarded as having reason and as being creative. In any society, the system of justice ought to treat them as having equal ability and opportunity. And, universal criteria like competition and qualification furnish the basis for recruiting officials into nonprivate and public positions, both high and low. Differences between persons collapse into the common denominator, equal capacity, which legally transforms into the status of rights-bearer.[8] On this level playing field, unequals are subjected to the same rules. What is the normative weight of this system of justice centering on the individual?

In his political theory, John Stuart Mill (1972) discusses the virtues of a society that worships individual ability. He argues that a society centered on the individual is one in which thought, initiatives, and the quest for something new, triumph over custom and tradition. The individual's mental and moral faculties are developed as one challenges orthodoxy.

Mentally the individual becomes creative and original, always seeking to improve her or his own state; morally one becomes an active, industrious and a kinder person. On the mental side, it is the creative character—the one that strives against common tendencies, not the one that gives way to them—that indirectly improves the lot of humanity. On the moral side, it is the character who employs his faculties in new challenges to improve his well being who sees no prospective enemies in others. The striving mind develops a feeling of goodwill and fellowship to other similar minds. On the other hand, the mind that does not strive, but depends on the circumstances of birth (such as ethnicity and class) to obtain what others possess, overflows with envy and ill will. A country regresses and decays when such minds predominate or are encouraged by public policy. So, Mill showed that a country progresses and develops in proportion to the way its people see success in life as a reward for individual initiative and hard work. He bases human progress and civilization on industry and the desire to accomplish, and celebrates a society that respects ability. Indeed, the proportional representation system he presents is meant to give political recognition to those with mental ability. The liberal principle of equal respect for persons translates into respect for ability.

A commitment to the claim that ethnic membership should be irrelevant in appointments and promotion would, therefore, have required the use of the merit principle for recruitment into elective and nonelective public offices. The problems with this principle in the Nigerian context have already been discussed in chapter 4 and need not be repeated here. What should be recognized is that in post-civil war Nigeria, the merit principle was meant to work within a structural framework different from that of the pre-civil war era. As the CDC members who argued about the irrelevance of ethnicity in appointment noted, several states and local governments had been created to accommodate groups more adequately than before, thus dispersing power to those who would not have had access to it previously. With groups having their own states, the operation of federalism requiring representation of the constituent units in the central legislature would have resulted in a greater amount of fair participation of groups in law-making. The consociationalists' arguments for proportional representation of groups would have been achieved without using the requisite electoral system. Similarly, the prescriptions of Walzer for internal self-determination for groups would have been realized.

However, there are some difficulties with this approach. First, the federal cabinet and its executive, as well as other important national institutions, would have been left open to those possessing power and ability, most of whom would be majority groups' elites who had controlled political power at various levels since the 1950s and 1960s. It would have been a straight case of power going into the hands of the powerful elites from the majority groups, who would then use their positions and resources to allocate goods and resources, just as it was in the 1960s. There is no doubt that elites from various states in the federation—states which stand as surrogates for ethnicity—would have been represented in national institutions including the cabinet, but this would have depended on the disposition of those in power.

The problem with human inclination is that it does not furnish a standard or set of principles for judgment but is fundamentally capricious, self-seeking, and mutable. In his discussion of a universal principle that would form the basis of law, Jeremy Bentham (1988: 15-17) rejected human dispositions, or what he called sympathy or antipathy, because they were sentiments produced by moods and the actions they give rise to are as arbitrary as they are unpredictable. Resting political representation in the cabinet and other important institutions on the goodwill of those in power would therefore amount to exclusion. That would have been the case in Nigeria because, without a constitutional agreement on equitable representation of the states, those in control of power would not have ceded part of it away by inviting rival group elites to share equally in key positions of national institutions. Representation would have been minimal and cosmetic, if at all.

This same problem would also have been reproduced in each of the minority states comprising several groups. Within those states, power would have fallen into the hands of ambitious elites of the numerically dominant group who, in turn, would have appointed able (and, perhaps, less able) members of their group into key state institutions. This is best illustrated by the case of Rivers State in the Niger Delta where the Ijaw people dominated key positions in government after the creation of that state in 1967. In effect, the problem of political domination that prompted the design of a new constitution would have remained unsolved, and the prospect of democratic equality would also have remained highly uncertain.

I will now consider the proposal that ethnic membership should be a criterion for recruitment into institutions (including executive committees of political parties) at the national and state levels. This claim, which emerged as the defining principle of the federal character policy, is similar to the arguments by Lewis, Nordlinger, Lijphart, and Rothchild, all of whom argue that democratic equality in ethnically plural states would require the proportional distribution of offices among groups. The problem with the use of ethnicity in the determination of membership in public institutions was hinted at while discussing the virtue of a society that respects ability. Mill (1972) argued that the moral character of a society suffers severe damage if most of its members seek advantages without self-improvement and initiative. Such members desire what others have obtained by dint of hard work, but they do not invest their energy and time to obtain what others have got. Instead, they grumble and are full of envy and malice. They become terrors, always pursuing achievers with hatred until they succeed in stifling the spirit of achievement. In effect, if we are to go by the argument made by Mill, then basing membership in national institutions on the basis of ethnicity was a submission to the complaints of weak and nonachieving Nigerians. The submission was a dethronement of the spirit of competition, a standard that made way for arbitrariness, that transformed mutual suspicion into a component of national character. The stage was set for the downward slide of the country. Some students of Nigerian politics have made this argument, but in a different way. For example, in an incisive analysis of the meaning of federal character, Peter Ekeh (1989: 37) argues that:

> First of all, federal character attacks standard and professionalism. Its unrestrained application in the civil service and other public services, usually without respect for minimum standards, has meant that professionalism is in danger in the public services of the Federation. . . . Secondly, the doctrine of federal character allows the elites from disadvantaged areas to exploit the political system without contributing to it in some other way. According to the meaning of federal character, it pays to hail from an impoverished area in terms of personnel. It inherently discourages attempts at promoting educational development in the same fashion in which communities were shot above educational thresholds in the post-war decades in Nigeria's history.

My characterization of the Millian argument above is a bit extreme, for it does not take account of recognition given to ability. Also, it does not address the justness or otherwise of the use of the ethnic criterion. Let me dwell briefly on these two issues.

The proposal that recruitment should be on the basis of ethnicity did not entail a complete rejection of principles based on achievement or merit. The proposal, which eventually emerged as one of the defining features of federal character strategy, assumed that the ability to govern was not a capacity exclusive to some groups, especially the numerically dominant. Rather, the presupposition was that every group could provide a competent candidate who could fill a key public position. The critical criteria for appointment, therefore, were ability *plus* ethnic membership; one without the other was not enough. In this respect, federal character was an express indictment of majoritarian democracy and its tendency to exclude minority groups from key public positions in government. It also differed from the quota system of the 1960s that reserved spots for regional groups until the groups were ready to fill them. I have earlier mentioned the Kantian-derived liberal principle that human beings are rational creatures capable of using principles to direct their lives. Here, we see the principle being given real democratic meaning through the insistence that all groups can equally furnish key public posts with individuals having the requisite ability.

If the proposal regarding the ethnic composition of members in public institutions, along with the policy that grew out of it, were just and fair, could one say the same of the electoral strategy for electing the president of the country and governors of the component states of the federation?

The electoral strategy was the chosen means to an end declared by the constitution makers, namely, to avoid political domination by a few groups. It could be regarded as having been informed by the pre-civil war political practice in which a numerically dominant regional group produced the political ruler by lining up at the polls behind its chosen candidate. In this older political practice, victory was preordained by numbers and minority groups knew their fate in advance of every election. The electoral strategy designed by the CDC was, therefore, an instrument for creating an equal ground for all group elites to compete for the offices of the president and governors. The representative ground had partly been leveled by the creation of states that separated minority groups from majority groups thereby reducing the majority to a number of smaller units. The electoral system completed this leveling by requiring that victory be contingent on both plurality (or, first-past-the-post) and distribution of votes. Unlike the pre-civil war electoral system, this one required candidates fielded by parties to go beyond their ethnic bases to win votes. It was not enough for candidates to have their groups behind them, even if they constituted more than half the national population or the electorate. In a world of ethnic politics in which parties and their candidates have secure bases, meeting the electoral conditions for victory would require crossing fault lines to obtain votes in alien domains. To do this, elites of rival parties have to be responsive to the concerns and interests of groups other than theirs, or accommodate each other by forming a broad national party to pool votes, or both. Thus, the reward for bridging ethnic divides was obtaining and sharing political power; the cost of not reaching out to other ethnic areas was electoral defeat.

Giovanni Sartori (1976: 343) argued that the public does not perceive political parties as being simply to the left or right ideologically. They are also perceived as more or less "alien" or "extraneous." This means that voters accept some parties as second or third choices, while other parties are not acceptable at all. Geo-ethnic areas where parties are rated as the second or third choices have to be the focus of attention because they will determine the outcome of elections. Parties and their candidates could, therefore, obtain victory by reaching out to areas where they are rated second, third, or fourth to negotiate coalition agreements with elites or with parties that have these areas as their support base. In this context, victory would be unpredictable because all contesting parties and their candidates would be attempting to reach out to geo-ethnic areas other than their own to accommodate other elites and to hammer out a deal up front concerning the equitable distribution of offices and resources.

Two important results can be expected from this electoral strategy: one is the creation of a politics of moderation as well as multiethnic accommodation arising out of the very self-interest of elites to gain power; the other is the equal hope of being elected, even if a candidate is from an ethnic minority group. The strategy could, therefore, be regarded as democratic, just, and conducive to stability. Horowitz equated it to the neutral and objective Rawlsian original contract in which representatives could not discern the status of the people with whom they negotiated about the nature of the society they were creating. According to Horowitz:

> The Nigerians had been through severe conflict and civil war, and they did not want a repetition. Since no one could be sure which group might be on the receiving end in any future round of ethnic conflict and civil strife, the Nigerians made, not a bargain but a real constitution, not a contract among groups that knew what their interests would be but a social contract among groups that were not sure what their interest might be the next time around. They made a blind, Rawlsian contract.

That is, one based on original position reasoning, not present
position reasoning. (Horowitz 1991: 150n.75)[9]

Horowitz was so impressed by this electoral strategy that he recommended it for other multiethnic societies, particularly South Africa. In his
words: "If one is looking for African democracy in a divided society, the
place to look is . . . Nigeria. . . . That is where many of the African lessons are, but they seem far away, little known and less understood in
South Africa" (1991: 136-37).

What rebuttal could be made to the argument that the electoral strategy for political inclusion was democratic and just? The problem to be
addressed is how members of both minority and majority groups can
have equal hope of winning executive power through the ballot box. In
dealing with this problem, one would concede that the electoral strategy
aimed at rewarding politicians for pursuing accommodative politics was
well thought out and well intentioned. However, a faulty assumption existed about the other element of the political inclusion package: namely,
state-creation. The assumption was that state creation had leveled both
majority and minority groups by dividing them into a smaller number of
small separate units. Those who controlled power by virtue of membership in numerically dominant groups were assumed to have been reduced
to the same level as those who suffered political exclusion by virtue of
their membership in numerically weak groups. What seemed to have
been forgotten was that the fragmentation of each of the three major
groups into a number of states did not automatically break the ties and
sentiments that held them together.

Thus, while aspiring presidential candidates from the dominant parties of the three largest groups could count on two, four, or even five
states as their home base, aspiring minority candidates could hardly boast
about securing one, as there was no single minority group that had a state
to itself. The confinement of their support base to a tiny fraction of the
state their groups occupied meant that minority presidential candidates
had to invest more time and energy to obtain recognition, and they had to
cover a greater part of the country to meet the challenges for victory.
Moreover, Nigeria's history has shown that minority parties and their
candidates are sometimes simply not acceptable (in the sense used by
Sartori) to the larger groups and, in consequence, cannot influence voters
in areas other than their own. Minority elites are therefore resigned to
playing the role of clients to their majority group counterparts.

The above argument finds some support in an empirical study by Omo Omoruyi, a leading Nigerian political scientist. In his study, Omoruyi showed that at the commencement of competitive politics in 1979, an ethnic minority elite led only one of the five registered political parties, that being the GNPP. Furthermore, that party dissipated its energies trying to set up shop in all parts of the country. He also showed that after 1979, the GNPP practically ceased to exist outside Borno State, the home state of Alhaji Ibrahim Waziri, its leader (Ekeh and Osaghae 1989: 214-15). Things worsened in the decades that followed, as none of the registered political parties in the late 1980s and 1990s were led by minority elites. Instead, the latter were condemned to client status.

Alternative Strategies

Perhaps one solution to the problem of unequal political competition discussed above would have been the creation of states for each minority group. In this manner, their elites could count on one or two constituent federal units as their electoral support-base as the majority group elites do. This would not have constituted an alternative to the inducement-based electoral strategy, but rather a rectification of the structural defect that disadvantaged ethnic minority parties and their presidential candidates. The problem with this solution is that every small group would have had its own state. Drawing the boundaries would have been a messy business, most of the units would not have been viable, and the outcome would have been a mockery of federalism as the number of states would be ludicrous and all would be dependent on the center.

Another solution to the problem would have been the adoption of an alternative strategy to the electoral approach. The alternative could have been a reversion to the classical liberal democracy inherited from the British and practiced in the pre-civil war era. It was a democracy characterized by census election. This form of democracy is what generated conflict between rival majority group elites during the 1950s and 1960s and accounted for the repression of ethnic minorities and their demands for separation from the then regions. But, to go back to that system would mean that the lessons of the past were not incorporated into the present or that the capacity to respond to contemporary challenges was lacking. It would amount to collapsing the present into the past and to regard society as a static reality, not a dynamic reality that is constantly refashioned by the energies of its members. This static, nonprogressive view of society is akin to the cyclical notion of history developed by the ancient historian Polybius and it led the Renaissance thinker Niccolò Machiavelli (1950: 271-75) to advise states and their rulers to look to the ancients and imitate their political institutions and mode of proceeding because humankind achieved excellence and glory during the period of classical antiquity.

Another alternative would have been the rotation of the office of the chief executive—an alternative that was initially contemplated by the CDC. Dividing the country into existing ethnocultural zones, and rotating the office in them, would have been a way of creating conditions for both majority and minority group elites to have equal hope of competing and winning. This is really not an alternative but a solution to the weakness of the electoral strategy and would have complemented, not led to the abandonment of, the strategy.

It might be objected that rotating the executive position deprives citizens of the rights and freedom central to liberal democracy. That is to say, it violates liberal values if, after every four years, the right to contest for the highest office is limited to members of a particular ethnocultural region. This is what made the CDC reject the notion of rotational presidency.

It might also be objected that such an innovation would elevate ethnic loyalty over national loyalty and create a fertile environment for "buccaneer" politics. In other words, it would risk the subordination of national loyalty to ethnic loyalty and prompt political incumbents to preoccupy themselves with the annexation of public wealth for themselves and their ethnic communities. The fear felt by incumbents and their geoethnic units that power would not rotate to them until after several decades would further fuel the corrupt use of power.

The first of the two objections discussed immediately above is certainly legitimate, but it ignores the multiethnic composition of the country and the systemic barriers that hinder members of disadvantaged groups from exercising the right to contest for the presidency. It is true that equality and freedom are the core values of liberal democracy, but a contradiction arises between form and content if different group members cannot exercise the same right. The classical social contract theorists—Hobbes, Locke, and Rousseau—showed that equality in modern society means individuals have the same faculties and advantages, that persons are not subordinated to one another, and that there is no right one person can claim that the other cannot. An important concept that emerged from their analysis of modern society is "hope." According to Thomas Hobbes (1968: 123-84), "hope" is the opinion that we might attain our ends and it is a consequence of equality. Where people are equal, they have equal hope of attaining scarce ends. The other side of hope is despair; it is the belief that we cannot attain our ends and is a consequence of inequality. For example, all six candidates competing for one teaching position in a university have equal hope of getting the job insofar as they have the same qualification. Where one is known to possess two or three Ph.D. degrees and has several publications, the rest will despair. Lose equality and the weak will become despondent and give up.

In Nigerian competitive politics, the hope of becoming president is limited to members (or elites) of the few numerically dominant groups. Elites or members of the several numerically inferior groups do not harbor such hopes because of the structural inequality discussed earlier on. Some might entertain the hope because of their personal wealth, but quickly give up at the early stages of party formation and registration. So a high school pupil cannot dream of becoming a national leader even if he or she possesses all the potential qualities, unless they belong to a numerically preponderant group. The principle of equality that liberalism cherishes requires that everyone should have hope of achieving one's ends. It would justify rotating the chair of the president if this would neutralize the structural inequality that prevents members of minority groups from exercising the right to compete for it.

Rotation, therefore, creates conditions for equality rather than negating it. The restriction of rights to compete to members of a particular geo-ethnic region in a four-year interval does not cancel out the rights of those in other areas. It only places them on hold until the chair rotates for their turn. What applies to one equally applies to the other. It is a case of mutual recognition in which each yields to the other in an orderly fashion. Absent mutual recognition and the result would be political subjection of some groups, as is currently the case.

Indeed, Charles Taylor has argued that a multiethnic country belongs equally to the ethno-national groups that comprise it, and the rules and norms that govern the political domain should reflect their interests and concerns in the same way. He endorsed a differentiated-citizenship regime that would allow for the survival of minority groups whose way of life is threatened by the pressures of the majority group, but he did not address the issue of equitable access to the executive chair. Will Kymlicka also did not address this issue. It was, however, Arend Lijphart (1985: 81) who prescribed a rotating prime ministership as part of his consociational measures. However, his electoral system of pure proportional representation in the legislature had little utility for the rotating chair in terms of pulling various groups together. In fact, Juan Linz noted in his discussion of regime breakdown that an electoral system such as one embodying pure proportional representation does not reward efforts at cooperation, it merely fosters division and crisis (Linz and Stepan 1976: 67-88). I follow Linz very closely by conceiving of the rotating chair as part of an inducement-based electoral package that facilitates the pursuit of accommodative politics. As part of an electoral package for accommodative politics, it is more qualitative than that of Lijphart, which stands on its own.

The second objection, namely, that power rotation enthrones ethnic loyalty and buccaneer politics, might be valid in the short term, but not in the long run. One of the advantages of this arrangement is its extension of the right to national leadership to sections of the country whose elites would not have had the chance to be at the apex of power under conventional democratic practices. The extension of the leadership right produces a sense of belonging in those who would otherwise be excluded and facilitates their identification with the state. Over time, people will develop mutual trust and confidence in the system and, as this works itself into the social fabric, ethical principles will take roots. As Arthur Lewis (1965: 75-83) rightly argued, mutual security created by the absence of adversarial politics encourages the habituation of democratic norms.

Summary

The objectives of this chapter were to evaluate the merits of the early 1970s demands for more states and to determine the desirability of the federal character policy as a strategy for ensuring equity in the composition of government.

With respect to the demands for more states, the forces that propelled these demands included competition for public wealth by groups and their elites and the desire of some groups for equal political accommodation. Wealth was found to be a weak basis for political claims, because to grant self-determination on that basis would have triggered endless demands for, and creation of, new units. On the other hand, demands for equal accommodation were found to have emanated from the unequal distribution of states during the 1967 state-creation exercise, and could properly be regarded as claims to redress injustice. Thus the demands were rooted both in economics and justice.

Denying the claims on account of their economic character had the advantage of avoiding the emergence of new and endless claims. But groups that felt cheated during the 1967 exercise would have been treated unfairly. Liberal equality, as theorized by Taylor, required that justice be done for those who were not properly accommodated. Meeting the claims on grounds of equity had one big risk: the proliferation of new units. Still, from the liberal standpoint, this option was better because groups would have been accommodated equally, the state would have emerged as a neutral body, and a framework for mutual trust would have been developed. On this account, the chapter endorsed the decision of the 1975 government panel to create new states.

With respect to the federal character strategy, it arose from the country's historical experience regarding the monopoly of power by elites from a few ethnic regions. For this reason, the use of the ethnic principle for recruitment at all levels of government became the cornerstone of the strategy. The disadvantage of this approach was that it had the tendency to sacrifice standards for arbitrariness in hiring for public offices. In turn, this had the tendency to foster mutual mistrust and, in turn, weaken political cohesion.

The alternative classical liberal strategy was equally open for adoption. This alternative emphasized individual ability and, theoretically, held the promise of improving the moral faculties and enhancing societal progress. However, it also held forth the prospect of simultaneously working toward the political exclusion of ethnic minorities at both the national and state levels.

Between the two strategies, the federal character approach was found to be normatively weightier, and for two reasons. First, the merit principle was not completely rejected; rather, all groups were assumed to contain some qualified individuals for public offices and their recruitment into government was not to be determined on grounds that would exclude minorities. The combination of group membership and merit ensured that those with ability were not drawn from a few geo-ethnic areas. Second, the use of an electoral instrument that induced elites to build complex networks of cross-ethnic alliances led to the acceptance of a politics of reciprocity while moderation had the prospect of countering any centrifugal tendencies. The electoral instrument offered an adequate solution to the fears of balkanization associated with the use of the ethnic principle for recruitment for public offices. However, the electoral mechanism that generated cross-cutting alliances disadvantaged minority group members (especially their elites) in terms of their ability to reach out to a greater part of the country that was home to majority groups. This disadvantage effectively excluded them from competing for the office of the president and in effect made them political unequals. To counter this effect, in addition to the already existing electoral mechanism, endorsement is given to the notion of a rotational presidency as a condition for political equality among majority and minority group members.

Notes

1. Under the 1953 agreement, each region received its full share of the contributions to federal revenues. This was known as the derivation principle and it applied 100 percent. However, it was criticized on grounds that it was too divisive. In response to the criticism, the Independence Constitutional Conference of 1958 set up another commission to examine the derivation principle. This resulted in the introduction of a Distributive Pool Account in 1959 to temper derivation by allocating some revenues among the regions on the basis of both equality and population. The growth in the importance of mining royalties during the late 1960s prompted the federal military government to reduce to 45 percent the proportion of revenue going back to the states from which they were sourced. This reduction increased the amount going to the Distributive Pool, 50 percent of which was shared among states on the basis of equality, and the other 50 percent on the basis of population. Money dispensed in this way accounted for 80 percent of the incomes of the then twelve states (Graf 1988: 139; Kirk-Greene and Rimmer 1981: 123-27).

2. Joseph (1987: 84) also notes that the pressure for the creation of more states was fueled by the unrelenting struggle for access to state offices with the aim of procuring material benefits for oneself and for one's communal group.

3. The circumstances that led to this panel's establishment go back to 1967 when the twelve states were created by military fiat. Government carried out the 1967 state-creation exercise without consulting those who were affected. The boundaries were, therefore, taken to be temporary pending the appointment of a Boundary Delimitation Commission that would look into their readjustment or confirmation. Delays in setting up the commission activated petitions from various parts of the country. Post-civil war economic developments (discussed above) provided a fertile condition for the conversion of these petitions for boundary adjustment into those for state creation. It was the intensity of the demands that forced government to make a statement of commitment in 1973 and to set up a panel in 1975 (Nigeria, 1976a: 8-9).

4. Incidentally, the eighth state rejected by government was the only one recommended for minority groups residing in the oil-generating areas.

5. Ten of the nineteen states were in the North, while the other nine were in the South. Of the ten states in the North, six were predominantly made up of

minority groups while the remaining four were made up of Hausa-Fulani. Of the nine states that emerged in the South, the Igbo occupied two, the Yoruba occupied four (including Lagos State), while various minority groups were grouped together in three. An extensive forest at the center of the country was designated the new federal territory, with the result that Lagos later ceased to be operational as the capital.

6. In the constitutional debates of the 1950s, delegates usually submitted issues they wanted to discuss (prior to the commencement of each conference) and, after lengthy arguments, terms of reference were agreed upon. In the post-civil war era it was different. The military was in office, the regions had been drastically reduced in size and power by increasing their number, and finance had been centralized. It was this supremacy that allowed Brigadier Murtala Mohammed's regime to avoid the preindependence procedures. According to Keith Panter-Brick (1978: 292), the committee "was not to carry out negotiations, nor even to discover what would be acceptable to entrenched interests: its task was more technical."

7. In dealing with competing claims to justice, Aristotle (1964: bk. II, chap. 9 1280b) argued that a political society is not a business venture that exists solely for the economic benefit of members. If it were only that, members would have nothing in common except economic exchanges.

8. For a discussion of how people emerge as juridical persons, see Claude Ake (1988: 45-60).

9. Similarly, Larry Diamond (1982: 655) notes that the federal character approach made for alliances that "cross[ed] ethnicity, region, and religion as impressively as any political coalition in modern history."

Chapter Six

The Revised Federal Character Approach

The mid-1980s marked the beginning of another phase in Nigeria's attempt to accommodate ethnic pluralism. The new phase entailed the revision of its federal character strategy to make it more inclusive. This phase involved the division of the country into a greater number of states to adequately reflect ethnicity, and the convening of a constitutional conference to resolve group-based claims and counter-claims to alternative political structures, power-sharing, and ownership of rich petroleum resources. The revision, which seems to have continued into the year 2000, has witnessed claims to, and actual adoption of, sharia (*Shari'a*) law by the predominantly Muslim states in the northern part of the country. This chapter will encompass a critical evaluation of the main strands of the latest revision and the adoption of sharia law, with a view to ascertaining the desirability of what was implemented.

The Revised Federal Character Approach

The Political Bureau and Federal Character

In the preceding chapter, I examined two interrelated elements of the federal character strategy for accommodating ethnic difference in politics: a) the separation of groups into several political subunits; and, b) accommodative policies requiring that political parties reach out to wide geo-ethnic areas and that governmental appointments reflect the multi-state structure. I defended the creation of new states on the grounds of equity and the need to build group trust and confidence in governance, but noted that state creation carried the potential risk of triggering new demands for, and endless creation of, new states. I also argued that these policy requirements were well intentioned but not sufficient enough to enable ethnic inclusion in government. In 1986, a government commission known as the Political Bureau was created to address some of these issues through its mandate, which was to identify the causes of past political failures and make recommendations for a new constitution that would guide a Third Republic.

The creation of states to accommodate groups, a central element of the federal character approach, became an issue for the Political Bureau because it triggered new and overwhelming demands by elites claiming to represent new groups. The 1976 exercise brought home to people the realization that state creation had a material windfall. It became clear that the creation of states was accompanied by the duplication of executive, legislative, and judicial offices. It also carried with it the duplication of the civil service, development of capital cities, contracts for construction projects, and guaranteed representation in federal institutions as required by the federal character policy. On top of all this were the federal government's appropriation of petroleum resources and the proportional allocation of its revenue among the states.[1] It was these material benefits that activated an overwhelming fifty-three new demands between 1979 and 1982, and seventeen formal requests from the Political Bureau in 1986.

Despite the view, articulated by some members of the public, that most of the existing states were not viable and should be either abolished, merged, or left as they were without further fragmentation, the Political Bureau found it necessary to recommend the creation of a few more. The ideal number was placed between a minimum of two and a maximum of six. The bureau felt it necessary to separate some groups that were in conflict in the North, and accommodate a minority group in the southeast that the government refused to group separately during the 1976 exercise, despite earlier recommendation by the 1975 government panel. It tried to respond to the slippery slope problem by suggesting that a constitutional provision prohibiting further creation of states for at least twenty-five years, starting from the date its proposed states would come into being, be included in the constitution.[2]

Back in 1957, the Minorities Commission judged that the multiplication of internal political units recognizing smaller groups would precipitate an endless process of recognition. However, post-civil war Nigerian governments regarded continued multiplication as necessary for justice and the Political Bureau's suggestion that a twenty-five-year moratorium be placed on further political fragmentation was not heeded. The minimum of two states was implemented but this was then followed by the creation of another nine in 1991. Some have argued that it was a strategy devised by General Ibrahim Babangida's regime to win group support for his planned prolonged stay in office. But the regime explained its decision to further recognize groups in new states as being based on three interconnected principles: the "principle of social justice, the principle of development, and the principle of balanced federation" (Babanginda quoted in Ilesanmi 1997: 142).

Furthermore, the constitutional conference convened in 1994-95 by General Sani Abacha's regime to craft a framework for good governance received thirty-five requests to create new states and one thousand and two requests for the creation of new local government units.[3] Some delegates to the conference thought that such demands were "motivated by the selfish ambition of those who aspired to rule them (the units) and should be ignored" (Nigeria 1995: 55). But the conference endorsed the calls saying that new units were necessary to "redress inequity," "guarantee justice and fair play," "give minorities a voice in local and national affairs," and "reduce the marginalization of disadvantaged areas or communities in national politics" (Nigeria 1995: 55). A subsequent commission that was called to examine the demands also recommended a new set of states. At first, the Abacha regime asserted that most of the existing ones were not capable of performing the functions of government, that they were completely dependent on the center, and that their proliferation had destroyed the principle of federalism. The regime made a decision to merge the proposed new states into a few large regions. However, this plan was quickly abandoned when it was realized that such an arrangement would unite Yorubas (who felt humiliated by the 1993 election result annulment) and encourage them to secede. Instead of a merger, the Abacha regime created six new states to further separate groups and ensure the continued existence of the country (*Tell* 1996: 8-14). Group separation had indeed become an endless process, but the need to achieve justice and ensure the continued existence of the country could not be divorced from this internal logic.

The second element of federal character, the ethnic origin policy that required membership in national institutions to reflect the constituent states and that states should also do the same by reflecting their local government units in political appointments, was also revisited. Section 277 of the 1979 constitution had defined state membership as "a person either of whose parents or any of whose grandparents was a member of a community indigenous to that State." This definition was also retained in Section 318 of the 1999 constitution. The parental criterion provided a basis for denying indigenous status to Nigerians resident in states not reflective of their biological and ethnic descent and also applied to their offspring who were born and had lived all their lives there. To claim indigenous status, they had to go back to their state of biological descent. Discriminatory practices emerged informally as state governments excluded non-indigenes from political appointments. Educational programs, housing schemes, access to health, and access to market stalls were not immune from the effects of this policy as those whose parental descent was not traceable to groups within the state were informally excluded (Bach 1997: 340). In some cases, positions in some federal agencies became exclusive preserves of those who were indigenous to the state where the agencies were located. This was particularly true of federal universities where appointments to positions such as the vice chancellor, registrar, dean, and departmental chair positions became sensitive to indigeneity.[4] To determine the indigeneity of candidates being recruited into positions, or being considered for university admissions or scholarships, authorities routinely asked for identification letters written by either a recognized chief in the village or a chairperson of the local government of one's ethnic origin. It must be noted that all of these practices were illegal, as the constitution did not demand the exclusion of citizens who were not indigenous to a state.

The 1986 Political Bureau, composed mostly of professors who may have witnessed or participated in rights violation in their universities, critically examined the problem. In a section of its report entitled "Citizenship and Nationality," the bureau noted: "[the] employment of Nigerians in certain states of the federation under alien conditions; and denial of employment opportunities to Nigerians on the basis of 'non-indigeneity,' 'alien' or 'outsider'" (Nigeria 1987: 196). The bureau's report tried to eliminate what it considered to be impediments generated by indigeneity to the development of Nigerian citizenship by recommending full residency rights for all citizens who lived in a state for at least ten years (1987: 197, 198). Nothing resulted from this report as the 1989 constitution and the Third Republic were stillborn efforts. The 1995 draft constitution did not address this recommendation and neither did the 1999 constitution. The problem remained and was expressed in June 1999 by the Lagos State House of Assembly under the Fourth Republic during its inaugural meeting. The legislature fought over the election of the Speaker whose parental descent was traced to a neighboring Yoruba state. This event occurred after the familial origin of the democratically elected governor had also been traced to a neighboring Yoruba state.

The 1994-95 Constitutional Conference and Claims concerning Power-Sharing and Resource Allocation

In chapter 5, I argued that the electoral inducement engendered by the federal character approach was not enough to democratize the executive chair, and that achieving the latter would require rotating the executive office. The 1986 Political Bureau did not really address this issue. Even worse, General Muhammadu Buhari's regime, which terminated the Second Republic, deviated from the federal character requirements by making unbalanced appointments and allocation of resources (Ibrahim 1991: 135). Babangida's regime, which succeeded Buhari's, tried to balance sectional and regional interests in political appointments, but the commitment fizzled and southern and middle belt elites lost out at the center.[5] This biased distribution of power, together with General Babangida's personal determination to be in office forever, generated competing claims regarding the political structure of the country, power-sharing, and ownership of revenue-producing resources.[6] These claims were further fueled by the annulment of the 1993 election results that would have transferred power to the southwestern part of the country.

A constitutional conference, convened to douse tensions arising from the annulment of the election results, received numerous claims and counter-claims for structural reforms. For example, the Council of Obas of Lagos, Ogun, Oyo, Osun, and Ondo States (the Yoruba states) put forth claims for a loose federation and the adoption of a rotational presidency (Committee of Afenifere 1994: 5-7; Council of Obas of Lagos, Ogun, Osun and Ondo States 1994: 7). Interest groups and elites in Igbo states of the East suggested regrouping the country into six regions within a federal framework and rotating the presidency among the regions. They also demanded the adoption of a revenue allocation formula emphasizing derivation ("A Memorandum on Behalf of the Igbo Speaking People" 1994: 77).[7] Counter-claims were made by the emirs and chiefs of the Northern States of Nigeria and by the Middle Belt Council for a "retention of the existing state structure" and a reduction in the "incessant demand for more states through a revenue allocation formula that de-emphasized equality of states" (The Middle Belt Council: 1994).[8] More radical were the claims made by various interest groups and elites representing the different oil producing ethnic minorities of the Niger Delta for political autonomy "outside the present Nigerian state and nation," the right to control and use their natural resources, and the right to protect their environment from further degradation (Movement for the Survival of the Ijaw Ethnic Nationality 1994: 28-29).[9]

The Constitutional Conference responded to the above claims by revising the federal character strategy that had been designed between 1975 and 1978 while simultaneously retaining its structural features. First, it recommended that the country continue with the federal structure after considering alternatives, such as confederation, to be "unsuitable for Nigeria" as well as political break-up, which was believed undesirable and lacking popular support. Federalism was considered to be suitable because "it would fit a heterogeneous society and sustain unity . . . provide opportunity for the people to participate in . . . governance . . . minimize . . . fears of domination . . . and inspire development" (Nigeria 1995 Vol. 2: 60-61). [10]

Second, the federal executive cabinet would be made more inclusive by implementing provisions requiring political parties with no less than 10 percent of seats in the National Assembly to be represented in proportion to their number of seats, very much in the manner prescribed by Arthur Lewis (1965: 74-84) during the first decade of independence. The arrangement was made more inclusive by having the office of the chief executive rotated between the North and South every five years.[11] The likelihood of ethnic minorities of both regions not having a fair chance at the office, and the possibility of violent competition between Igbos and Yorubas in the South, prompted the Abacha regime to make a modification. Instead of two regions (the North and South), power would rotate every five years among each of six zones—northeast, northwest, east-central, southwest, middle-belt, and southern-minority—reflecting the country's divisions. [12] This form of sharing mechanism would also apply to each of the constituent states and local government units.[13]

Regarding claims to rich natural resources, the conference stopped short of addressing them by devising provisions requiring the president, on the advice of a National Revenue Mobilization Allocation and Fiscal Commission, to make proposals to the National Assembly for revenue allocation. The assembly was expected to use the principles of population, equality of states, and derivation in determining an allocation system, but with the proviso that at least 13 percent derivation be constantly reflected in the allocation system (1995 Vol. 2: 142).

The 1995 draft constitution embodying these innovations did not come into effect on account of the fall of Abacha's regime in 1998 and public resentment against everything associated with the dictator. A Constitutional Debate Coordinating Committee (CDCC), appointed in November 1998 to canvas the various views held by the public for a review of the draft document, rejected all innovations except the one concerning revenue allocation (Nigeria 1999: §162: 1 and 2; §133-35).

The Crisis of Secularism

One of the greatest constitutional tests Nigeria has confronted in the last few years is the adoption of sharia as public law by several states in the northern part of the country. The adoption of sharia conflicted with the federal level's commitment to liberal constitutionalism entailing the separation of state from religion and relegating religion to the private practice of citizens with which the state ought not to interfere.

The historical origins of the conflict go back to the colonial era when the British used Islamic rule in the emirate as the cornerstone of their policy of indirect rule. The Islamic legal system operating in the region in the nineteenth century was given official support as sharia courts administered justice at the local level, but they were stripped of their harsh system of punishment. Official recognition of the Muslim religion was carried into the independence era when the government of the Northern Region of Sir Ahmadu Bello adopted the sharia penal code for the region, following recommendations by an international panel of jurists that was set up for the purpose of examining the sharia penal code. This penal code operated alongside modern law, and its scope was limited to family cases such as marriage and inheritance. To resolve appeal cases, a Muslim Court of Appeal that had been in existence since colonial times was renamed the Sharia Court of Appeal (Agbaje 1990: 299; Coalition for Peace 2000: 25-31; Ilesanmi 1997: 132-36). However, these courts, which operated in conjunction with modern courts, were not competent to make judgments on criminal cases, as their jurisdiction was limited to family matters and to consenting Muslims only.

Legal pluralism ran into difficulties in the late 1960s and early 1970s when the former Northern Region was fragmented into several states and each new state created its own Sharia Court of Appeal. With the Northern Region gone, there was no longer a united court of appeal and to demand one for these states alone would have meant acknowledging the continued existence of the Northern Region (Laitin 1982: 411-12). It was in the context of this legal anomaly that representatives of the predominantly Muslim states of the North demanded a Federal Sharia Court of Appeal during the drafting and debate of the 1979 constitution. Opposition by representatives of predominantly Christian states to what they considered an attempt at making Islam a state religion resulted in a constitutional provision for a Sharia Court of Appeal for any state that wished to have it.[14] This compromise arrangement, which was also kept in the 1989 and 1999 constitutions, has been considered consistent with the federal character policy that aims at giving political recognition to the various groups in the country (Sklar 1999: 16).

This arrangement encountered severe problems soon after the return to democratic rule in 1999. Several states in the former Northern Region, including those having a sizable proportion of Christians and animists and were hotbeds of violent religious conflicts in the 1980s, adopted sharia as public law. Whereas in the 1970s and 1980s, Muslims aimed at enlarging the operational scope of the sharia from the state to the federal level, what was done in the year 2000 was to limit it to the state level, but broaden its jurisdiction from personal matters to include criminal cases. This effectively made the Muslim religion a state religion.

Political rulers of the Muslims states have given a number of reasons for the adoption of sharia law. One reason is that the affected states are predominantly Muslim and that the people demand it.[15] A second reason is that the country's legal system is heavily Christian and even the calendar is Gregorian and that adopting sharia law recalibrated the imbalance. A third argument is that the federal arrangement is explicitly designed to respect difference and this permits a state to adopt a legal system that is consistent with the wishes of its people. An ancillary argument is that the country is currently rife with moral decay and the morality embedded in sharia law is the best solution to the problem (Madugba 2000: 19-20).[16]

Would the arguments above be compelling enough to defend the legal adoption of sharia as state law? This question will be addressed in the section below.

Evaluation of the Revised Federal Character Strategy

The relevant issues that emerge from the narrative above are: 1) the tension between the political necessity to separate groups into different states and the slippery slope this engenders; 2) the federal character policy requirement and the impediments it presents to national citizenship; 3) the claims and agreements regarding political structure, power-sharing, and natural resource ownership; and, 4) the place of sharia in Nigeria's federalism. This part of the chapter will encompass an analysis of these issues and consider whether or not alternative policy choices were both desirable and feasible.

Recognition in Separate Units and the Problem of the Slippery Slope

It is manifestly evident from the historical account given above that Nigeria's adoption of polyethnic federalism has produced endless demands for, and multiplication of, political subunits. The historical account shows that continuous division is being carried out with some concern for equity and national unity, but the question is for how long should it go on?

Nigeria is without doubt highly heterogeneous, and constitutional instruments have deliberately been used since the 1970s to take that fact into account. The multiplicity of groups can be best appreciated when it is considered that most groups have subgroups differentiated by dialect and customs. Subgroup rivalry and conflict tend to be as intense as, and some times more violent than, those between groups. Subgroup conflict is, however, overshadowed by, and subordinated to, the intergroup conflict because of the narrow geographic scale and political level at which they occur. For example, conflict between Yoruba subgroups is as violent as conflict between Igbos and Hausa-Fulanis, just as conflict between Igbo subgroups is as intense as that between Yorubas and Igbos. Separate a group and the difference and conflict within it become more pronounced and visible.

The multiplicity of subgroups within a group does not help matters. For example, the Ijaw, who do not rank among the three major groups in the country, consist of over forty subgroups, some of whom have little in common except similarity in language. Adopting polyethnic federalism as a solution to difference entails being confronted by groups who are internally differentiated into multiple parts. While the need to accommodate diversity requires that territorial units be created for those who are different, as successive Nigerian regimes have done since the late 1960s, prudence will also dictate that not all subgroups of larger groups or every small group can be separately accommodated. The line must be drawn at some point. Duchacek (1991: 30) made this point when he noted that "no polyethnic system in the world can integrally implement the federal ethno-territorial principle according to which every ethnic community, however microscopic it may be, should administer its own self-contained autonomous area."

Perhaps one way of dealing with the ethno-territorial problem is to adopt a policy that prohibits further fragmentation of units. This might be considered a reactive and vexatious policy and new regimes might set it aside, as was the case during the regime of Alhaji Shehu Shagari. Recall that the 1975-76 Constitution Drafting Committee (CDC) reacted to pressures for new states by drafting constitutional provisions requiring that certain procedures be followed. The CDC technically prohibited further multiplication of units by making the procedures difficult and complex, yet the civilian regime that was installed in 1979 tried to undermine the committee's goal by slowly navigating its way around. Similarly, the 1986 Political Bureau prescribed a twenty-five-year moratorium after it recommended the creation of a few states, but the prohibition was set aside by the very regime that set up the bureau. A prohibitive policy may not endure because different regimes will regard it as failing to reflect the social circumstances with which they are confronted.

A second option is to listen to and evaluate separatist claims in order to determine those that merit attention. This is what successive government commissions in Nigeria have been doing since the mid-1970s. The advantage of this option is that it steers the state away from an authoritarian policy approach to ethnic demands by providing institutional mechanisms for the expression and peaceful resolution of grievances.[17] This facilitates a feeling of security to groups and confers legitimacy on the process and the system. However, this approach does not resolve the problem entirely because the readiness of regimes to listen and evaluate claims for their merit stimulates new demands by new groups. It was precisely the willingness of successive Nigerian regimes to receive and consider new claims that produced an endless state-creation exercise.

A third alternative is to emphasize the viability requirement. While it is fair to listen to claims and resolve them in light of the requirements of justice, it is also fair that economic viability not be sacrificed. Duchacek made this point when he noted that, for a new state to be created out of an existing one, it must have the necessary economic means to provide for its existence. He cited Mexico as a country that has a stringent economic condition for the creation of new states within the national territory (Duchacek 1970: 239-42, 314-15). Surely if the various government commissions had given weight to the viability requirement, it is likely that the demand for states would not have continued endlessly. To pay little or no attention to this requirement is to be willfully blind to the need for self-sustenance and financial autonomy of the units that groups demand. The 1976 government panel, for example, noted that "all the existing states except possibly Lagos were heavily dependent on the Federal Government" (Bach 1997: 335). The marginal attention paid by successive Nigerian regimes since the 1970s to the notion of economic self-reliance in their treatment of group claims may have been responsible for the dramatic increase in the number of units. In fact, the government panel that examined claims in 1976 did emphasize that economic viability was not relevant because:

> each state was not, and should not be required to function as self contained or self sufficient unit. In other words, the country as a whole constitutes a single economic system and so long as this system is viable, the viability of the component units can be assured through the normal process of exchanges and distributive actions of the Federal Government. (Nigeria 1976a: 13)

Subsequent government commissions adopted the same attitude, an exception being the 1994-95 Constitutional Conference that gave critical weight to economic viability but went on to undercut it by recommending the creation of eleven states, all of which were to be dependent on central revenue for their survival.[18]

The economic viability option seems reasonable but, at the end of the day, would be fruitless because, in the Niger Delta for example, every village that has rich oil resources under its soil could easily meet the requirement. Every village in the Niger Delta would then claim statehood and meeting such claims would not only trivialize federalism but also be unjust to the millions of people living in the rest of the country.

On the other hand, the normative argument for the political recognition of groups collapses if the economic requirement is not one that can be easily met. If more emphasis had been placed on self-sufficiency in the past, it is likely that the nineteen-state structure would not have emerged as it did in 1976, and the adoption of a federal character would have been severely compromised. Emphasizing it would seriously question the multistate structure that has been used to separate groups and has served as the basis for nurturing difference in politics.

Perhaps a better alternative is to adopt a policy that would allow the existing state structure to stabilize. In the first twenty years after independence, political subunits were created on the average of every seven years and, in the last fifteen years, the average has been five years. After each round of division, the units barely began operations before being subjected to another round. One good thing that emerged from the rapid and successive fragmentation is that groups have been significantly separated and accommodated within the thirty-six states and 768 local gov-

ernments units that have emerged, at least when compared with the existence of merely three regions in the 1950s. Multiplication of states has
gone a long way toward accomplishing the objective for which it was
conceived and what is now required is a consolidation, not a trivializa-
tion, of the accomplishment. Consolidation could be achieved if the units
are given time to operate. A policy requiring the existing units to remain
intact for some decades would lead to an adjustment process whereby
ethnic elites and their followers would become accustomed to operating
within the framework of the states in which they are grouped. Over time,
they would adjust and accommodate themselves by creating networks for
political, social, and economic exchange. To the extent that they get used
to living in, and develop a sense of attachment to, the units in which they
are grouped, the present demand syndrome would fizzle out and the state
system would stabilize.

The Midwest State, for example, was created in 1963 and was not
fragmented until 1990. It was one of the few states that remained intact
for about thirty years even though demands to create a new state out of it
began in the early 1970s. At some point its name changed to Bendel
State but nevertheless, while it lasted, its inhabitants were used to living
together. A dense network of exchange and interactions was forged and
when the state finally fell to the forces of fragmentation in 1990, there
was much public lamentation. Headlines in the local press read "Good
Old Bendel" and "The Demise of Sweet Old Bendel." It is this type of
adjustment, continued interaction and emotional connection, that can
make for stability in the state system.

Federal Character and the Problem of National Citizenship

As we have seen in the first part of this chapter, the problem of citizenship rights derives from the commitment to ensure uniform access to
political and economic resources through the creation of political units
around groups and the policy requirement for appointment at each of the
three levels of government. The policy recognized group rights alongside
constitutional commitments to liberal individualist rights. The policy did
not expressly call for the displacement of individual rights by group
rights, but its operation elevated the latter over the former and constrained it. Constraints can best be appreciated when it is understood that
the progressive reduction in the territorial span of the constituent states
through the creation of new units also increased the number of citizens
living outside units of their parental descent. Thus, a greater number of

citizens were subjected to second-class treatment. This problem exists, then, along with that of naturalized citizens and their offspring who could not trace familial descent to an indigenous community within any state of the federation and, as a consequence, were not in a position to enjoy the same rights as other citizens.

Perhaps one way of dealing with the appointment problem should have been to abandon the indigeneity requirement for appointment and recruitment and to adopt competition and achievement as the basis for treating citizens equally. This would have meant the abandonment of federal character and the adoption of the undiluted merit principle that was the subject of much dispute in the 1950s and 1960s. The merit principle had been recognized as unjust since it worked to the political exclusion of some group members. It was the quest for justice that prompted the adoption of the proportionality principle in the appointment and allocation of resources during the early 1970s. Returning to the pure merit principle would have been a retrogressive option, as it would have generated real conflict.

Another alternative could have been to use group membership, as was done, and to accept the unintended infractions as unavoidable inconveniences. After all, the indigeneity requirement does not deny to citizens their rights. It only requires that certain rights be enjoyed by citizens through their states of biological origin. It is a requirement that applies generally, and its inconveniences could have been regarded as an unavoidable cost of equitable access to public institutions. The inconveniences could have been accepted with regret, but because they affect the real life chances of some individuals, regretfully accepting them is really not the best way of dealing with the problem.

Another option would be to use language competence as the main criterion for the definition of state membership. From a liberal point of view, this option is superior to parental descent as it allows migrants in a state (or those who have married into an internal community) to have access to the benefits of membership. This would certainly have alleviated the problem of migrants since language is ethnically inclusive while descent is inherently exclusive. The problem here is that language competence does not translate into open attachment to the community. Internal migrants have very strong bonds with their original ethnic communities where they may have invested their life savings (such as in building homes), visit frequently every year, and wish to be buried when they die. They regard themselves as economic sojourners who would return home upon attaining success. Language competence becomes an economic instrument, then, and not a measure of attachment to the local community. Another problem is that subgroups of the larger groups have their own states and their language could be spoken by rival related subgroups in different states. This is particularly true of western Nigeria where Yoruba subgroups have their own states, or of eastern Nigeria where rival Igbo subgroups have their own units. People could pass the language test without having lived in the states where they want to claim membership benefits.

Given these difficulties, the alternative should be a substitution of residency for indigeneity. Instead of defining state membership in terms of familial descent, residence in a relevant unit should serve as the criterion. Competence in the local language could be a consequence of residency, especially for migrants in a state, their offspring, and for those who have married into it. From a liberal perspective, this is far superior because it allows migrants to enjoy political and social rights wherever they live. This is what the 1986 Political Bureau opted for when it recommended that citizens should have full residency rights in any state in which they have lived for ten years.

Some might argue that migrants could find themselves in the most important positions within their resident state (for example, Igbos could occupy key positions in Rivers State) and, as a consequence, undercut the very objective of the federal character approach. Some members of the 1978 Constituent Assembly had also argued that, at the national level, the president might end up appointing people who belonged to a few ethnic groups if indigeneity was diluted (Nigeria 1978: 357). This fear is taken far too seriously as migrants do not usually constitute a significant percentage of the population of the communities where they live and are therefore not in a position to displace original members from public service jobs. If the opposite is true (and this would be a rare case), the fear of domination could be addressed by placing limits on non-indigenous appointments.

The 1995 Constitutional Agreements and 1998-99 CDCC Decision Regarding Political Arrangements

I will begin this section by acknowledging the dubious origin of the Constitutional Conference—dubious in the sense that it was really a ploy by General Abacha to divert attention from the illegitimacy of his regime by preoccupying Nigerians with a Babangida-cloned endless transition program (Soyinka 1996: 11). Despite its questionable origin and status, the conference provided an outlet for aggrieved groups (such as cultural groups, interest groups, elite groups, and traditional chiefs) to express their concerns about ethno-regional power imbalances. It also provided an institutional basis for addressing competing claims regarding alternative political structures and power-sharing arrangements. The conference may have been intended to serve only a diversionary purpose in the sense that it was used to serve a hidden political agenda. Nonetheless, important normative claims were made and constitutional arrangements were negotiated equally, which possessed normative importance. The constitutional agreements set up a framework for the revisions that were implemented by the 1998-99 Constitutional Debate Coordinating Committee (CDCC). It would, therefore, be worthwhile to evaluate the claims for their normative relevance, and to analyze the negotiated arrangements to determine if they were the best possible and, if not, what feasible alternatives could have been viable given the claims and conditions on the ground. This would also enable one to determine if the course taken by the 1998-99 CDCC was indeed the best.

Structural Arrangements

What would justify claims to abandon federalism in Nigeria for alternatives like confederation or political dissolution? What conditions could justify the parting of ways by the various ethnic regions in Nigeria?

One might argue that the monopoly of power by one section of the country or its treatment as a birthright could justify claims for dissolution of the polity. To hold power permanently is to deny citizenship status to others. Citizenship, in its unqualified sense, means legal membership in a state. The most important criterion for determining citizenship is legal possession of a political right, or what Aristotle (1964: bk. 3, chap. 1 1275b) referred to as the "right to rule." People lacking the formal right to rule are subjects, not citizens, and are perhaps best exemplified by people in colonial territories who were denied the right to participate in government. Long-term political subjection is enough to justify confederation and political calls for dissolution.

Some might object to the above by invoking the platonic division of powers in Nigeria. Objectors would argue that the eastern part of the country commands economic power, that the west controls bureaucratic power, and that the North has political power. Power is therefore fragmented and allocated to each of the regions and this must be maintained in order to prevent any region from possessing it all (Abdullahi 1994:

140-42; Akinterinwa 1997: 275). This objection fails when arguments about citizenship, such as those made above, are considered. To parcel out political power to one section of a country and exclude others from it constitutes a violation of citizenship rights. It is self-contradictory for different groups of people to form a political union only to have the right to rule limited to a few. This limitation undermines the entire project of forming a self-governing political union. Political power is a primary good that could be used to annex other spheres of power—economic, bureaucratic, and so on—if not subject to democratic terms. This is actually the case in Nigeria where power has been used to elevate members of some geopolitical regions into dominant positions. The so-called control of economic power by the east turns out to be a fallacy since people from that geopolitical region are more active in the informal sector than in the formal economy. The lack of natural resources and the defeat of the Biafran project have driven most easterners into the informal sector where they dominate, as opposed to the big businesses in the formal sector where they are marginally represented.

The second factor that would provide reasonable grounds for political separation is insecurity of life. Social contract theorists all identified generalized insecurity as the primary condition that provoked people to form a commonwealth. They also identified the point at which people, in their right senses, would meaningfully quit the commonwealth. This is when security of life can no longer be guaranteed, as when the commonwealth comes under the subjection of a foreign power, or the regime becomes tyrannical and people can no longer tolerate it. The chief reason for constituting political society is defeated if the vulnerability of citizens to arbitrary power cannot be reduced, and more so if agents of the state are the very ones unleashing terror on the people. Political developments in the country during the late 1980s and early 1990s certainly met the conditions for the dissolution of the body politic. The 1995 Constitutional Conference expressed this view when it noted that public fears about the possible political disintegration rested on "unfairness, inequity and injustice in the governing of Nigeria" (Nigeria 1995 Vol. 2: 59).

Given the reasonableness of the claims, would it have been best to have a structural arrangement different from what the conference decided on? Confederation and/or a structure in which groups enjoy complete autonomy were the alternatives that were demanded but these were neither desirable nor practical for a number of reasons.

First, confederation and group autonomy entailed the weakening of the center and the conferment of sovereign status on ethno-regional units.

This would have amounted to a political separation, which the Ijaw actually demanded, and most Nigerians were not prepared for the incoherence and chaos that would have ensued. Memories of Biafra were not yet dulled and most people did not want a repeat experience. In fact, it is generally believed that Nigeria's existence after the annulment of the June 12, 1993, election results was saved by the Biafran experience.[19]

Second, the interdependence among various parts of the country made confederation or political breakup unrealistic. Over the years, networks of social and economic interactions had developed between different geo-ethnic regions that together have made the country a complete system with interdependent parts. The functioning and progress of one part has become tied to exchanges and interactions between all the parts and a break-up would spell disaster for this system. For example, the landlocked northern part of the country is as dependent on the coastal ports for sea transport as it is dependent on oil revenue derived from the Niger Delta.[20] Also, the South has become increasingly dependent on the North and the middle belt for food and beef requirements, but this is blunted by the reliance of the country on oil revenue derived from the Niger Delta. There are also people from various ethnic regions who reside in and conduct their business from places other than their own and, in consequence, their economic survival is tied to the continued existence of the country. The remark made by Governor Donald Cameron in the 1930s that, for geographic and economic reasons, no part of the country would likely become a separate, self-contained political and economic unit in the future is as valid today as it was when he made it.

Third, it would have been quite difficult to draw agreed upon boundaries in order to arrive at acceptable political units for a confederal arrangement or for political breakup. The northern part of the country housed and continues to house multiple and mutually antagonistic groups of different religions. Not only have religious and communal conflicts have been endemic, but some minorities believe that they are the victims of political oppression by the Muslim power elite. Frequency of conflict and the related loss in human lives have always featured in global statistics on violent communal and ethnic conflicts (Gurr 1993: 361, Table A 17; Rothchild 1997: 10). Mutual suspicion would, therefore, have made it difficult to find groups willing to live together in the same polity.

The problem of drawing determinate boundaries would have been as difficult in the South where Igbos and Yorubas are internally differentiated and hardly act as unitary actors. For example, Abiola's claim to the presidency was betrayed by some of his kinsmen who volunteered to head the puppet interim national government set up by General Babangida. Rivalry and conflict between Yoruba subgroups is historical but is overshadowed in contemporary times by the larger conflict between the main groups. With the Igbo, I have already made reference to the memorandum submitted on their behalf, but that was unsigned by some representatives who claimed to be representing both Imo and Igbos of Rivers and Delta States. Minorities were not free from the problem of disunity either. For example, on the eve of the constitutional conference of 1994, an interest group called the Southern Minorities Group held a series of meetings to decide on one large territorial unit in which ethnic minorities of the Niger Delta would be grouped. A splinter body quickly developed to express fears that "if minorities are granted independence, as is being canvassed by Akobo and Ken Saro Wiwa, president of the Movement for the Survival of the Ogoni People, the rate of ethnic domination may be worse" (*Newswatch* 1994: 10-11). These examples highlight the difficulties in drawing boundaries if the country were to be broken into confederal units. Walzer may have been justified when he stated that his arguments for the right of cultural groups to self-determination do not provide a single best answer to all situations.

On the whole, reasonable grounds existed on which to base claims for confederation and the political dissolution of the country, but these arrangements did not constitute better alternatives to a federal system. Anthony Birch (1989: 63-64) argued that temporary grievances, no matter how strongly felt, should not be used as plausible grounds for breaking up a state unless they have a history and the state does not provide mechanisms for peaceful adjustment of policies. Nigeria meets the first requirement because grievances regarding monopoly of power and domination by a few groups date back to the 1950s. One cannot say the same about the second requirement since the country has adopted several constitutional strategies from the 1970s on for avoiding political domination by a few powerful groups; unfortunately, these strategies have not been effective. In this respect, the 1995 conference was justified in rejecting claims for arrangements other than federalism and the 1998-99 CDCC also had reasonable grounds for endorsing the retention of a federal structure.

Power-Sharing

Was the 1995 negotiated strategy for power-sharing a desirable means of ensuring equity among various groups? Was the CDCC right in excluding the rotation of the executive chair and proportional representation in cabinet from the 1999 Constitution?

Proportional representation of parties in the executive cabinet and rotation of the office of the president were the elements of the strategy negotiated by the 1995 conference. I had argued for the rotation of the executive chair in chapter 5 when I noted that the country's federal structure not only disadvantaged minority group members in the competition for the office of the president but also discouraged them from doing so. I invoked the liberal principle of equality in defense of rotation, and also showed that such an arrangement was not at odds with democratic principles. The arguments would fully defend the 1995 constitutional conference agreement on rotation as meeting the requirements of justice in a multiethnic society, but would condemn its exclusion from the 1999 Constitution as a reversal of democratic gains.

Some might argue that the Nigerian Fourth Republic started off as a true competitive democracy, that the three registered political parties competing for power were inclusive of various group elites, and that power shifted from the Muslim north to the Yoruba west without resorting to rotational arrangement. It might also be objected that the demand for rotational presidency was generated by the terrible developments of the mid-1990s and that those dark moments might not be witnessed again.[21] There are still others who would object that Nigerian political parties have informal arrangements for rotating the office of the chair among various cultural zones in the country, and that it would be better to leave the arrangement at the informal level rather than legalize it in the constitution (Suberu and Diamond 2000: 18). This objection regards a constitutional entrenchment of the arrangement as a violation of conventional democratic principles.

Regarding the first objection, I concede that some of the parties were inclusive, especially the People's Democratic Party (PDP), which could properly be regarded as a party of the Nigerian bourgeoisie. It is also true that power shifted from one ethnic section of the country to another without a constitutional provision for rotation that would have temporarily suspended the rights of some citizens to contest for it. However, power shifts occurred not because of the ability of some Yoruba elites to successfully compete for power but because of tactical decisions made by the northern power elite. Yoruba-based opposition to the existing structural arrangement, especially the unified command of the military, and violent campaigns by pan-Yoruba cultural groups for an Oduduwa Republic brought the northern Muslim elite to the realization that their future hold on power depended on redressing the injustices of 1993. Their collective long-term interest demanded that they allow the southern part of the country, especially the southwest where the Yoruba reside, to produce the leader. They temporarily suspended their right to contest for the office, making it possible for a Yoruba elite to win the presidential elections.[22] What obtained was a de facto rotation that may not continue into the future. But justice will require that rotation continue so that every group member will have an equal chance to compete for it. The best assurance of its continuation is an entrenched constitutional provision that would move the executive chair from one geo-ethnic area to another during every national election.

The second objection is weak because it does not take into account the country's political history. Arguments about rotating the office of the president date back to the drafting of the 1979 Constitution when the Constitutional Drafting Committee debated and abandoned the idea. The termination of the Second Republic in 1983 generated mild comments from academics meeting in international conferences that the error the Nigerian constitution makers made was throwing out rotational arrangement. The arrangement was proposed and demanded by a cross-section of Nigerians when the Political Bureau met in the mid-1980s to work out a political blueprint for the country, but, as discussed earlier, it was rejected.

The problem with the third objection is that it implicitly accepts rotating the office but wants to keep it hidden. If rotation is desirable, why not bring it into the open by resting it on law? Why hide it? The danger with the informal arrangement is that it rests on the disposition of those in control of power, as was argued in the preceding chapter. Power is the chief good in society and those in control of it will not desire to part with it unless they are compelled by law to do so. It is a historical fact that the NPN had an informal rotational arrangement during the Second Republic, but it is also true that Moshood Abiola had to quit the party in 1982 because power did not shift when the time came around.

The suggestion that a rotational arrangement should be informal and secret is not helpful as it looks to universalist liberal principles that do not fit the cultural specifics found in Nigeria. There is the general recognition today that over two-thirds of the 184 countries in the world are multiethnic and that classic liberal democratic principles are not appropriate for them. For example, an international conference organized by the Swiss Peace Foundation on the occasion of the 50th anniversary of the United Nations issued the Charter of Basel, which noted that "only democratic solutions, which take account of group specific matters will hold in the long run" (Bachler 1997: 314). In addition, at a December

1999 Conference on Constitutional Design at the University of Notre Dame attended by experts from all over the world, a consensus emerged that multiethnic societies require democratic arrangements facilitating political inclusion, not those arrangements tailored to homogeneous societies. The point here is that principles derived from a particular cultural context might not be helpful if they are used as standards to judge what is best for another country that is fundamentally different.

Now, to the issue of proportional representation of parties in the cabinet which the 1995 conference agreed to and which was provided for by the 1995 draft document, but excluded from the 1999 Constitution. One of the problems of the federal character strategy when it was devised in the mid-1970s was that majority group members were systemically advantaged in terms of winning presidential elections and appointing a cabinet. I argued this point in chapter 5 and showed that one solution to the structural problem would be to rotate the office of the president. But this solution is not enough because it does not ensure balanced representation in the cabinet. Although federal character was supposed to generate inclusive political parties that would translate into an inclusive federal cabinet, this benign expectation was not realized. Parties that emerged and operated between 1979 and 1983 were all ethnic-based. Although dissenting elites emerged to join forces with rival ethnic parties (as in the case of some Yoruba or Igbo elites joining the Hausa-Fulani controlled National Party of Nigeria), these elites were often regarded as spoilers or sell-outs. They had less legitimacy and whatever roles they played in government were regarded as marginal. In the Nigerian Fourth Republic that began in 1999, the ethnic orientation of some parties was unmistakable. The Alliance for Democracy (AD), for example, was predominantly comprised of Yoruba elites and had firm electoral hold on the entire southwest. The ethnic outlook of the People's Democratic Party (PDP), a party of Hausa-Fulani elites in alliance with Igbo elites, was blunted by the northern establishment's adoption of Olusegun Obasanjo, a Yoruba, as the presidential candidate and eventual winner of the elections. Obasanjo was considered a sell-out by his kinsmen and women, and his inability to win votes in the southwest partly informed the AD's call for a government of national unity that would provide legitimate representation of Yoruba voters in government (*Vanguard* 1999a: 13; *Vanguard* 1999b). What measures, then, would ensure legitimate representation of groups in cabinet?

The requirement of section 147 subsection 3 of the 1999 Constitution that at least one indigene of each state in the federation be appointed a minister is a sure way to go. However, this is not enough if parties sweep up the electoral votes in their respective areas (as the AD did in the southwest in 1999) but are excluded from office. Excluding them would amount to excluding the legitimate representatives of the voters from government and punishing the parties for not being able to capture votes from areas controlled by rival parties. These problems could probably be addressed by combining the incentive-based electoral formula devised in the mid-1970s with the consociational coalition technique that requires parties to be represented in cabinet in proportion to the votes they have received.

An inclusive cabinet engineered in this way has more depth than the classic consociational coalition. In the case of the latter, political parties may not adequately or legitimately represent ethno-regional groups that are fractured into rival groups. But in the case of this innovative model, the reward of legitimate representation in government encourages factional groups to support parties representing their interest. In addition, the emphasis on cross-ethnic appeal as a condition for occupying the highest office of the land (the most violently contested office in sub-Saharan Africa) prompts even the most extreme factional groups and elites to adopt moderate and reconciliatory postures and positions. All these measures provide assurance to both majority and minority groups, ensure adherence to established procedures, legitimize outcomes, and assist the cultivation of democratic norms.

One difficulty with an inclusive cabinet generated by a combination of electoral instrument and consociational technique is that it rules out the institution of opposition that is a central feature of liberal democracy. Another difficulty is that ministers will be divided on policy issues and goals, making it difficult for government to proceed smoothly. Technically, there will be opposition within the cabinet as its members take conflicting party positions on policy issues. This might not be a problem if John Calhoun's (1953: 28-30) concurrent majority principle or what Lijphart (1977) and Nordlinger (1972: 24-26) differently prescribed as the mutual veto are accounted for. The concurrent majority principle requires mutual agreement of all parties as a condition for the adoption of policy decisions. But a mutual veto that prevents the party with numerical strength in cabinet from having its way would generate real crisis, and the inclusive government would hardly last.

Do these difficulties undermine the argument for the type of inclusive government described above? I argue that they do not, and for a number of reasons. First, the prescribed cabinet should not translate into the absence of opposition that is a vital part of liberal democracy. The institution has the great virtue of being a watchdog of the government in office, forcing the latter to act within the limits of its powers and be accountable for what it does. Its readiness to displace the ruling government at the end of four years further ensures a more robust accountability. Now, bringing members of different parties into government helps strengthen the institution of opposition. In Nigeria, as in most other multiethnic societies, the executive chair is regarded as the main seat of power; it is the office that interests both politicians and the public most. For example, in Nigeria the president is also the commander-in-chief. This individual appoints and dismisses service chiefs such as the police chief. The incumbent also appoints the chairpersons and members of the Federal Judicial Service Commission, the National Police Council, the National Defense Council, the National Economic Council, the Code of Conduct Bureau, and so on without Senate confirmation (Nigeria 1999: §154). The executive also has the power to appoint and dismiss ministers, including the Attorney General, though appointment is subject to confirmation by the Senate that the president's party dominates (Nigeria 1999: §147). There are also juridical powers including the power to appoint members of the justices of the Supreme Court, president and justices of the court of appeal, and the chief judge and judge of the federal high court, on consultation with the National Judicial Council whose members the president had earlier appointed.

In the office of the president we see an enormous concentration of power. It is therefore not surprising that a party which is not in control is considered to be out of power, even if it has 40 percent of seats in the national assembly. So, appointing a few ministers from the losing parties (in proportion to their electoral vote) does not invest the latter with the real seat of power. Their role as parties in opposition is moderated by their being represented in cabinet, but that role remains solid by virtue of their not controlling the most valued office. The latter would be particularly true when one considers that representation in government rests on constitutional provisions, not postelection agreements between majority and minority parties for the pooling of legislative seats. This instills the understanding that in a democracy, the losing party is in dialectical unity with the winning party and that, in their contradictory unity, they effect good governance. An inclusive cabinet, therefore, is not a negation of opposition; rather, it addresses the problem of intolerance and intense hatred between the losing and winning parties, a problem that contributed to the political tragedies in the 1960s and early 1980s. In short, an inclusive cabinet nurtures a culture of toleration that is central to the operation of the institutions of government and opposition.

Second, a cabinet including various parties does not necessarily translate into one with conflicting and contradictory policy goals. Cabinet members are political heads of departments who carry out the government functions directed by the chair who is their boss. Their relationship to the chair makes it less likely that they would go off and independently execute policies not sanctioned by the chair or that they would challenge him or her. At any rate, since the 1970s when the federal character policy was adopted in Nigeria, conflict between ethnoregional elites and their parties has erupted over issues other than policy differences. It is quite unlike the early 1960s when disagreement over policy issues such as affirmative action, a unitary versus a federal system, regional security, representation in the federal legislature and so on occupied the center of politics. In contemporary times, the issues have to do with the entrenchment of democracy, subordination of the military to civil authority, transparency in governance, and securing a good deal for the oil-producing communities, none of which generates disagreements as to their desirability. The determination of various group elites to end military rule during the late 1990s combined with the absence of ideological differences among the parties that competed for the 1999 elections, demonstrate that there could be a commitment to the pursuance of unifying policy options rather than contentious and damaging ones. Indeed, the absence of ideological and policy differences is such that all the parties that officially emerged in 1999, including the ruling PDP, have practically dissolved and political opposition is found not between parties but between the legislature and the executive. This form of opposition that departs from the classic one between parties is a true reflection of contemporary Nigerian politics in which the public demands transparency and accountability after years of military oppression and institutionalized corruption. Under this pressure, the executive and legislative arms of government actively check each other's tendency to either loot public wealth for private purposes or exercise power arbitrarily. This form of opposition makes for transparency and accountability and is what Nigeria is likely to witness in the years ahead, rather than the traditional type of opposition that prompted the executive to "buy off" legislative members of opposition parties and to cultivate and tolerate corruption.

Claims and Agreements Regarding Revenue Allocation

I now turn my attention to claims and agreements regarding natural resource ownership, a contentious issue that has generated violence in the Niger Delta since the early 1990s. I will make normative judgments about these claims and then assess the fairness of the 1994-95 constitutional agreement and its endorsement by the 1998-99 CDCC.

The key issue at stake in the Niger Delta is who should own the rich petroleum resources located there. Those contesting ownership claims, as seen from the narrative presented earlier in this chapter, involve the state on the one hand and, on the other, ethnic communities on whose land oil is located. It will be necessary to spell out the grounds on which each makes its claims, beginning with the communities, who invoke the derivation method of revenue sharing operative in the 1950s and 1960s to support their claims.

The communities argue that, in the pre-civil war years when agricultural exports were the principal source of revenue, federal allocations to the then regions were disbursed on the basis of their relative contribution to the central purse. This arrangement, it is argued, benefited the three major ethnic groups who were the major producers of export crops. The emergence of oil as the principal source of revenue also required an application of the same method. Instead, the federal government elected to abandon it because the rich resources are not extracted from areas inhabited by the major groups. Land ownership has also served as a premise for claims. It is argued that the land from which oil is derived is the ancestral home of ethnic communities across the delta and, as such, they have rights to whatever comes from it.

On the other hand, notable public figures, especially those from the northern part of the country, have argued that Nigeria belongs to all of its citizens as do the resources within it (Aminu 1994: 187-88; West 1994). On the eve of his election as president, Olusegun Obasanjo made a similar statement while brokering peace with Ijaw youths.

Liberal arguments can be invoked to justify the Nigerian state's claim to resource ownership. These arguments affirm the equal rights of citizens and require the state, as a guarantor of these rights, to treat every one with equal respect. This is the dominant liberal view of citizenship. It is a view that regards political society as formed by free individuals who share equally in the rewards and burden of citizenship. John Locke and Jean-Jacques Rousseau (who argued for a highly tempered liberalism) articulate this view clearly.

In the social contract doctrines of these two thinkers, the act by which individuals unite in a political society also entails submission of their possessions to the community brought into being by the union. This submission is not alienation; rather, it creates the basis for the legitimate exercise of ownership right (Locke 1980: 120-21; Rousseau 1968: bk. 1, ch. 9). Upon such submission, the state (which I take to be institutional manifestation of the political community) guarantees the right, and this transforms possessions into property. As the guarantor of right, the state has jurisdiction of the territory over which it presides and regulates every one within it. Also, as a guarantor of right, the state ought not to invade what it guarantees because doing so would amount to tyranny. As a body that has the legitimate monopoly of force, it guarantees right not only by ensuring compliance to its laws but by warding off external invasion, thereby ensuring jurisdiction of its territory relative to other states. Indeed international law recognizes the jurisdictional right of states to their territory.

Now, it is the act of constituting a society that gives birth to a territorial unit known as a country, large enough for all its members to live and enjoy in common. With Rousseau the contractors are sovereign, as is the case with Locke, except that, in the latter, sovereign power is delegated to the legislature, which is a key institution of the state. The Lockean notion of sovereignty approximates our contemporary idea of it. With each of the two philosophers, it is the sovereign body that has jurisdictional right to the country. It makes rules by which members can enjoy the country in common, and this includes rules that govern the acquisition and sale of land (Hume, "Treatise of Human Nature," part II, §iii). The right of members to their acquisitions is subordinate to the right of the sovereign to the entire country (Rousseau 1968: bk. 1, ch. 9). For this reason, the property right of members could be subordinated when it is expedient to do so. If, for example, a planned river dam would submerge a number of villages (such as the Three Gorges Dam in China), or some private buildings would stand in the middle of a proposed highway, it would be expedient to subordinate private rights to the larger interest of the national community, in which case those who suffer loss of right will receive compensation in proportion to the value of what they lose. Some countries, such as Canada and Great Britain, call this the right of eminent domain. On this basis, the state could make claims to resources in its territory if they are not the creation of private labor. In fact, the right of the sovereign to its national territory partly explains why foreigners carrying out economic transactions first seek its permission. Thus, a foreign firm coming to explore oil has to negotiate with the government for permission and also pays taxes to it. These arguments could justify the control of oil by the Nigerian state.

What principled objections can be raised against the above argument as applied to the issue under discussion? First, the social contract theorists in their writings assumed political society to be formed by individuals living the same cultural life. They assumed individuals would have the same values and that a national political community would be instituted to defend these shared values. This basic assumption should not be applied to the Nigerian case where people with different ethnic backgrounds have consistently argued for two levels of political community—the national and the subnational. The several preindependence constitutional negotiations approximated social contract meetings for the institution of a desirable political community, but what emerged was a tri-regional federal arrangement that did not accommodate minority groups very well. Objections to this arrangement eventually resulted in the current multistate structure in which a national political community exists alongside several subnational political communities that are themselves not meaningful units of self-government. Here, the center has appropriated the rights of the states with the effect that the latter are units of administration rather than of self-government.[23]

Second, social contract theorists founded the legitimacy of the agreements that produced political society on the consent of the governed. Agents of the state were expected to act justly by sticking to the terms of the contract (as with Rousseau) or by governing in accordance with the laws of nature prescribing equality and freedom (Locke 1980: 69-75, 111). Obligation ended when public officials acted unjustly. These conditions would trouble the application of social contract ideas to the Nigerian case. Consider the constitutional negotiations that produced the political arrangements Nigeria had at independence. Ethnic minority groups dissented from the start in 1950 through the Independence Conference of 1958. Their protests, conference boycotts, and slogans indicating that they would oppose independence unless they were given political recognition like the majority groups were evidence of active resistance to the constitutional agreements. Moreover, the 1966 armed rebellion and the declaration of the Niger Delta People's Republic by Ijaw youths attests to the resistance to political arrangements that emerged from the preindependence negotiations.

Third, argument concerning the right of eminent domain does not destroy a right; rather, it recognizes a right by making room for compensation for what is expropriated. To compensate, the state has to negotiate the value of the property with its owner. In this respect, there is actually no loss of right. Instead right is reproduced in something else. The affirmation of right is akin to what happens in contract when parties are recognized as property owners and their right gains universal objectivity through exchange (Hegel 1952: 57 ¶71).

Let us turn to claims by groups across the delta and the theoretical arguments that could be invoked to support them. Arguments advanced by contemporary theorists of group recognition, discussed at length in chapter 1, state that ethnic minority groups suffering injustice should be granted rights to internal self-government. In this perspective, rights to resources are implicated because internal self-determination would not exclude rights to them. For example, Will Kymlicka's prescription for a variety of special rights that include internal self-government, guaranteed representation on intergovernmental bodies, and veto rights would recognize minority ethnic communities as having rights to resources in their homeland (Kymlicka 1995: 139-44 and chapters 2, 3; 1989: chapters 7, 9). He calls this the equality argument and relates it to resource claims by arguing that vulnerability to the political and economic decisions of the majority calls for minority protection in the form of the right to control resource development that would otherwise undermine their way of life (Kymlicka 1996: 46). This argument might support the position of the oil communities that the federal government has been able to appropriate oil resources because it is dominated by elites of the three major groups.

Another argument would be Hume's (1948: 76) discussion of the rules that should determine property rights in a newly formed human society. Hume established several orders of principles, one of which is the accession principle. It holds that individuals have a right to objects that are intimately connected to their property. For example, the orange tree on my land or the offspring of my cattle are mine because they are derived from what I already possess. Hume's principle applied to individuals but it could be used to support communities' claims. Shifting it from individuals to groups might be justified by the system of land ownership—such as family, village, and clan—obtainable in the Niger Delta as in most parts of sub-Saharan Africa. So, by virtue of land ownership, the communities have a right to resources on their property. What objections could be raised against these arguments, including the one concerning the derivation method that applied during the 1950s and 1960s?

First, it might be objected that the pre-civil war revenue allocation method applied to the then political regions comprising the present-day oil communities, not to ethnic communities. The objection here is that the derivation rule did not follow naturally from group ownership of resources and should not provide an adequate ground on which to base ethnic communities' claims. It might also be objected that ethnic communities have indeterminate boundaries and it would be difficult to enforce rights among them. For example, an oil well might be located in the territory of one village and not in the territory of the other, as is often the case, yet both villages might belong to the same ethnic community and share common local boundaries. An ethnic elite might then be championing the right of their community to oil, but their village probably has no oil well while the neighboring sister village has two or three.[24] So, the problem of ownership rights rears its head at a lower level. The problem, some might argue, is palpable in the case of the lower Niger Delta where some ethnic communities live either along the coastline or on pieces of land surrounded by sea, with oil wells located not on land but in the sea offshore and deep shore. It would be absurd if coastal and island communities were to be assigned ownership of what is in the sea and, if so assigned, arguments would arise over territorial sea boundaries, thus reproducing the ownership problem anew.

The first objection is not as strong as it appears. Political regions of the 1950s and 1960s had strong ethnic characters and their derivation claims were made on behalf of the dominant group in each. The point has already been made about ethnic minorities entering independence as second class-citizens whose interests were not reflected in the political arrangements that were instituted. Indeed, it is more accurate to regard conflict over resources as having been initiated by the majority group elites when they fought over who should get what during the pre-independence constitutional negotiations.

The second objection is even weaker as it does not affect the merit of the argument. The objection raises the practical problem of recognizing right, not the question of right itself. To argue that territorial boundaries of villages or towns are not in fact coextensive with ethnic communities does not invalidate the right. Rather, it endorses the right by showing that its enforcement would raise boundary problems between villages and towns.

What rights does the state have? The earlier argument that the state has sovereign jurisdiction over the territorial area comprising the country is certainly valid in an ethnically homogeneous country where members agree to institute a single national political community. However, this scenario changes if those who decide to unite in one country have different ethnic backgrounds and wish to have differentiated political communities—a large one embracing everyone at the national level *plus* other lower ones for which people have primary affection and in which they have authority over their own local affairs. In this situation, certain authority is delegated to the center while the region (state) is also delegated certain authority (Sawer 1969: 118). Numerous philosophical arguments have been made about the divisibility of sovereignty in federalism and they need not be discussed here. The point I wish to make is that when people unite in a political society that is federal, they (the sovereign body) delegate authority to both the center and the regions. The center represents the people of all the regions (the entire people in the country) while the regions represent people within their respective local areas. Jurisdictional right to the country is therefore shared between the two levels. This means that the communities that constitute the second level of government have as many rights as the federal level does. This equality, however, should not give rise to wholesale control of resources by either of the two levels; instead, it would require that both have ownership rights that are equal or near equal. Neither ought to exercise an absolute right that would eliminate the other's. Nigeria has been *de facto* unitary precisely because the federal government's exercise of absolute powers abolished the states' rights.

It is this exercise of absolute powers that has generated violent protests across the Niger Delta and has raised national consciousness about the need for a true federal system in which jurisdictional rights of the center coexist with those of the states. Indeed, it was with the aim of achieving this goal that the National Constitutional Conference of 1994 made a provision in the 1995 Draft Constitution requiring the National Assembly to work out revenue allocation criteria that combine the derivation principle with several other principles (Nigeria 1995 Vol. 1: §153; 1995 Vol. 2: 142). The general framework set out in the 1995 Draft Constitution is very much akin to the 1951 allocation framework produced by the Hicks Commission, which I have earlier argued constituted a perfect balance of principles. The draft document required the constant reflection of the derivation principle in any formula approved by the assembly and should not amount to less than 13 percent of the revenue accruing to the federation account from natural resources. This arrangement was endorsed by the Constitutional Debate Coordinating Committee (CDCC) set up by the regime of General Abubakar in late 1998 to review the 1995 draft document, and it is entrenched in Section 162 (2) and (3) of the 1999 Constitution.

While the 1994 constitutional framers and the 1998 CDCC did recognize the states as having rights to revenue generated from their domains, it is unclear how the 13 percent derivation base was determined. The Sub-Committee on Revenue Allocation in the 1994 Constitutional Conference that worked out the allocation criteria did not explain if the figure was derived from some principle or if it was arbitrary. The 1998 reviewers did not provide any rational grounds either. In the absence of known principles, one can safely conclude that the figure is arbitrary. The figure is actually lower than it appears because Section 163(2) of the 1995 Draft Constitution endorsed by the CDCC states that "the figure of the allocation for derivation shall be deemed to include any amount that may be set aside for funding any special authority or agency for the development of the State or States of derivation." This provision draws a whole range of entitlements into the 13 percent baseline. If you will recall, the Minorities Commission of 1957-58 reported that the Niger Delta had suffered governmental neglect because of its inaccessibility. The commission noted that providing infrastructure in the region was prohibitively expensive, as it would cost £69,000 to build a hospital bed compared to £1,000 in other parts of the country (Nigeria 1958: 42). It was on this ground that it recommended the declaration of the region as a "Special Area" for which a Federal Board should be appointed to oversee its development (Nigeria 1958: 94-95). Nothing tangible came out of it. In 1976, the government panel on creation of states recommended that: "the problem of the Riverine peoples should be seen in terms of national emergency and the Federal Government should therefore set up an authority to develop the . . . area" (Nigeria 1976a: 23). Government's responsibility to pay attention to special development was not derived from and, in fact, did not in any way relate to oil production. It was a social responsibility owed to the people as citizens, not as inhabitants of oil-producing areas. That is to say, the central government has the responsibility of providing social infrastructures for the region, just as it does in other parts of the country. But the conference factored the cost into the 13 percent by including the funds for special agencies such as the Oil Mineral Producing Areas Development Commission (OMPADEC). Also, President Olusegun Obasanjo's bill for the establishment of the Niger Delta Development Commission (NDDC) followed the spirit of the 1995 draft document by proposing that the development plan of the impoverished Niger Delta region be funded with half of the 13 percent derivation revenue. When funds for such responsibilities are subtracted, the derivation share falls drastically below the 13 percent base. Thus, the figure is no more than a charitable concession to the right of oil-producing states to share the wealth derived from their domain.

Nigeria's Federalism and Sharia

There are two major issues to be evaluated in this section: the first is whether secularism in Nigeria is too closely tied to Christianity to have any claim to even-handedness toward Muslim groups; the other is whether Nigeria's polyethnic federalism creates space for the states to adopt a legal system that is consistent with the cultural practices of their members.

To begin with the first issue, it is true that the values of the Nigerian state, like those of all modern liberal states, are genealogically linked to Christianity and even to Stoic thought. It was the Stoics who declared the moral equality of persons by invoking reason as the common human attribute. In the early stoicism of Chrysippus, equality was limited to individuals who used reason to live above earthly concerns by interpreting whatever came their way as good, not evil. However, the middle stoicism of Panaetius universalized equality by drawing on Plato to argue that the individual's soul consisted of rational and irrational parts, and that reason is a possession of all, not just the wise (Oates 1940).

The universalization of equality by middle stoicism was given a moral grounding by Christianity. In Christian doctrine, everyone emerged as a creation of God and stood equally before Him through Christ the redeemer. According to Paul: "There can be neither Jew nor Greek . . . neither bond nor free . . . no male and female, for ye are all one man in Christ Jesus" (Dumont 1982: 11). This moral equality of persons was given an individualist cast when the Reformation movement rejected institutions (such as the Catholic Church and all its dignitaries) as mediators with God. With this rejection, God became accessible to individual consciousness through faith and justification became private, not requiring external good works and practices (Luther 1961: 21-22, 64-66). Two consequences flowed from the Protestant notion of the individual's assumption of responsibility for her salvation. One was the privatization of religious life, for which John Locke was later to make intellectual arguments in his *Letters of Toleration* (Madan 1993: 671-72). The other was that, because of the privatization of religion, the Christian moral equality of persons before God became part of a common consciousness and arguments about inequality and privileges were no longer defensible. Hegel (1953: 24) glorified this when he noted that, "only the

Germanic peoples [who Hegel saw as the originators of the Reformation movement] came, through Christianity, to realize that man as man is free and that freedom of Spirit is the very essence of man's nature." The consciousness of freedom had to be made real through practical struggles.

Like equality, human rights also date back to stoicism and Christian thought. Middle and late stoicism regarded individuals as subject to law, the law of reason. Everyone possessed it by nature and it was the standard for justice everywhere in the world. Ethically, positive law had to be in accordance with this law of nature. Cicero (1929: 215-16) developed this view further by arguing that the law of states must approximate it or be found null and void. The transition to Christianity brought a modification of this view. Natural law was presented by St. Thomas Aquinas as the imprint of God's wisdom in His creatures and its first precept was to seek good and avoid evil. Here natural law was subordinated to eternal law or the wisdom of God by which the whole universe is preordained. In turn, positive law was regarded as a specification of natural law for the purposes of setting standards for just behavior (Aquinas 1992: 11-96). In Christianity, we see a transformation of natural law into God's law, a change that was carried into the seventeenth century by Richard Hooker.

Two objections might arise here. First, some might object that liberalism divorced itself from Christian thought by first accepting the material reality of objects and proceeding scientifically to derive a state that had no bearings with unknown forces. For example, it might be argued that Hobbes forever severed the affinity between church and state by presenting human beings as matter in perpetual motion and the state as being constituted to permit the maximization of motion. This objection would insist that the liberal state is completely secular and has no relationship whatsoever with Christian religion. Second, and related to the first, some might argue that the early social contract theorists made a clean break with religion by showing that free and equal individuals rationally constitute a political society, that legitimate authority is based on the consent of the people, and that no edict by any power whatsoever will have the force of law unless it is promulgated by the authority that has been instituted by the people. Accordingly, the state owes nothing to religion and has no relationship with it.

Regarding the first objection, it is true that Hobbes was a materialist who used the law of physics to explain human behavior and the constitution of political society. Indeed, Hobbes showed that human beings are motivated by fear and desire and they optimize motion by ceaselessly striving for objects of desire and running away from those of aversion.

However, the political society that he arrived at was one that interfered with motion. Hobbes's social contract generated a powerful ruler that was at once legislator, executive, and judge. The ruler was also the commander in chief, could not be deposed, and was self-perpetuating. Hobbes' ruler was all in all. The people had no citizenship rights; instead, they were reduced to subjects who had to be taught what is good for peaceful coexistence. Hobbes's theory is illiberal because the motion that he began with could not be maximized in the political society where the ruler is absolute.[25] In discussing liberalism, one would discount his version of it.

To the second objection, despite the seeming secularity of the liberal state, Christian natural law in fact provides the moral basis for individual equality. John Locke showed that all individuals are creatures of God and, as a consequence, have the same advantages of nature and the same capacity to reason. Advantages of nature referred to equal natural rights in life and liberty while reason was cosmic law, the law of nature. The latter "teaches all mankind, who will but consult it, that being all equal and independent, no one ought to harm another in his life, health, liberty or possessions: for men being all the workmanship of one omnipotent, and infinitely wise maker . . . sent into this world by his order, and about his business; they are his property . . ." (Locke 1980: chapter 2, ¶4-6). Liberal rights and freedoms are grounded on the Christian understanding that we are all created by God. And Locke, the father of liberalism, presents the defense of these rights as the ends for which society and government are constituted. Hence, as Rousseau also argued, any government that acts contrary to these ends is guilty of tyranny and has to be removed. It is easy to see that the fundamental liberal values constituting the bedrock of the modern state are structurally linked to Christianity. These values informed the French Declaration of the Rights of Man and of the Citizen and the U.S. Declaration of Independence. In turn, these two documents were reflected in the 1948 United Nations Universal Declaration of Human Rights. As Virginia Leary (1990: 17-22) has rightly noted, the Universal Declaration of Human Rights was drafted by Westerners and reflects values believed fundamental to European and American culture since the dawn of liberalism.

It is this Christian-derived liberal norm that was exported to the colonial territories, including Nigeria. Although the British colonial administration in Nigeria gave official support to Islamic religion by using it as the basis for indirect rule in the northern part of the country, this did not affect the fact that the state was instituted at the national level. Instead, what operated were the liberal values closely associated with the Christian moral equality of persons and the natural law that reaches back to Aquinas, Cicero, and Panaetius. Christian-flavored liberal norms have been entrenched in the various constitutions the country has adopted since 1960. For example, sections 33-46 of the 1999 Nigerian Constitution spell out the fundamental rights and liberties of the individual. These were also spelled out in the 1979 Constitution as well as in previous ones, including the 1960 Independence Constitution (sections 17-32).

Would this argument about the historical ties between Christianity and liberal constitutionalism justify the adoption of sharia by the northern states of Nigeria? Answering this question will require drawing attention to the ongoing debate in political theory over the issue of whether marginalized ethnic groups have claims to special recognition in liberal constitutional regimes. The argument, first popularized by Will Kymlicka and already discussed earlier on, presupposes that there is a *prima facie* plausible claim on the part of ethnic minorities that their cultural distinctiveness should be accommodated in law (Kukathas 1992: 105-39). The ground for this accommodation is the non-neutrality of the existing legal system and its tendency to marginalize them. According to the argument, federalism provides a mechanism for grafting both liberal and nonliberal orders into a constitutional whole. The nonliberal order has to be tolerated insofar as rights are not violated blatantly and herein lies the important qualifications for recognition of minority status and legitimate claim to oppression or marginalization.

In the Nigerian context, Muslim groups comprise the largest in the country; they outnumber other groups in all the northern states and are roughly equal in number to Christians in the Yoruba states of the west (Sklar 1999: 16). In political terms, the dominance of the state and the determination of national policy by elites of the Muslim north are well known, so marginalization cannot provide a moral basis for their claims. However, the federal character policy that was devised in the 1970s required that political recognition be given to all groups at either the state or national level. Fairness required that Muslim norms and practices be accommodated, as was done in the pre-1999 constitutional grant of sharia law. This constitutional recognition was given not on grounds that the constitutional order was rooted on Christian-related liberal values.

Admittedly, the liberal principles that govern the state are genealogically tied to Christianity, but take out the Christian ties and we find the principles to be valuable for their own sake. Freedom, equality, and tolerance are principles that are universally accepted regardless of their origins. Because of their intrinsic value, these principles are generally accepted as standards for evaluating public institutions and the way people relate to them. Thus, non-Western countries have since accepted the Universal Declaration of Human Rights that was influence by these principles. All African countries, both Muslim and non-Muslim, have affirmed their commitment to these principles through the African Charter on Human and Peoples Rights that was designed to be reflective of African legal philosophy and to be responsive to the continent's needs (Gittleman 1984: 152; Leary 1990: 23).

Also, the Charter of the Organization of Islamic Conference reaffirmed all Muslim states "commitment to the UN Charter and fundamental Human Rights," despite the evasiveness of the 1990 Cairo Declaration on Human Rights in Islam and its divergence from international standards (Mayer 1999: 179). In most, if not all, Muslim states, grassroots and popular movements have emerged to press for full adherence to international law on human rights where the latter is not respected. Thus, a Roundtable on the Universality of Human Rights held in Amman, Jordan, in December 1994 reached the conclusion that there is a recognizable human rights norm in the unique features of different faiths and cultures. The roundtable presented "equality" as the very "essence of human rights" and proceeded to resolve that "our various faiths and cultures need to cooperate in affirming and strengthening commitment to the universality of human rights" (Armouto: 1996: 47-52). Also exemplary are developments in contemporary Iran where civil society has revived and is successfully pressing for the freedom and equality of persons.

Now I turn to the issue of Nigeria's polyethnic federalism as a device for accommodating groups. Truly, equal political accommodation is the goal of the Nigerian federal device. Most, if not all, of the constituent states have boundaries that coincide with ethnicity and membership is defined in terms of familial descent. Legally, Nigerian constitutions have not prescribed the exclusion of citizens who are not indigenous to a particular state from enjoying certain citizenship rights within it. But, the definition of state membership on familial terms has made it possible to exclude anyone whose descent is traceable to another state. Thus claims to indigeneity take the form of ownership claims to the state and the adoption of sharia is one such claim. The actual adoption of sharia law by Muslim groups in the northern states could be seen as part of the general and ongoing practice of using rights of indigeneity to trump national citizenship rights. In all of this, the real victim is the individual who is denied basic rights of citizenship and left without a constitutional defense.

What should be done? The official federal government's response to the adoption of sharia is to regard the latter as a political project by "overzealous politicians" that should be ignored (*Guardian* 2000a). President Obasanjo strongly believes that if the federal government goes to court, the judges would be divided along religious lines and the issue would tear the country apart. This position seems pragmatic when viewed in light of justifications for sharia given by some political entrepreneurs.

Some have argued that President Olusegun Obasanjo, a Christian from the Yoruba ethnic group, is targeting the North in his political reforms and that the region is increasingly becoming marginalized.[26] Claims to marginalization turned out to be inaccurate, for the Senate's Federal Character Committee on Political Appointments that looked into the case reported that, beginning on May 29, 1999, the northwest got forty top positions, the northeast thirty-five, the north-central thirty-three, the southwest thirty-five, the south-south thirty-two, and the southeast thirty-one (*Guardian* 2000b). There is also the argument that President Obasanjo was chosen by the northern power elite to appease the Yoruba for the awful events of the mid-1990s, and that he was expected to be a loyal agent, just as he was in the 1970s, but that he has sold out. In effect, power seems to have slipped from the North and the sharia is a strategy for reintegrating the region into a coherent community that will ensure the political victory of its elites in the national power game (*Sunday Guardian* 2000).

Given the strategic power game behind the adoption of sharia law, the federal government would be playing into the hands of power seekers if it goes to court to seek an interpretation of the relevant sections of the country's constitution. A court ruling that upholds the adoption of sharia will severely weaken the commitment to liberal constitutionalism or whatever variety of it that exists in Nigeria. On the other hand, court nullification will be regarded as anti-Muslim politicking and may have to be implemented by force. In both scenarios, the government will be delivering itself to political mercenaries and the reaction and subsequent outcome would do more to destabilize constitutionalism than strengthen it. So, the federal government faces a huge dilemma: on the one hand, it is difficult to let apparent violations of the constitutional order to occur without a response; on the other, neither a mere court order nor government force would have sufficient legitimacy to compel a retreat. But an avoidance or do-nothing strategy is not the best route to stability, for it amounts to an abandonment of the commitment to defend liberal constitutionalism.

However, resolving the problem should not require full resistance by the federal government, for reasons discussed above. Rather, it might require three responses. The first and immediate response is for the government to react at the point when the promise not to enforce sharia upon non-Muslims is violated. There was the initial pledge that sharia will not apply to non-Muslims, and pledges are not automatically false. But they turned out to be, given the case of Livinus Obi, an Igbo trader, who was publicly whipped in Kano State for selling alcohol. Or the case of Chinedu Christian, another Igbo trader, who was sentenced to six months imprisonment with an option of fine by a magistrate court in Gusau, Zamfara State, for possession of sixty bottles of beer (*Guardian* 2001). When promises are violated, as in these two cases, the federal level could react. It could also react when *hudud* punishments become widely used, at which point some northern opinion might support intervention.

A second response is to address the clash between claims to indigeneity rights and national citizenship rights and the triumph of the former over the latter within the states. This has already been discussed and need not be repeated here. Addressing the indigeneity problem will reveal that the post-1999 adoption of sharia law is a gross anomaly, even to those who supported it. This solution might be appealing because, in the short term, it avoids the dilemma of taking action against the ten offending northern states. But to focus exclusively on this second strategy without the first will not help very much because the dilemma will not go away in the short run. The federal level will still have to confront the problem of sharia as an infringement upon common citizenship rights, unless the first strategy precedes the second.

The third response is to address the issue of who should exercise national political power, the very problem that is at the bottom of the crisis of secularism. Attempts to break the platonic division of powers (as discussed earlier on) through the federal character constitution of 1979, as well as the subsequent constitutions of 1989 and 1999, have proved elusive. The 1999 informal power shift to the Yoruba was meant to placate them, and this planned temporary shift is not likely to reoccur in the near future should the northern elites regain what is regarded to be theirs. The current expression of regret over the power shift is a clear indicator of what is in stock for Nigeria's democracy. A constitutional solution to the problem of secularism will inevitably bring Nigerians to the principle of rotation of office because the fundamental problem that threatens the corporate existence of Nigeria is that of the right to power.

Summary

In conclusion, Nigeria's fourth approach to its problem of ethnic difference was informed by the inadequacies of the federal character strategy adopted in the mid-1970s and consequent group-based claims for a more equitable arrangement. What emerged was not really abandonment but rather a revision of federal character.

One aspect of the revision involved the successive creation of more states and local government units to further accommodate groups. The creation of new units was generally regarded by segments of the Nigerian public as an endless exercise that had to be stopped, but, as this chapter showed, the need to achieve group equity was part of its inner logic. This justification does not amount to a call for endless multiplication of units but, at the same time, one would not argue for a specific and arbitrary number of units that would best accommodate groups. However, the current structure of thirty-six states and close to 800 local government units should be given some time to function. There is really no point in creating new units if they cannot stabilize, or if those for whom they are meant cannot learn to accommodate themselves to them. It is in this respect that I argue for a policy requiring the existing units to function for some decades, with the hope that elites and their groups will get used to living within the structure currently in place and, over time, the demand syndrome will fade.

Another aspect of the fourth stage of revision was the attempt to address the problems that arose from the constitutional definition of state membership on the basis of familial descent. The definition gave rise to the informal, but illegal, use of indigeneity as the basis for political appointment and recruitment and for the distribution of social benefits, thereby discriminating against citizens residing in states not of their biological descent. The 1986 Political Bureau felt that this was a violation of citizenship rights, for which reason it prescribed the redefinition of state membership on residency terms. Nothing was done about this, as the 1999 Nigerian Constitution (Section 318) still defines state membership on familial terms. This chapter found the Political Bureau's prescription to be superior to the indigeneity requirement because it permits migrants and their offspring to enjoy membership rights in the communities where they reside and to whose development they contribute, either directly or indirectly.

Federal character revision also involved constitutional agreements on competing claims to alternative political structures, power-sharing arrangements, and ownership of natural resources. Claims to confederation and political dissolution as alternative forms of structural arrangement were defensible on the grounds of a monopoly of power by a few ethnic sections of the country and the denial of rights of members of several other ethnic sections to exercise political leadership. However, confederation or political breakup posed frightening political and social costs. These were not alternatives that offered hope for peace and stability. It is in this respect that this chapter defended the 1995 agreement to divide the country into six geo-ethnic regions for the purposes of rotating the office of the president.

The biggest challenge to the quest for a just and stable constitutional order is the post-1999 adoption of sharia law by most states in the northern part of the country. The basis for the adoption was the charge by Muslim groups that the Nigerian state is structurally rooted in Christian values. The chapter found this claim to be valid, but argued that Muslim groups are not marginalized within the country's constitutional structure, and the Muslim legal system cannot be reconciled with the commitment to liberal constitutionalism at the federal level.

Notes

1. The derivation share fell from 20 percent in 1975 to 10 percent in 1980 and, when the oil market crashed in 1983, it was further reduced to 1.4 percent.

2. A minority report emerged from the bureau dissenting from the above position. It opted for retention of the nineteen-state system on the grounds that the existing federal structure was already sufficiently decentralized to cope with the challenges of federalism (Nigeria 1987: 178-79).

3. Local governments had already increased from 301 in 1978 to 593 at the time of the conference

4. A particular case was a university in Port Harcourt in Rivers State where there was an attempt to murder the nonindigenous registrar in 1980. The incident led to a formal protest by the Legislative Assembly of Bendel State (the registrar's indigenous state) and an apology from the then Rivers State Legislature.

5. The palace coup that brought this regime to power in 1985 was believed to have been motivated by the need to address grievances about power imbalances.

6. The discontent caused a failed military coup in 1990 by some southern and middle belt military officers who made a radio address on the monopoly of

power by people from the Muslim North and announced the temporary excision of five Muslim northern states from the country (Ibrahim 1991: 135).

7. This document was not signed by five of the eleven representatives listed on it, in particular those who were claimed to represent Imo State and the Igbos of Rivers and Delta States.

8. Northern chiefs regarded the charge of political domination by one part of the country as a delusion arising out of the fear of the unknown (Emirs and Chiefs of the Northern States of Nigeria 1994: 4-5; The Middle Belt Council 1994: 12-13).

9. Similar but less radical claims were made in a memorandum submitted on behalf of the Ogoni, an ethnic minority group living in the oil-rich Niger Delta. The memorandum demanded political autonomy for the Ogoni within Nigeria and proposed that each ethnic group that can viably exist on its own should constitute a political unit within a loose federation, while those without economic resources to support statehood should negotiate to live with their neighbors (Movement for the Survival of the Ogoni People 1994: 2). In a document released by other communities in the Niger Delta, it was noted that, "the three big brothers, the Hausa/Fulani oligarchy, the Yoruba, and the Igbo, sought the use of the minorities and the resources of the minorities to enhance their way of life and to force them to serve willy-nilly. . . . The area considers itself as alienated territory and worse still, the people are evidently regarded as second-class citizens whose talents and natural wealth must go to service the well being of the three big brothers" (Urhobo Oil Mineral Communities 1994: 3).

10. To quote the conference report:

> "At the time the Constitutional Conference was inaugurated, the tension in the country was so high that many people thought the Conference would not last. There were in fact some who believed that blows would be exchanged inside the Conference hall. To the pessimists the end for Nigeria was in sight. Contrary to these fears, however, the conference began so well and through out the general debates no member called for the disintegration of Nigeria. When Committee No. 1 began its sittings, it commenced on a position where it was not necessary to consider the disintegration of Nigeria. It proceeded from a position of one united Nigeria and then progressed with its deliberations. . . . As has been stated above, there was not a single call for the disintegration of the country; most of the complaints were centered around the manner the country was governed. There were cries of neglect by certain areas and of inequity in sharing power and resources. More than anything else it was this unfairness, inequity and injustice in the governance of Nigeria that worried a num-

ber of people who nonetheless did not opt for a break-up of the country." (Nigeria 1995 Vol. 2: 59)

11. The North was defined as "the States, including the Federal Capital Territory, Abuja, carved out from the former Northern Region of Nigeria as at 1 October, 1960." The South was defined as "the States carved out from the former Eastern and Western Regions of Nigeria including the Territory of Lagos as at 1st October 1960." (Nigeria 1995 Vol. 1: §229, sub.4)

12. Some feared that, under a north-south rotation, minorities would have no chance of producing a president and, in the South, warfare would arise from the competition between the Igbo and the Yoruba (Akinola 1996: 14).

13. Recall that the Constitutional Drafting Committee (CDC) of 1975 rejected proposals by its Sub-Committee on the Executive and Legislature Committee for the rotation of the office of the president among four geographic zones. The Constitutional Conference of 1994 not only adopted what was rejected in 1975 but went on to borrow the South African system of power-sharing. Known to some as the "Slovo formula" (the brain child of Joe Slovo, the late leader of the South African Communist Party), the South African power-sharing agreement required proportional representation in both regional and central legislatures. It also entitled a party that held at least 5 percent of seats in the National Assembly to have cabinet portfolios in proportion to the number of seats it has in the assembly. Negotiated between 1991 and 1993, the formula enabled power-sharing between the African majority and the White minority, and, at another level, between the African National Congress and several other parties, both racial and nonracial. It is this formula that the Constitutional Conference copied and combined with rotational presidency (de Villiers 1994).

14. For an extended discussion of the face-off between Christians and Muslims during the 1997-98 Constituent Assembly meetings, see Laitin (1982: 411-30).

15. For an extended discussion of the adoption of the Shari'a by some states in the North, see Abdul Raufu Mustapha (2000: 41-47).

16. Other political entrepreneurs in the region have also sought to defend the adoption of sharia law by making arguments to justify it. For example, some argued that ethnic groups in the Niger Delta region and in the eastern and western parts of the country are fighting for ethnic republics and that sharia is our own response from the North. It was also argued that the political reforms of the elected president Olusegun Obasanjo, a devout Christian, had disproportionately affected the North and that the leader was gradually handing over government to the Christian Association of Nigeria.

17. In the 1960s and 1970s authoritarian African regimes developed an avoidance policy for dealing with ethnic claims. This avoidance policy entailed insulating the state from groups and, in most cases, this took the form of outright repression or the imposition of a one-party or no-party system as in Sudan, Chad, Ethiopia, Ghana, and Sierra Leone.

18. All except two of the nineteen states of the Second Republic were dependent on federal grants for their survival; these two were Kano and Lagos States.

19. For example, in Port Harcourt (Rivers State), people were in solidarity with the Ogoni activists during the early 1990s and, in fact, regarded military occupation of Ogoni land as an open declaration of war by the government. However, the demand for political autonomy was regarded as extremist and politically remote. The demand split the Ogoni ethnic group and helped to fuel the crisis that ended with the execution of Ken Saro Wiwa and seven others (*Newswatch* 1995: 14-16; *Tell* 1994: 10-17).

20. Dependence on the coastal seaports led to disputes over the status of Lagos during the preindependence period and inflamed northern threats to overrun the South if the seaports were closed.

21. In June 2000, participants in a colloquium to forge an alternative constitution for Nigeria rejected my expert advice for the rotation of the office of the president because, in their view, the conditions that generated the demand for it in the 1990s will not reoccur.

22. Local press reports in Nigeria during the months of January and February 1999 indicated that northern elites were united in the decision not to contest the office of the president, and attempts at flouting it were quickly condemned by the Turaki Committee, one of the fora in which they were organized.

23. This is partly because of the military command that went with military rule and partly because of the absolute dependence of the states on the center for oil revenue to be distributed equally among them. Even the 1999 Constitution has centralizing tendencies (Suberu and Diamond 2000: 13-14).

24. In a conference held in Wilberforce, Ohio, a participant noted that Ken Saro Wiwa's right to speak for the Ogoni was challenged because his village contained no oil well.

25. The excellent scientific foundation that Hobbes built in chapters 1-12 of *Leviathan* was undermined in chapters 17-30 in which he created an absolute ruler that constitutes an impediment to motion.

26. The local press reported that the eleven permanent secretaries who were retired were all from the North. Balarabe Musa, a one-time governor of Kaduna State in the North, notes that only five northerners are left out of the forty-five brigadier-generals in the army. Moreover, the anticorruption investigation has focused on the family of the late general Abacha, the former head of state, and on General Mohammadu Buhari, head of the Petroleum Trust Fund, who also briefly ruled in the early 1980s (Post Express 1999; *Sunday Guardian* 1999; *Today* 1999).

Chapter Seven

Group Recognition: Lessons from the Nigerian Experience

Analysis of the constitutional negotiations in Nigeria reveals that the country has adopted five institutional strategies for coping with ethnic difference and reducing conflict. The strategies discussed in the preceding chapters were: 1) a federal system where differences among the three major groups were given political expression while those between majority and minority groups were suppressed; 2) legislative districts whose boundaries closely followed group boundaries; 3) a federal system in which the subunits were restructured and an affirmative action program instituted to enable greater political expression of difference among both majority and minority groups; 4) more state status for groups within a federal system to ensure that central government offices and material resources were distributed evenly across the states and, in turn, state governments distributed offices and resources across groups within their jurisdictions; and, 5) more state status for more groups in a federal system where the central government affirmed the right to distribute resources evenly among the states but with some attention to source of derivation.

Some of these institutional strategies were morally defensible in the circumstances in which they were negotiated, but they either were not deep enough to make for adequate political inclusion or were not adequately combined with different counter-strategies to minimize problems of group proliferation and institutional instability. This is especially true of the last two strategies listed above. Other strategies were morally defensible even though they generated tension among groups or were driven by strategic considerations for power. This was the case with the second strategy listed above involving an affirmative action program and the political separation of minorities in the 1960s. Others may also have been pragmatic at the time they were negotiated and in the circumstances of the period, but they were ultimately not morally defensible. This is true of the first strategy negotiated in the 1950s.

Overall, the concrete case-by-case analysis of these strategies shows that constitutional recognition of groups in Nigeria has offered greater promise for stability than would otherwise have been the case if differences were suppressed or recognition was limited to only the three major ethnic groups. Indeed, it would not be an overstatement to say that the little unity that exists today is the result of the group expressive strategies adopted since the 1970s. However, my case-by-case analysis also shows that the institutional expression of difference has generated many difficulties, some of which were anticipated at the outset, but countermeasures were not taken to tackle them. The difficulties include institutional instability arising from group proliferation, ethnicity as the basis for citizenship rights, and conflict arising from the ownership of natural resources. In what follows, I use the difficulties that have arisen in Nigeria to evaluate some of the prescriptions of the philosophical and empirical thinkers examined in chapter 1.

A central theme in consociational arguments is that classic liberal democracy facilitates majoritarian rule that is dangerous in plural societies because it permanently denies minorities access to power and causes them to lose their allegiance to the state. What is required is a democracy that emphasizes group inclusion and consensus. With the philosophical arguments, the central theme is that in multicultural states, individuals stand as equals in the political public if institutions reflect their diverse cultures. This theme is argued in a variety of ways. For example, Charles Taylor argues that our identity is shaped by the recognition we receive from others, and that the demand for equal recognition requires a model of liberal society in which culturally diverse groups are treated as equal partners. For his part, Kymlicka argues that in liberal democracies, minority groups require special rights to enable their members to exercise the autonomy and freedom that is taken for granted by majority group members. In all of these arguments, the unit of analysis is the group, which ought to be recognized and considered a relevant moral unit in constitutional design.

However, the Nigerian experience shows that the design of political arrangements around groups triggers group proliferation rendering the arrangements unstable. This problem was recognized in 1958 when the Minorities Commission in Nigeria used this rationale to justify its refusal to meet demands by some minority groups for recognition in separate political units. But recognition had to be granted in the 1960s to avert imminent disintegration of the country. The 1967 redrawing of internal political boundaries provoked the emergence of new groups with new political demands. The design of a federal character strategy in the mid-1970s further stimulated the proliferation of groups with new demands. A slippery slope was inevitable because the use of the ethnic principle led to the duplication of state offices, created access to power and wealth for elites, and gave symbolic value to groups in need of esteem and honor. These results have since fueled endless demands for recognition, stimulated countless multiplication of units, and rendered national institutions unstable every time they are reproduced.

We have seen that the consociationalist Eric Nordlinger holds a low opinion of federalism precisely because of the problems it generates when its units are constructed around groups. He reasoned that the drawing of internal boundaries would create new minorities with ties to another group from which it has been separated. Worse still, federalism, with its grant of internal self-determination, might promote secession and civil wars (Nordlinger 1972: 31-32). For all of these reasons, he discounted federalism as a strategy for accommodating groups. But Kymlicka and Taylor have tried to provide ways of dealing with the problem. They have argued that constitutional recognition be given to groups that are tied to homelands. In the case of immigrant countries, this requirement limits recognition to nonimmigrant groups that are few in numbers. But Nigeria is not a country of immigration and in Nigeria minority groups are countless in number while majority groups are comprised of sub-groups, all of which make the normative theorists' arguments less useful to the country and less compelling theoretically. Thus, the solution is helpful if applied only to immigrant societies (including modern-day Britain), but not to those with different ethnic relations. What this means is that in most Western democracies there is a limited number of ethnic groups claiming territories who can be given official recognition. In this respect, the argument will encounter obstacles if applied to African countries.

This is not to suggest that the normative arguments are not relevant to Nigeria. The country's response to the problem of institutional instability indicates that arrangements in which groups have no recognition do not constitute better alternatives. Its strategies for coping with ethnic pluralism have been publicly debated and revised on a number of occasions and each time the key elements of federal character survived because this strategy was found to be the best way to ensure equity. The problem that continues to nag is how to end the proliferation of subunits.

A second issue the Nigerian case raises is the question of citizenship rights. One common thread that runs through the theoretical arguments is that a liberal commitment to political equality requires a constitutional order in which citizenship is differentiated. Iris Marion Young (1990: 104) and other democratic equality theorists argue that liberal universal rules are actually the rules of the strong who share a common way of life, not the weak who share different ways of life and cannot make their voices heard. As a remedy, she proposes "a democratic public" that provides "mechanisms for the effective representation and recognition of distinct voices" (1989: 261). Joseph Carens takes a similar position when he argues for a genuinely shared citizenship in Canada. According to Carens, the best way of achieving justice for Aboriginal peoples in Canada who do not have a sense of common political bond with non-Aboriginal Canadians is to "recognize the inevitable injustice of a deliberative process that effectively excludes or overrides Aboriginal cultural perspectives on what justice requires" (Carens 1996-97: 120). He proposes dialogue as a means of arriving at arrangements that combine mutual compromises and mutual understanding about justice. Also, Taylor argues for a model of liberal society in which the collective rights and goals of disadvantaged and threatened cultural communities are recognized.

Recognizing the interests of the weak in constitutional instruments and political processes was a major issue that defined Nigerian politics during the late 1950s and early 1960s. The bitter civil war that was fought over recognition in the late 1960s finally led to the statutory adoption of ethnicity as a principle for ensuring equitable access to power and resources. For three decades now, this principle has been used to create states, make cabinet appointments, constitute political parties, and make selections for the army, the universities, the civil service, and government parastatals. It has also been used as the basis for legislative representation during periods of civil rule, and it has been revised to ensure that the office of the president and governors are rotated among groups at the national and state levels, respectively. The latter mechanism, however, was abandoned even before it was put into effect.

The "boomerang effect" on citizenship rights has emerged clearly. Although citizenship is defined in legal terms, membership in the political subunits is defined by the constitution in terms of parental descent. This has led to sensitivity in the ethnic/state origin of people competing for political offices and of those appointed into or selected for national institutions. Ethnicity has become the basis for citizenship identification, as individuals relating to national institutions have to first submit letters of identification from the chairpersons of their local government areas attesting to their ethnic origin. Indeed, the government commission that was instituted in 1986 to revise the federal character strategy noted that the definition of membership of the subunits of the federation constituted an impediment to the development of Nigerian citizenship and encouraged attachments to "home communities" (Nigeria 1987: 197). But nothing has been done to redress this situation. In June 1999, the Lagos State House of Assembly gave expression to the problem during its inaugural session. Members brawled over the election of the Speaker whose origin was traced to a neighboring Yoruba state. Physical conflict was hastened by the realization that the democratically elected governor also belonged through parental descent to a neighboring Yoruba state.

The problem shows that arguments for the recognition of difference in constitutional and political processes run the risk of elevating ascriptive group membership to be the major determinant of citizenship. Ronald Beiner (1995: 6) has referred to this effect as the "ghettoization of citizenship," meaning that each group in a state will withdraw behind the boundary of its identity. Critics like Alvin Schmidt and Arthur Schlesinger Jr. regard ascription as portending danger for stability. They emphasize what Steven Rockefeller has referred to as the danger of elevating ethnic identity over universal human potential (Taylor 1994: 89).

In fairness, theorists like Kymlicka and Taylor are particularly interested in opening up a space in liberalism for minority group rights. They each argue that departures from liberal individualist rights are justified only to the extent that they are needed to rectify inequality. In a chapter on apartheid Kymlicka (1989: 249) shows that "the notion of cultural membership and the principle of equalizing cultural circumstances" would not justify "petty apartheid."

But, as the Nigerian experience shows, and as the country's Political Bureau of 1986 reported, a deep sense of ascriptive inclusion and exclusion are possible outcomes of the principle of equalizing cultures. These are the very fears that the critics of multiculturalism in North America harbor. Yet the Nigerian experience, especially the fears held by successive governments and their reluctance to abandon the use of indigeneity in the definition of membership for political subunits, would also suggest that no better alternative to the ethnic principle currently exists.

A third issue the Nigerian case raises is the tension around and confusion associated with groups' control of resources within their domain. Lijphart and Nordlinger have argued for the proportional distribution of resources among groups in accordance with their numerical size. Kymlicka, on the other hand, argues that national minorities who are vulnerable to political decisions made by the majority should be granted rights to internal self-government. In addition, they should have substantial control over the use of resources on or in their land (Kymlicka 1996: 44-49). In this case, government is expected to be coextensive with ethnic groups so that their unit government can control resources. In the Nigerian case, where internal boundaries have been redrawn numerous times to take into account ethnic difference, rights to natural resources have been vested in the sovereign body with the central government acting as its agent. The vesting has to do with the disastrous outcome of the winner-take-all politics that was practiced in the pre-civil war years. The system produced political domination by a few ethnic groups' elites and ensured the unequal distribution of public goods. It was the determination to do away with this inequity that prompted the federal government to declare state ownership of the petroleum industry and share its revenue equally among the various ethnic sections in the country. The civil war taught Nigerian constitutional engineers that the vesting of resource rights to ethnic units generates grievances among other ethno-regional groups that would consider them to be either excessive privileges or state partiality. It seems, then, that the arguments of Lijphart and Nordlinger for the distribution of resources among groups according to their numerical size might appear to be justified in the Nigerian case.

On the other hand, the violent uprising by communities spread across the Niger Delta over the federal government's absolute claim to oil wealth shows that the arguments of Lijphart, Nordlinger, and Rothchild for proportional sharing of resources do not provide the sure route to a stable normative order. The uprising which, at its early stages, resulted in the state execution of eight minority rights activists, including Ken Saro Wiwa and is presently threatening the stability of Nigeria's Fourth Republic invites the need to examine minority claims to share in the resources in their areas. Perhaps Kymlicka's argument that oppressed minorities should have substantial control is the equitable way to go. The difficulty is that it could set a dangerous precedent for every other national group in the country who would take this cue by attempting to exercise similar rights to important resources in their territories. This would, of course, encroach on and severely constrain the jurisdictional right of the sovereign state to its national territory. However, in a federal system where jurisdictional rights are shared between levels of government, profitable resources ought to be shared between the center and the states in which they are located. Justice requires that minority states have some sort of entitlement to the natural resources located in their areas, regardless of the effects that the granting of such a right will have on national cohesion. Arthur Lewis recognized this when he argued that, in a deeply divided country, the transfer of wealth from richly endowed regions to poorer ones inflames the passions that flare into rebellion and secession. It was for this reason that Lewis advised West African states to adopt a federal system that would enable each regional group to obtain control in the development and use of the resources found in its area. All of this suggests that Kymlicka's arguments for the right of oppressed minorities to share in the control of resources located in their land is in order, even if such a right would trigger similar claims by nonthreatened groups in other parts of the country.

In sum, the Nigerian experience of the invention of constitutional structures to accommodate multiethnic groups and the determination to revise and improve on these structures would validate the main theme of both the philosophical and empirical theorists. The theme is that a commitment to liberal equality (democratic equality, in the case of the empirical thinkers) requires principles that treat groups as equal political partners and, as a consequence, institutional arrangements recognizing difference. However the Nigerian case also demonstrates that political projects of this sort have their own particular problems and, thus, the theoretical arguments should not be seen as providing magical political solutions to the problems endemic to Africa's multiethnic states. Indeed, the problems generated by Nigeria' constitutional arrangements serve to highlight the main weaknesses of these theories. Despite this, the appropriate normative route, as the country's history has shown, is not the abandonment of group expressive strategies by those that deny recognition, for this promises more intense conflict and instability than recognition does. What is required is the retuning of the underlying theoretical arguments to address their shortcomings in light of the Nigerian experience.

Bibliography

Abdullahi, Ango. "Agriculture and Nigeria's Political Crisis." In *Nigeria: The State of the Nation and the Way Forward*, edited by Abdullahi Mahadi, George Kwanashie, and Mahmood Yakubu. Kaduna, Nigeria: Arewa House, 1994.

Ackerman, Bruce. *Social Justice in the Liberal State*. New Haven, Conn.: Yale University Press, 1980.

Ademoyega, Adewale. *Why We Struck*. Ibadan, Nigeria: Evans Brothers, 1981.

Agbaje, Adigun. "Travails of the Secular State: Religion, Politics, and the Outlook on Nigeria's Third Republic." *Journal of Commonwealth and Comparative Politics* 28, no. 3 (1990): 288-306.

Ake, Claude, ed. *Political Economy of Nigeria*. London: Longman, 1985.

————. "Theoretical Notes on the National Question in Nigeria." Port Harcourt, Nigeria: University of Port Harcourt, 1987. Mimeographed.

————. "The State As a Capitalist Phenomenon." Unpublished Manuscript. Port Harcourt, Nigeria: University of Port Harcourt, 1988.

————. "The Feasibility of Democracy." Unpublished Manuscript. Port Harcourt, Nigeria: Centre for Advanced Social Science, 1994.

————. *Democracy and Development in Africa*. Washington, D.C.: Brookings Institution, 1996.

Akinola, Anthony. *Rotational Presidency*. Ibadan, Nigeria: Spectrum Books, 1996.

Akinterinwa, Bola. "The 1993 Presidential Election Imbroglio." In *Transition without End: Nigerian Politics and Civil Society under Babangida*, edited by Larry Diamond, Anthony Kirk-Greene, and Oyeleye Oyediran. London: Lynne Rienner, 1997.

Akinyemi, Bolaji, et al., eds. *Readings on Federalism*. Lagos: Nigerian Institute of International Affairs, 1979.

Alagoa, E. J. *A History of the Niger Delta*. Ibadan, Nigeria: Ibadan University Press, 1972.

Aminu, Jibril. "Oil and the National Debate." In *Nigeria: The State of the Nation and the Way Forward*, edited by Abdullahi Mahadi, George

Kwanashie, and Mahmood Yakubu. Kaduna, Nigeria: Arewa House, 1994.

Anderson, Benedict. *Imagined Communities: Reflections on the Origins and Spread of Nationalism*. London: Verso, 1990.

An-Na'im, Abdullahi Ahmed. "A Modern Approach to Human Rights in Islam: Foundations and Implications for Africa." In *Human Rights in Africa*, edited by Abdullahi Ahmed An-Na'im and Francis M. Deng. Washington, D.C.: Brookings Institution, 1990.

Aquinas, Saint Thomas. *Treatise on Law*. With an Introduction by Stanley Parry. Washington, D.C.: Gateway Editions, 1992.

Aristotle. *The Politics of Aristotle*. Translated with an Introduction by Ernest Barker. Oxford: Clarendon Press, 1964.

Armouto, Mazen, ed. *The Encounter: Islam, The West and Human Rights*. Amman, Jordan: Institute of Diplomacy, 1996.

Awolowo, Obafemi. *Path to Nigerian Freedom*. London: Faber and Faber, 1947.

———. *Awo: The Autobiography of Chief Obafemi Awolowo*. Cambridge, U.K.: The University Press, 1960.

Ayandele, Emmanuel. *Nigerian Historical Studies*. London: Frank Cass, 1979.

Bach, Daniel. "Indigeneity, Ethnicity and Federalism." In *Transition without End: Nigerian Politics and Civil Society under Babangida*, edited by Larry Diamond, Anthony Kirk-Greene, and Oyeleye Oyediran. London: Lynne Rienner, 1997.

Bächler, Günther, ed. *Federalism against Ethnicity*. Zurich: Verlag, 1997.

Bayart, Jean-François Rüegger. *The State in Africa: The Politics of the Belly*. London: Longman, 1993.

Beiner, Ronald. "Introduction." In *Theorizing Citizenship*, edited by Ronald Beiner. Albany: State University of New York Press, 1995.

Bello, Ahmadu. *My Life*. Cambridge, U.K.: Cambridge University Press, 1962.

Berman, Bruce. "Ethnicity, Patronage and the African State: The Politics of Uncivil Nationalism." *African Affairs* 7, no. 388 (1998): 305-41.

Birch, Anthony. *Nationalism and National Integration*. London: Unwin Hyman, 1989.

Calhoun, John. *A Disquisition on Government*. New York: Liberal Arts Press, 1953.

Cameron, Donald. "Memorandum: The Principles of Native Administration and Their Application." In *The Principles of Native Administra-*

tion in Nigeria: Selected Documents, edited by Anthony Kirk-Greene. London: Oxford University Press, 1965.

Carens, Joseph. "Democracy and Respect for Difference: The Case of Fiji." *University of Michigan Journal of Law Reform* 25, nos. 3 and 4 (1992): 547-631.

————, ed. *Is Quebec Nationalism Just? Perspectives from Anglophone Canada.* Montreal and Kingston: McGill-Queens University Press, 1995.

————. "Dimensions of Citizenship and National Identity." In *Philosophical Forum* 28, nos. 1-2 (1996-97): 111-24.

Chabal, Patrick. *Power in Africa. An Essay in Political Interpretation.* New York: St. Martin's Press, 1994.

Chandos, Oliver Lyttelton [Viscount Chandos]. *Memoirs.* London: Bodley Head, 1962.

Charnock, Martin. *Law, Custom and Social Order: The Colonial Experience in Malawi and Zambia.* Cambridge, U.K.: Cambridge University Press. 1985.

Chazan, Naomi, et al. *Politics in Contemporary Africa.* Boulder, Colo.: Lynne Rienner, 1988.

Cicero, Marcus Tullius. *On the Commonwealth.* Translated with an Introduction by George Sabine and Stanley Smith. New York: Bobbs Merrill, 1929.

Coalition for Peace. "The Position of the Coalition for Peace on the Sharia Legal System." In *Equal Justice,* a quarterly publication of Human Rights Monitor (April 2000): 25-31.

Coleman, James. *Nigeria: Background to Nationalism.* Berkeley: University of California Press, 1958.

Committee of Afenifere. "The Position of the Yoruba People." 1994, Nigeria.

Council of the Obas of Lagos, Ogun, Oyo, Osun, and Ondo State. "Memorandum Submitted to the National Constitutional Conference," 7 February 1994, Nigeria.

de Villiers, Brutus, ed. *Birth of a New Constitution.* Kenwyn, South Africa: Juta, 1994.

Diamond, Larry. "Cleavage, Conflict, and Anxiety in the Second Nigerian Republic." *Journal of Modern African Studies* 20, no. 4 (1982): 629-68.

Diamond, Larry, Anthony Kirk-Greene, and Oyeleye Oyediran, eds. *Transition without End: Nigerian Politics and Civil Society under Babangida.* London: Lynne Rienner, 1997.

Duchacek, Ivo D. *Comparative Federalism: The Territorial Dimension of Politics*. New York: Holt, Rinehart and Winston, 1970.

———. "Comparative Federalism: An Agenda for Additional Research." In *Constitutional Design and Power-Sharing in the Postmodern Epoch*, edited by Daniel J. Elazar. Lanham, Md.: University Press of America, 1991.

Dudley, Billy. *Instability and Political Order: Politics and Crisis in Nigeria*. Ibadan, Nigeria: Ibadan University Press, 1973.

Dumont, Louis. "A Modified View of Our Origins: The Christian Beginnings of Modern Individualism." *Religion* 12 (1982): 1-27.

Dworkin, Ronald. "Liberalism." In *Public and Private Morality*, edited by Stuart Hampshire. Cambridge, Mass.: Cambridge University Press, 1978.

———. "What Is Equality? Part II: Equality of Resources." *Philosophy and Public Affairs* 10, no. 4 (1981): 283-345.

———. "In Defense of Equality." *Social Philosophy and Policy* 1, no. 1 (1983): 24-40.

Ekeh, Peter. "Citizenship and Political Conflict: A Sociological Interpretation of the Nigerian Crisis." In *Nigeria: Dilemma of Nationhood: An African Analysis of the Biafran Conflict*, edited by Joseph Okpaku. New York: Third Press, 1972.

———. "Colonialism and the Two Publics in Africa: A Theoretical Statement." *Comparative Studies in Society and History* 17, no. 1 (1975): 91-112.

———. "Social Anthropology and Two Contrasting Uses of Tribalism in Africa." *Comparative Studies in Society and History* 32, no. 4 (1990): 660-700.

Ekeh, Peter, and Eghosa Osaghae, eds. *Federal Character and Federalism in Nigeria*, Ibadan, Nigeria: Heinemann, 1989.

Ekekwe, Eme. *Class and State in Nigeria*. London: Longman, 1986.

Emirs and Chiefs of the Northern States of Nigeria. "A Memorandum to the National Constitutional Commission." 5 March 1994.

Ezera, Kalu. *Constitutional Developments in Nigeria*. Cambridge, U.K.: University Press, 1964.

Fenno, Richard F. *The President's Cabinet: An Analysis in the Period from Wilson to Eisenhower*. Cambridge, Mass.: Harvard University Press, 1959.

Galanter, Marc. *Competing Equalities*. New Delhi: Oxford University Press, 1984.

Geertz, Clifford, ed. *Old Societies and New States*. New York: Free Press, 1963.

Gittleman, Richard. "The Banjul Charter on Human and Peoples' Rights: Legal Analysis." In *Human Rights and Development in Africa*, edited by Claude E. Welch Jr. and Robert I. Meltzer. Albany: State University of New York Press, 1984.

Glazer, Nathan. *Ethnic Dilemmas, 1964-1982*. Cambridge, Mass.: Harvard University Press, 1983.

————. *We Are All Multiculturalists Now*. Cambridge, Mass.: Harvard University Press, 1997.

Glickman, Harvey, ed. *Ethnic Conflict and Democratization in Africa*. Atlanta, Ga.: African Studies Association, 1995.

Graf, William. *The Nigerian State: Political Economy, State, Class and Political System in the Post Colonial Era*. London: James Currey, 1988.

Green, M. M. *Ibo Village Affairs*. London: Sidgwick and Jackson, 1947.

Guardian (Lagos). 29 September 2000.

————. 16 October 2000.

Gurr, Ted Robert. *Minorities at Risk: A Global View of Ethnopolitical Conflicts*. Washington, D.C.: United States Institute of Peace Press, 1993.

————, with Barbara Harff. *Ethnic Conflict in World Politics*. Boulder, Colo.: Westview Press, 1994.

Gutman, Amy, and Dennis Thompson. *Democracy and Disagreement*. Cambridge, Mass.: Belknap Press, 1996.

Heater, Derek. *Citizenship: The Civic Ideal in World History, Politics and Education*. London: Longman, 1990.

Hegel, George Wilhelm Friedrich. *Philosophy of Right*. Translated with notes by T. M. Knox. Oxford: Oxford University Press, 1952.

————. *Reason in History*. Translated with an Introduction by Robert S. Hartman. Indianapolis, Ind.: Bobbs Merrill, 1953.

Hobbes, Thomas. *Leviathan*. Edited by C. B. Macpherson. Harmondsworth, U. K.: Penguin Books, 1968.

Hobsbawn, Eric, and T. Ranger, eds. *The Invention of Tradition*. Cambridge, U.K.: Cambridge University Press, 1983.

Horowitz, Donald. *Ethnic Groups in Conflict*. Berkeley: University of California Press, 1985.

————. *A Democratic South Africa?* Berkeley: University of California Press, 1991.

————. "Constitutional Design: An Oxymoron?" Corrected version of a paper presented at the annual meeting of the American Society for Political and Legal Philosophy, San Francisco, 5-6 January 1998.

Hume, David. "Treatise of Human Nature" and "Enquiry Concerning Principles of Morality." In *Moral and Political Philosophy*, edited with an Introduction by Henry D. Aiken. New York: Hafner Press, 1948.

Hutchful, Eboe. "Texaco Funiwa-5 Oil Well Blow-out, Rivers State, Nigeria." *Journal of African Marxists* 7 (1984): 51-62.

Ibrahim, Jibrin. "Religion and Political Turbulence in Nigeria." *Journal of Modern African Studies* 29, no. 1 (1991): 115-36.

Igbo Speaking Peoples of Nigeria. "Memorandum on Behalf of the Igbo Speaking Peoples of Nigeria." 8 February 1994.

Ige, Bola. *People, Politics and Politicians of Nigeria (1940-1979)*. Ibadan, Nigeria: Heinemann, 1995.

Ilesanmi, Simeon O. *Religious Pluralism and the Nigerian State*. Athens: Ohio University Center for International Studies, 1997.

Janoski, Thomas. *Citizenship and Civil Society*. Cambridge, U.K.: Cambridge University Press, 1998.

Jennings, Ivor. *Cabinet Government*. Cambridge, U.K.: Cambridge University Press, 1959.

Jones-Quartey, K. A. B. *A Life of Azikiwe*. Baltimore, Md.: Penguin Books, 1965.

Joseph, Richard. *Democracy and Prebendal Politics in Nigeria*. Cambridge, U.K.: Cambridge University Press, 1987.

Kaltefleiter, W., and U. Schumacher. "Constitutional Engineering As an Instrument for Conflict Management in Societies with Changing Cultures." In *Multicultural Conflict Management in Changing Societies*, edited by Louise Nieumeijer and Renée du Toit. Pretoria: HSRC, 1994.

Kearney, Robert. *Communalism and Language in the Politics of Ceylon*. Durham, N.C.: Duke University Press, 1967.

Keyes, Charles F. *Ethnic Change*. Seattle and London: University of Washington Press, 1981.

Kirk-Greene, Anthony, ed. *The Principles of Native Administration in Nigeria: Selected Documents*. London: Oxford University Press, 1965.

Kirk-Greene, Anthony, and Douglas Rimmer. *Nigeria since 1970: A Political and Economic Outline*. London: Hodder and Stoughton, 1981.

Kukathas, Chandran. "Are There Any Cultural Rights?" *Political Theory* 20, no. 1 (1992): 105-39.

————, ed. *Multicultural Citizens: The Philosophy and Politics of Identity.* St. Leonards, Australia: Center for Independent Studies, 1993.

Kymlicka, Will. *Liberalism, Community and Culture.* Oxford: Clarendon Press, 1989.

————. *Multicultural Citizenship: A Liberal Theory of Minority Rights.* Oxford: Clarendon Press, 1995.

————. "Concepts of Community and Social Justice." In *Earthly Goods: Environmental Change and Social Justice,* edited by Fen Olser Hampson and Juddy Reppy. Ithaca, N.Y.: Cornell University Press, 1996.

Laitin, David. "The Sharia Debate and the Origins of Nigeria's Second Republic." *The Journal of Modern African Studies* 20, no. 3 (1982): 412-30.

Leary, Virginia. "The Effect of Western Perspectives on International Human Rights." In *Human Rights in Africa,* edited by Abdullahi Ahmed An-Na'im and Francis M. Deng. Washington, D.C.: Brookings Institution, 1990.

Lewis, Arthur. *Politics in West Africa.* London: Oxford University Press, 1965.

Lijphart, Arend. *Democracy in Plural Societies: A Comparative Explanation.* New Haven, Conn.: Yale University Press, 1977.

————. *Democracies: Patterns of Majoritarian and Consensus Government in Twenty-One Countries.* New Haven, Conn.: Yale University Press, 1984.

————. *Power-Sharing in South Africa.* Berkeley: University of California Institute of International Studies, 1985.

————. "The Alternative Vote: A Realistic Alternative for South Africa." *Politikon* 18, no. 2 (1991): 91-101.

————. "Prospects for Power-Sharing in the New South Africa." In *Elections '94 South Africa,* edited by Andrew Reynolds. New York: St. Martin's Press, 1994.

————. "Consensus and Consensus Democracy: Cultural, Structural, Functional, and Rational-Choice Explanations." *Scandinavian Political Studies* 21, no. 2 (1998): 99-108.

————. "Power-Sharing and Group Autonomy in the 1990s and the 21st Century." Paper read at the conference on Constitutional Design 2000, University of Notre Dame, South Bend, Ind., 9-11 December 1999.

Linz, Juan. "Crisis, Breakdown, and Re-equilibration." In *The Breakdown of Authoritarian Regimes,* edited by Juan Linz and Alfred Stepan. Baltimore: Johns Hopkins University Press, 1976.

Lloyd, Peter Cutt. *Classes, Crisis and Coups.* London: MacGibbon and Kee, 1971.

Locke, John. *Second Treatise of Government.* Edited by C. B. Macpherson. Indianapolis: Hackett Publishing Company, 1980.

Lugard, Frederick. *Lugard and the Amalgamation of Nigeria: A Documentary Record.* Compiled with an Introduction by A. H. M. Kirk-Greene. London: Frank Cass, 1968.

———. *Political Memoranda.* London: Frank Cass, 1969.

Luther, Martin. "Preface to Romans" and "Freedom of a Christian." In *Selections from His Writings,* edited with an Introduction by John Dillenberger. New York: Anchor Books, 1961.

Machiavelli, Niccolò. "The Discourses." In *The Prince and the Discourses.* New York: Modern Library, 1950.

Mackintosh John P. *Nigerian Government and Politics.* London: George Allen and Unwin, 1966.

Madan, T. N. "Whither Indian Secularism?" *Modern Asian Studies* 27, no. 3 (1993): 671-93.

Madugba, Agaju. "The Nigerian Constitution and Sharia Law." In *Equal Justice*, a quarterly publication of Human Rights Monitor. Kaduna, Nigeria: April 2000, 25-31

Mamdani, Mahmood. *Citizen and Subject: Contemporary Africa and the Legacy of Late Colonialism.* Princeton, N.J.: Princeton University Press, 1996.

Marshall, T. H. *Citizenship and Social Class and Other Essays.* Cambridge, U.K.: Cambridge University Press, 1950.

Mayer, Ann Elizabeth. "Islamic Law and Human Rights: Conundrums and Equivocation." In *Religion and Human Rights: Competing Claims?* edited by Carrie Gustafson and Peter Juviler. Armonk, N.Y.: M. E. Sharpe, Columbia University Seminar Series, 1999.

Meek, Charles. *Tribal Studies in Northern Nigeria.* Vol. 2. London: Paul Kegan, Trench, Truber and Co., 1931.

———. *Law and Authority in a Nigerian Tribe.* London: Oxford University Press, 1937.

Melson, Robert, and Howard Wolpe, eds. *Nigeria: Modernization and the Politics of Communalism.* Ann Arbor: Michigan State University Press, 1971.

Middle Belt Council. "The Middle Belt Position for the Proposed National Constitutional Conference." Final Communique. 3 March 1994.

Mill, J. S. *Utilitarianism, On Liberty, Considerations on Representative Government,* edited by H. B. Acton. London: Everyman's Library, 1972.

Miller, David, and Michael Walzer, eds. *Pluralism, Justice and Equality.* Oxford: Oxford University Press, 1995.

Movement for the Survival of the Ijaw Ethnic Nationality. "A Memorandum." 4 February 1994.

Movement for the Survival of the Ogoni People. *Ogoni Bill of Rights.* Port Harcourt, Nigeria: Saros International, 1992.

———. "A Memorandum to the National Constitutional Conference." 30 January 1994.

Mustapha, Abdul Raufu. "Ethnicity and the Politics of Democratization in Nigeria: Structures, Transformations and Processes." Paper presented at the Workshop on Ethnicity and Democracy in Africa, Queens University, Kingston, Ont., Canada, March 2000.

Ndegwa, Stephen. "Citizenship and Ethnicity: An Examination of Two Transition Moments in Kenya." Paper read at the annual meeting of the American Political Science Association, San Francisco. Revised version. 1996.

Newswatch (Lagos). 28 February 1994.

———. 13 November 1995.

Nieumeijer, Louise, and Renée du Toit, eds. *Multicultural Conflict Management in Changing Societies.* Pretoria: HSRC, 1994.

Nigeria. *Proceedings of the General Conference on Review of the Constitution.* Lagos: Government Printer, 1950.

———. "Commentary on Sir Louis Chick's Report on Financial Effects of Proposed New Constitutional Arrangements." In *Record of the Proceedings of the Resumed Conference on the Nigeria Constitution.* Lagos, 1954.

———. Her Majesty's Stationery Office. Commission Appointed to Inquire into the Fears of Minorities and the Means of Allaying Them. *Report.* 1958.

———. Federal Ministry of Information. *Federal Military Government Views on the Report of the Panel on Creation of States.* Lagos: Government Printer, 1976a.

———. Federal Ministry of Information. *Report of the Constitution Drafting Committee Containing the Draft Constitution*. Vols. 1 and 2. Lagos: Government Printer, 1976b.

———. Federal Ministry of Information. *Constituent Assembly Report.* Vol. 2. Lagos: Government Printer, 1978.

———. Federal Ministry of Information. *Nigeria: 1978-1979 Official Handbook*. Lagos: Government Printer, 1979.

———. Federal Ministry of Information. *Constitution of the Federal Republic of Nigeria 1979*. Lagos: Government Printer, 1980.

———. Federal Ministry of Information. *Report of the Political Bureau*. Lagos: Government Printer, 1987.

———. National Assembly. *Report of the Constitutional Conference Containing the Draft Constitution*. Vols. 1 and 2. Abuja: Government Printer, 1995.

———. National Assembly. *Constitution of the Federal Republic of Nigeria 1999*. Lagos: Government Printer, 1999.

Nordlinger, Eric. *Conflict Regulation in Divided Societies*. Occasional Paper. Cambridge, Mass.: Center for International Affairs, Harvard University, 1972.

Norrie, Kenneth, Richard Simeon, and Mark Krasnick. *Federalism and Economic Union in Canada*. Toronto: University of Toronto Press, 1986.

Northern Nigeria. "A Review of the Constitution." NC/B2A. 1949.

Nwabueze, Ben O. *Federalism in Nigeria under the Presidential Constitution*. London: Sweet and Maxwell, 1983.

Oates, Whitney Jennings. *The Stoic and Epicurean Philosophers: The Complete Extant Writings of Epicurus, Epictetus, Lucretius [and] Marcus Aurelius*. New York: Modern Library, 1940.

Okin, Susan Moller. *Justice, Gender and the Family*. New York: Basic Books, 1989.

Okpu, Ugbana. *Ethnic Minority Problems in Nigerian Politics, 1960-1965*. Uppsala, Sweden: Almqvist and Wiksell, 1977.

Olaloku, F. Akin. "Nigerian Federal Finances: Issues and Choices." In *Readings on Federalism*, edited by A. B. Akinyemi, P. C. Cole, and Walter Ofonagoro. Lagos: Nigerian Institute of International Affairs, 1979.

Onoh, Christian. "Igbos Are Not Prepared for Another War." *Sunday Guardian* (Lagos), 6 August 2000.

Orr, Charles. *The Making of Northern Nigeria*. London: Frank Cass, 1969.

Ottaway, Marina. "Ethnic Politics in Africa: Change and Continuity." In *State, Conflict and Democracy in Africa*, edited by Richard Joseph. Boulder, Colo.: Lynne Rienner, 1999.

Otubanjo, Femi. "The Citizen and the State: The Balance of Obligation." *African Philosophical Inquiry* 2, nos. 1 and 2 (1988): 83-95.

Paden, John N. *Ahmadu Bello, Sardauna of Sokoto: Values and Leadership in Nigeria*. London: Hodder and Stoughton, 1986.

Panter-Brick, Keith, ed. *Soldiers and Oil*. London: Frank Cass, 1978.

Parekh, Bhiku. "British Citizenship and Cultural Difference." In *Citizenship*, edited by Geoff Andrews. London: Lawrence and Wishart, 1991.

Perham, Margery. *Native Administration in Nigeria*. London: Oxford University Press, 1962.

Porter, John. *The Measure of Canadian Society: Education, Equality, and Opportunity*. Toronto: Gage Publishing Limited, 1979.

Post Express (Lagos). 13 October 1999.

Pye, Lucian. *Aspects of Political Development*. Boston and Toronto: Little, Brown and Company, 1966.

Rabushka, Alvin, and Kenneth Shepsle. *Politics in Plural Societies: A Theory of Democratic Instability*. Columbus, Ohio: Charles E. Merrill, 1972.

Ranger, Terence. "The Invention of Tradition in Colonial Africa." In *The Invention of Tradition*, edited by Eric Hobsbawn and Terence Ranger. Cambridge, U.K.: Cambridge University Press, 1983.

———. "The Invention of Tradition Revisited: The Case of Africa." In *Legitimacy and the State in Twentieth Century Africa*, edited by Terence Ranger and Olufemi Vaughan. London: McMillan Press, 1993.

Rawls, John. *A Theory of Justice*. Cambridge, Mass.: Harvard University Press, 1971.

———. "Kantian Constructivism in Moral Theory." *Journal of Philosophy* 77, no. 9 (1980): 515-72.

———. "Justice As Fairness: Political Not Metaphysical." *Philosophy and Public Affairs* 14, no. 3 (1985): 223-51.

———. *Political Liberalism*. New York: Columbia University Press, 1993.

Raz, Joseph. *The Morality of Freedom*. Oxford: Clarendon Press, 1986.

Robertson, James. *Transition in Africa from Indirect Rule to Independence: A Memoir*. London: C. Hurst and Company, 1974.

Rothchild, Donald. *Safeguarding Nigeria's Minorities*. Pittsburgh, Pa.: Duquesne University Press, 1964.

————. *Managing Ethnic Conflict in Africa*. Washington, D.C.: Brookings Institution, 1997.

————, ed. With Victor Olorunsola. *State versus Ethnic Claims: African Policy Dilemmas*. Boulder, Colo.: Westview Press, 1993.

Rousseau, Jean-Jacques. "The Social Contract." In *The Social Contract and Discourses*. Translated by G. D. H. Cole. London: Everyman's Library, 1968.

Sartori, Giovanni. "Political Development and Political Engineering." *Public Policy* 27 (1968): 261-98.

————. *Parties and Party Systems*. Cambridge, U.K.: Cambridge University Press, 1976.

Sawer, Geoffrey. *Modern Federalism*. London: The New Thinkers Library, 1969.

Schlesinger Jr., Arthur. *The Disuniting of America: Reflections on a Multicultural Society*. New York: W. W. Norton, 1998.

Schmidt, Alvin. *The Menace of Multiculturalism: Trojan Horse in America*. Westport, Conn.: Praeger, 1997.

Shapiro, Ian. *Democracy's Place*. Ithaca, N.Y.: Cornell University Press, 1996.

Shklar, Judith. *American Citizenship*. Cambridge, Mass.: Harvard University Press, 1991.

Simeon, Richard, and Ian Robinson. *State, Society, and the Development of Canadian Federalism*. Toronto: University of Toronto Press, 1990.

Sklar, Richard. "Contradictions in the Nigerian Political System." *Journal of Modern African Studies* 3, no. 2 (1965): 201-13.

————. "Nigerian Government in Perspective." In *Nigeria: Modernization and the Politics of Communalism*, edited by Robert Melson and Howard Wolpe. Ann Arbor: Michigan State University Press, 1971.

————. "Foundations of Federal Government in Nigeria." Paper read at the 42nd annual meeting of the African Studies Association, Philadelphia, 11-14 November 1999.

Soyinka, Wole. *The Open Sore of a Continent*. Oxford: Oxford University Press, 1996.

Stremlau, John. *People in Peril: A Report to the Carnegie Commission on Preventing Deadly Conflict*. New York: Carnegie Corporation, May 1998.

Suberu, Rotimi T. "The Travails of Federalism in Nigeria." In *Nationalism, Ethnic Conflict, and Democracy*, edited by Larry Diamond and Marc F. Plattner. Baltimore, Md.: Johns Hopkins University Press, 1994.

Suberu, Rotimi, and Larry Diamond. "Institutional Design, Ethnic Conflict Management and Democracy in Nigeria." Paper presented at the international conference on Constitution Design 2000, the Kellogg Institute Conference, University of Notre Dame, Ind., 9-11 December, 1999.

Sunday Guardian (Lagos). 27 June 1999.

————. 6 August 2000.

Szeftel, M. "Ethnicity and Democratization in South Africa." *Review of African Political Economy* 60 (1994): 185-99.

Taylor, Charles. "Shared and Divergent Values." In *Options for a New Canada,* edited by Ronald L. Watts and Douglas M. Brown. Toronto: University of Toronto Press, 1991.

————. *Multiculturalism: Examining the Politics of Recognition.* Edited by Amy Gutmann. Princeton, N.J.: Princeton University Press, 1994.

————. "The Dynamics of Democratic Exclusion," *Journal of Democracy* 9, no. 4 (October 1998): 143-56.

Tell (Lagos). 10 January 1994.

————. 29 July 1996.

————. 10 August 1998.

Today (Lagos). 25-31 July 1999.

Udogu, Emmanuel. "National Integration Attempts in Nigerian Politics 1979-1984." *Canadian Review of Studies in Nationalism* 27, nos. 1-2 (1990): 157-71.

Udoma, Udo. *History and the Law of the Constitution of Nigeria.* Lagos, Nigeria: Malthouse Press, 1994.

Urhobo Oil Mineral Communities. "The Nigerian Petroleum Industry and Urhobo Oil Mineral Communities." Paper presented on the occasion of the Ministerial Committee Visit, The Petroleum Training Institute, Warri, Nigeria, 1994.

van Gelder, Willem, and Jos Moerkamp. "The Niger Delta: A Disrupted Ecology. The Role of Shell and Other Oil Companies." A Discussion Paper by Greenpeace. Amsterdam, Netherlands, October 1996.

Vanguard (Lagos). 13 April 1999a.

————. 20 April 1999b.

Walzer, M. *Spheres of Justice: A Defense of Pluralism and Equality.* Oxford: Martin Robertson, 1983.

————. *Interpretation and Social Criticism.* Cambridge, Mass.: Harvard University Press, 1987.

————. "The New Tribalism." *Dissent* (spring 1992): 164-71.

————. *Thick and Thin.* Notre Dame, Ind.: University of Notre Dame Press, 1994.

Welsh, David. "The Provincial Boundary Demarcation Process." In *Birth of a New Constitution,* edited by Bertus de Villiers. Kenwyn, South Africa: Juta, 1994.

Wente-Lukas, Renate. *Handbook of Ethnic Units in Nigeria.* Stuttgart, Germany: Franz Steiner, 1985.

West, Tam David. "Yakassai's Blackmail." *Tell,* 31 January 1994.

Wheare, K. C. *Legislatures.* London: Oxford University Press, 1963.

Williams, Melissa. "Group Inequality and the Public Culture of Justice." In *Group Rights,* edited by Judith Baker. Toronto: University of Toronto Press, 1994.

————. "Justice towards Groups: Political Not Juridical." *Political Theory* 23, no. 1 (1995): 67-91.

Wiwa, Ken Saro. "1989 Constitution Is against Minority Rights." *Constitutional Rights Journal* (October-November 1993): 5-7.

Young, Crawford. *The Politics of Cultural Pluralism.* Madison: University of Wisconsin Press, 1976.

————. "The National and Colonial Question and Marxism: A View from the South." In *Thinking Theoretically about Soviet Nationalities: History and Comparison in the Study of the USSR,* edited by A. L. Motyl. New York: Columbia University Press, 1992.

————. "The Dialectics of Cultural Pluralism: Concept and Reality." In *The Rising Tide of Cultural Pluralism.* Madison: University of Wisconsin Press, 1993.

————. "Evolving Modes of Consciousness and Ideology: Nationalism and Ethnicity." In *Political Development and the New Realism in Sub-Saharan Africa,* edited by David Apter and Carl Rosberg. Charlottesville: University of Virginia Press, 1994.

————. *The African Colonial State in Comparative Perspective.* New Haven, Conn.: Yale University Press, 1995.

Young, Iris Marion. "Polity and Group Difference: A Critique of the Ideal of Universal Citizenship." *Ethics* 99, no. 2 (1989): 250-74

————. *Justice and the Politics of Difference.* Princeton, N.J.: Princeton University Press, 1990.

Index

Abacha, Sani, 139, 142, 150
Abiola, Moshood, 153, 156
Ackerman, Bruce, 14, 18, 117
Action Group (AG), 61-63, 66, 68-70, 79, 84-85, 94n6, 101-102
African Charter on Human and People's Rights, 171
Ake, Claude, 37, 135n8
Alliance for Democracy (AD), 157
alternative vote, 27-28, 33. *See also* plurality plus distribution method; federalism: electoral strategy; electoral method
Althusser, Louis, 57n16
Anderson, Benedict, 35; imagined community and, 35
Aquinas, Thomas, 169
Aristotle, 78, 120, 135n7, 151
Awolowo, Obafemi, 48, 94n2
Azikiwe, Nmamdi, 48

Babangida, Ibrahim, 138, 141, 155
Beiner, Ronald, 185
Bentham, Jeremy, 124
Berman, Bruce, 50, 54
Biafra: and secession, 3, 9, 102, 108, 109, 152, 153
Birch, Anthony, 154
Bourdillon, Bernard, 46
Buhari, Muhammadu, 141, 179n26

Cairo Declaration on Human Rights in Islam (1990), 172
Calhoun, John, 158
caliphate, 43, 55n3, 55n5, 55n6. *See also* Islam

Cameron, Donald, 153
Canada: Meech Lake Accord and, 18; Aboriginal peoples and, 18, 184; multiculturalism and, 13, 19, 22. *See also* Charles Taylor; Reg Whitaker
Carens, Joseph, 39n3, 184
Chabal, Patrick, 52-53
Christianity, 43, 81, 107, 143-44, 168-71, 173-76, 178n14. *See also* Islam; secularism
Chrysippus, 168
Cicero, 78, 169, 171
Coleman, James, 45
consociationalism, 8, 25-26, 28-29, 31-33, 119, 123, 131, 158, 182-83. *See also* Arend Lijphart
constitutions: the Richards Constitution (1946), 48; Macpherson Constitution (1951), 49; Independence Constitution (1960), 100, 107, 171; Republican Constitution (1963), 100, 107; 1995 Draft Constitution, 140, 142, 166-167
constitutional conferences: Independence Constitutional Conference (1958), 9, 100, 134n1; Resumed Lagos Conference (1954), 60, 66, 67; General Conference (1950), 60-62, 64-66, 82, 89; London Conference (1953), 61-62, 68; Resumed Conference (1958), 69; Ad Hoc Constitutional Conference (1966), 102, 108; 1994-95 Con-

About the Author

John Boye Ejobowah holds a Ph.D. in political science from the University of Toronto where he currently teaches comparative politics of the developing areas (with an emphasis on Africa). His research interests include contemporary normative theory, constitutionalism, and institutional arrangements for conflict reduction within states.